*W*hat
You Weren't Taught
in Sunday School

Dr. Jerald F. Dirks

amana publications

© 2011AC /1432AH
amana publications
10710 Tucker Street
Beltsville, MD 20705-2223 USA
Tel. 301-595-5777, 800-660-1777
Fax 301-595-5888, 240-250-3000
Email: amana@amana-corp.com
Website: www.amanapublications.com

First Edition
2011AC /1432AH

Reprint
2017AC /1438AH

Library of Congress Cataloging-in-Publication Data

Dirks, Jerald.
  What you weren't taught in Sunday school / Jerald F. Dirks.
    p. cm.
  Includes bibliographical references (p.   ).
  ISBN 978-1-59008-069-6
  1. Christianity--Miscellanea. 2. Bible--Miscellanea. I. Title.
  BR121.3.D57 2011
  270.09--dc23
                                                2011024830

Printed by Mega Printing in Turkey

TABLE OF CONTENTS

PREFACE

ACCORDING TO A TELEPHONE POLL on religious knowledge conducted in 2010 by the Pew Forum on Religion and Public Life,[1] out of 3,013 adult Americans who answered the survey, fully 2,528 self-identified as being Christians. Assuming a random sampling of the American population, this finding suggests that approximately 84% of the American population is at least nominally Christian. Despite this and other findings suggesting "that America is among the most religious of the world's developed nations,"[2] the survey found that the average American has a very poor knowledge of the religious teachings and practices of the major world religions. More specifically, the poll results indicated that many Christians are frighteningly uninformed about their own religion of Christianity.

This lack of knowledge about Christianity among American Christians can be best illustrated by reviewing some of the aforementioned poll results. (1) The doctrine of transubstantiation, i.e., that the bread and wine of the Eucharist actually turn into the body and blood of Christ, is a central tenet of Roman Catholicism. Nonetheless, 45% of the surveyed Catholics did not know that their church teaches transubstantiation! (2) A majority (53%) of Protestants were not able to identify Martin Luther as being the person who inspired the Protestant Reformation! (3) Only 42% of Roman Catholics were able to name Genesis as being the first book in the *Bible*! (4) Only 67% of white evangelical Christians, 63% of white Roman Catholics, and 49% of white mainline Protestants and black Protestants correctly identified the Golden Rule as not being one of the Ten Commandments!

---

[1] --- (2010).
[2] --- (2010).

As concerning as the above results are, they should not be surprising. The fact of the matter is that the average Christian has never read the entire *Bible* and has very little knowledge of all the information that is contained therein. Likewise, the average Christian has a very poor working knowledge of early Christian history and is typically unaware of the controversies about and evolution of Christian doctrine and dogma during the first few centuries of the Christian era. Clearly, American Sunday schools are doing a poor job of educating Christians about their faith.

As such, the topic of what is not being taught in Sunday school is timely and relevant. While this modest volume cannot address all the deficits in Christian education that are currently plaguing American Christians, it can begin the job by focusing on a few areas that are typically ignored in Sunday school. Among those areas, one can list the following. (1) How was the *Bible* formed, and how many different *Bibles* are recognized by one or another branch of Christianity? (2) What was the actual historical role of Paul in the formation of Christianity, and what was the nature of the conflict between Paul and the actual disciples of Jesus? (3) To what extent are the concepts of Holy War and genocide part and parcel of Biblical history? (4) Who were the non-Israelite Israelites? (5) Where was Mt. Sinai? (6) Who was Moses' first wife? (7) How many different people does the *Bible* credit with killing Goliath? (8) Was "Doubting" Thomas the brother of Jesus? (9) Who actually wrote the canonical gospels? (10) How many different lists of Jesus' 12 disciples does the New Testament give? (11) What are the major additions to, deletions from, and misleading translations to be found in the *Bible*? (12) How is Jesus portrayed in traditional Jewish and Islamic literature? (13) Was America really founded as a Christian nation?

The answers to these questions may be disturbing to many Christians. Perhaps that is the reason why they are not taught in Sunday school. Welcome to the world of *What You Weren't Taught in Sunday School.*

Jerald F. Dirks, M.Div., Psy.D.

April, 2011

CHAPTER 1

A MULTITUDE OF DIFFERENT *BIBLES*

The *B-i-b-l-e,*
Yes, that's the book for me.
I stand alone on the word of God—
The *B-i-b-l-e.*

INTRODUCTION

GENERATIONS OF CHILDREN HAVE MEMORIZED the above ditty in Sunday school and in vacation *Bible* school. The implicit implications of this children's song are that there is only one *Bible* and that this book is the revealed word of God. Further, drawing their authority from THE *Bible* that they hold aloft, countless pulpit pounders and *Bible* thumpers have harangued their Sunday morning congregations, both those in their churches' pews and those they reach via local, regional, and national telecasts, about whatever topic they are addressing. Once again, the unspoken assumptions are that there is only one *Bible*, that Christianity agrees on what constitutes that one Bible, and that they are in possession of that one *Bible.*

In reality, there are numerous different *Bibles.* When confronted with such a statement, the average Christian will probably respond that he is aware that there is a King James Version, a Revised Standard Version, a New Revised Standard Version, etc., but that these are merely different translations of the one and only *Bible.* While it is true that the aforementioned versions are merely different translations, albeit ones that variously rely on earlier or later manuscripts of the *Bible*, which reliance results in some differences in content in places, as witnessed in chapter five of this book, this is not what is meant by different *Bibles*. Rather, despite what the average Christian assumes to be the case, Christianity has never agreed on what books actually belong in the *Bible*, resulting in different Christian churches having different books in their various *Bibles*. Further, as is illustrated below, such disagreements exist with regard to both the Old Testament and the New Testament.

FORMATION OF THE OLD TESTAMENT CANON

THE *TANAKH*

To understand how the various Christian churches ended up with differing Old Testaments, one has to start with the story of the formation of the *Tanakh*, the book that constitutes the Jewish holy scriptures. It is only after understanding the formation of the *Tanakh* that one can begin to appreciate how the Protestant, Roman Catholic, and Greek Orthodox churches ended up with such mutually discrepant Old Testaments.

As noted above, the 24-book *Tanakh* is the official canon of authoritative Jewish scripture and basically conforms to the Protestant Old Testament. The only real differences between the two sets of scripture concern issues of: (1) whether or not a book is presented as one book, as in the Judaic *Tanakh*, or divided into two or more books, as in the Protestant Old Testament; (2) the names or titles assigned to the various component books; (3) the order in which the books are presented in the *Tanakh* vs. their order in the Protestant Old Testament; and (4) language, with the *Tanakh* being in Hebrew, and the Protestant Old Testament being translated into a variety of modern vernaculars.[3]

---

[3] (A) Silberman LH (1971); (B) Reumann J (1971).

The *Tanakh* is named after a neologism, which was artificially contrived from the first letter of each of the three component parts of the *Tanakh*. These three parts of the *Tanakh* are the: (1) Torah, i.e., "teaching," but often translated as "law;" (2) Nevi'im, i.e., "prophets;" and (3) Ketuvim, i.e., "writings."[4] Utilizing the names and division of books as found in the Protestant Old Testament, Figure #1 presents the three divisions within the *Tanakh*.[5]

Figure #1

THE COMPOSITION OF THE *TANAKH*

TORAH	NEVI'IM	KETUVIM
Genesis	Joshua	Psalms
Exodus	Judges	Proverbs
Leviticus	I Samuel	Job
Numbers	II Samuel	Song of Solomon
Deuteronomy	I Kings	Ruth
	II Kings	Lamentations
	Isaiah	Ecclesiastes
	Jeremiah	Esther
	Ezekiel	Daniel
	Hosea	Ezra
	Joel	Nehemiah
	Amos	I Chronicles
	Obadiah	II Chronicles
	Jonah	
	Micah	
	Nahum	
	Habakkuk	
	Zephaniah	
	Haggai	
	Zechariah	
	Malachi	

---

[4] Silberman LH (1971).

[5] Figure #1 is based upon the following references: (A) Silberman LH (1971); (B) Sundberg AC (1971); (C) Sarna NM (2003).

The five books of the Torah were each constructed in a cut-and-paste manner by combining prior sources known as J (circa 950 BCE), E (circa 750 BCE), P (sixth or fifth century BCE), and D (seventh century BCE),[6] and the Torah did not reach something approaching its current form until approximately 410 BCE.[7] In that regard, Genesis was constructed by combining such prior written sources as J, E, and P with editorial glosses and other material, with J being the most heavily used literary strand.[8] Exodus was constructed from J, E, P, D, and editorial glosses, with P being the most heavily used literary strand.[9] Leviticus was almost totally dependent on P, but also has some editorial glosses.[10] Numbers was compiled from J, E, P, and various editorial glosses, with P being the most frequently used literary strand.[11] Finally, Deuteronomy was primarily based on D, especially chapters five through 28, but also included some P and other material, as well as editorial glosses.[12]

The first place that the Torah is referred to as scripture is in the Letter of Aristeas, which was written in the late second century BCE.[13] Nonetheless, it is certain that the Torah was considered scripture well before that. For example, the Samaritans split away from Judaism circa 335 BCE,[14] and the Samaritans also hold the Torah to be revealed scripture. Thus, it appears that the Torah as we basically now have it was

---

[6] (A) Hyatt JP (1971); (B) Marks JH (1971); (C) Duncan GB (1971a); (D) Leslie EA (1929).
[7] Duncan GB (1971a).
[8] Marks JH (1971).
[9] Gray J (1971).
[10] Milgrom J (1971).
[11] Guthrie HH (1971a).
[12] Gottwald NK (1971).
[13] McDonald LM (2005).
[14] Leslie EA (1929).

accepted as scripture within Judaism no later than the fourth century BCE and probably nearer to the year 400 BCE. However, given that the Torah was still in the process of change during the time of Ezra (circa 397 BCE) and Nehemiah (circa 445 BCE), it is likely that some earlier form of the Torah (e.g., the core of Deuteronomy that is generally identified with the "book of the law" found by Hilkiah, the Israelite high priest during the reign of King Josiah circa 621 BCE[15]) was accepted as scripture prior to 400 BCE.[16]

The Nevi'im or "prophets" may be divided into two main groupings, i.e., the Former Prophets and the Latter Prophets. Using the book divisions as found in the Hebrew *Tanakh*, the Former Prophets consists of four books (i.e., Joshua, Judges, Samuel, and Kings) of allegedly historical narrative concerning Israel from the time of the Exodus from Egypt until the start of the Babylonian captivity. In the Christian Old Testament, Samuel is divided into I and II Samuel, and Kings is divided into I and II Kings. In the *Tanakh*, the Latter Prophets consists of Isaiah, Jeremiah, Ezekiel and the Book of the Twelve. In the Christian Old Testament, the Book of the Twelve is further divided into the books of the so-called Minor Prophets, including Hosea, Joel, Amos, Obadiah, Jonah, Micah, Nahum, Habakkuk, Zephaniah, Haggai, Zechariah, and Malachi.[17]

---

[15] II Kings 22:8-13.
[16] McDonald LM (2005).
[17] (A) Silberman LH (1971); (B) Hyatt JP (1971).

Figure # 2

COMPOSITION OF THE NEVI'IM IN THE *TANAKH**

FORMER PROPHETS	LATTER PROPHETS
Joshua	Isaiah
Judges	Jeremiah
Samuel	Ezekiel
(I Samuel)	Book of the Twelve
(II Samuel)	(Hosea)
Kings	(Joel)
(I Kings)	(Amos)
(II Kings)	(Obadiah)
	(Jonah)
	(Micah)
	(Nahum)
	(Habakkuk)
	(Zephaniah)
	(Haggai)
	(Zechariah)
	(Malachi)

*Listings that are indented and enclosed within parentheses indicate the corresponding books in the Christian Old Testament to the single book in the Jewish *Tanakh*. Thus, Kings in the *Tanakh* corresponds to I and II Kings in the Old Testament.

Before considering when the Nevi'im was accepted as scripture within Judaism, a slight digression is needed to consider the role of some of the different religious sects within Judaism in the centuries leading up to the common era. This digression is necessary because not all Jewish sects accepted the Nevi'im as scripture.

The first Jewish sect to be considered was known as the Sadducees, aka the Zadokites, whose name can be translated as "righteous ones." The Sadducees were composed primarily of members of the Jewish upper class and aristocracy and were mainly congregated in and around Jerusalem. In that regard, it is noted that they were the sect within Judaism from which the high priests were traditionally selected and that they were personally invested in maintaining the prerogatives and lifestyle of the priestly class. They were heavily focused on the re-established temple cult within Jerusalem and on the associated rites and practices of temple sacrifice. In fact, it can be maintained that their entire religious life was centered on temple practice. In terms of theological constructs, they apparently did not believe in the coming of a messiah, in the concept of resurrection after death, or in the existence of angels. Their philosophical rationale centered on a belief in a theocratic government, which was to be vested in the descendants of Zadok, the high priest during the reign of King Solomon, i.e., in themselves. Given these political goals, they were often political opportunists who were willing to accommodate to other cultures and governments, including the Roman Empire, in order to keep their political ambitions alive. As noted previously, their religious life was almost completely focused on the temple cult and ritual. As such, with the destruction of the Second Temple in August, 70 CE, their reason for existence basically vanished, and they ceased to exist as a viable sect within Judaism.[18]

---

[18] (A) Leon-Dufour X (1983); (B) Schonfield HJ (1967); (C) Sandison GH (---); (D) Josephus F (1988).

With regard to the scriptural orientation of the Sadducees, they focused rather exclusively on the written law, refusing to recognize the Pharisaic creation of the oral law, i.e., what would later coalesce as the *Talmud*. (See chapter six for a discussion of the *Talmud*.) They also refused to recognize any written scripture outside of the five books of the received Torah, i.e., Genesis, Exodus, Leviticus, Numbers, and Deuteronomy.[19]

A second Jewish sect was the Hassidim, whose name can be translated as "the pious." This sect arose about the beginning of the second century BCE and shortly thereafter split into two main groups: the Pharisees and the Essenes.[20] Because of the importance and prominence of each of these two subgroups of the Hassidim, each will be considered separately.

The Pharisees were probably the dominant Jewish sect at the time of Jesus and have been estimated to have numbered about 6,000 members at that time. Unlike the more aristocratic Sadducees, the Pharisees were not just congregated in and around Jerusalem, but were spread out and dispersed throughout the whole of Palestine. If the Sadducees were the aristocracy, then the Pharisees were a populist "people's" movement. The Pharisaic contribution to the evolution of Judaism was quite profound and far reaching, as can be seen by the fact that the Pharisees: (1) gave birth to the various rabbinical schools and to rabbinical Judaism; (2) were associated with the synagogue movement in Judaism, which began to challenge the over focus of the Sadducees on the temple cult and on the rite of temple sacrifice; (3) were the great proponents of the oral law, i.e., the *Talmud*, which attempted to interpret, if not alter via interpretation, the Torah, and which resulted in nearly endless ritual; and (4) readily

---

[19] (A) McDonald LM (2005); (B) Schonfield HJ (1967); (C) Sandison GH (---); (D) Josephus F (1988).
[20] Schonfield HJ (1967).

accepted as authoritative scripture the various books of the Nevi'im and the Ketuvim, which today find their place beside the Torah in the *Tanakh*. In terms of theological constructs, the Pharisees awaited the coming of a messiah and believed in a resurrection after death, in a final Day of Judgment, and in the existence of angels. They resisted assimilation to Hellenistic influences and were more nationalistically oriented than were the Sadducees.[21]

The Essenes, numbering about 4,000 members, tended to withdraw from society and established "monasteries," such as that at Khirbet Qumran on the shore of the Dead Sea, or closed communities in and around Jerusalem or in Damascus. In terms of their scriptural orientation, the Essenes accepted the Nevi'im and the Ketuvim, although apparently not giving them the same level of authority as they accorded to the Torah. The Essenes also utilized a number of books that were not acceptable to the Pharisees and that never were accepted as part of the *Tanakh*. By and large, these books can be found in various collections of the pseudepigraphical writings, appear to have had a great influence on the early Christian churches, and are frequently quoted without reference in the New Testament. In terms of religious practice, they avoided the temple and the temple cult and refused to recognize the legitimacy of the ruling high priests of Judaism. They were further characterized by their great emphasis on ritual ablution, on the repetitious use of immersion in water, by their wearing of white, by a frequently communal and ascetic lifestyle, by extremely strict marital limitations, and by a refusal to even defecate on the Sabbath. In terms of theological constructs, the Essenes awaited the coming of a messiah (if not two messiahs, one being priestly and from the line of Aaron, and one being kingly and from the line of David). The Essenes

---

[21] (A) Schonfield HJ (1967); (B) Leon-Dufour X (1983); (C) Sandison GH (---); (D) Josephus F (1988); E) Mack BL (1995).

believed in a resurrection after death, in a final Day of Judgment, and in the existence of angels. They also believed in a final, cosmic battle between good and evil, which gave a dualistic and markedly apocalyptic coloring to their theology and writings. Like the Pharisees, the Essenes resisted Hellenistic influences. After the destruction of the Second Temple in August, 70 CE, various Essenic communities either ceased to exist, e.g., the community at Khirbet Qumran, or were absorbed by the nascent Christian churches, e.g., the Damascus group, and possibly by the early Mandaean movement, which alleged its origin from John the Baptist.[22]

The Zealots comprised yet another Jewish sect. The Zealots were primarily a political group with extremely nationalistic ambitions that was fragmented into a variety of sub-sects, including the Galileans and the Sicarii, i.e., "dagger men" or "assassins." The Galileans claimed their origin with the aborted military uprising of Judas of Gamala (aka Judas the Galilean) in the year six CE. Thereafter, they engaged in isolated acts of guerrilla warfare against Rome that were punctuated by armed uprisings, e.g., in 66 CE and in 132 CE. While Josephus, the first-century CE Jewish historian and apologist, claimed that the Zealots' religious orientation was like that of the Pharisees, it may be more likely that their nationalistic platform masked a variety of different religious practices, beliefs, and sects. To the extent that they looked for the arrival of a messiah, they pictured the messiah as a warrior and king, one who would deliver them from all aspects of foreign control. The Zealots ceased to exist as a sect within Judaism after their final, unsuccessful uprising under Simon bar Kochba in 132 CE.[23]

---

[22] (A) Josephus F (1988); (B) Mack BL (1995); (C) Sandison GH (---); (D) Leon-Dufour X (1983); (E) Stegemann H (1998); (F) Dupont-Sommer A (1967).

[23] (A) Duncan GB (1971a); (B) Josephus F (1988); (C) Sandison GH (---); (D) --- (2003f); (E) Leon-Dufour X (1983); (F) Dupont-Sommer A (1967).

Finally, one must consider the Samaritans, a group arising out of the Assyrian conquest of the northern Kingdom of Israel in 723/722 BCE. Having conquered the northern kingdom, the Assyrian Empire placed numerous Assyrian colonists in northern Palestine. These colonists intermarried with the remnants of those Israelites in northern Palestine who had not been taken off into captivity and exile and thus gave rise to the ethnically mixed group of people known ever since as Samaritans. These Samaritans considered themselves to have maintained the ancient religion of the Israelites as it had been practiced in the northern Kingdom of Israel, a religious practice which differed in several ways from that of the southern Kingdom of Judah.[24] Despite these differences, the Samaritans actively welcomed the return of the Judaean exiles from the Babylonian captivity, offered to help build the Second Temple in Jerusalem—an offer that was disdainfully rejected by the return-ing exiles, and accepted the Torah provided by Ezra as their own scriptural guide. Nonetheless, they were consistently rejected as being ethnically and religiously impure by the returning captives from Babylonia. As such, they withdrew into their own community, established their own sites of religious practice, i.e., at Mount Gerizim near modern Nablus (Shechem), Palestine, preserved their own independent version of the Torah, and began to call themselves the Shamerin, i.e., "observant ones." The final rupture between the Shamerin and the rest of the Jews took place in the fourth century BCE. Since then, they have maintained a closed and isolated existence, in which they acknowledge only their own version of the Torah and of the Biblical book of Joshua as the scriptural basis of their religious life. They reject all other books of the *Tanakh*. Currently, the Shamerin number only about 500 adherents, but they maintain their own temple and high priest in Nablus.[25]

---

[24] One of the most noticeable differences had to do with the relative lack of emphasis given to the temple cult practice of Jerusalem by the northern Kingdom of Israel. After all, the temple was located in Jerusalem, which was the capital of the southern Kingdom of Judah.

[25] (A) Epstein I (1966); (B) --- (2003g); (C) Duncan GB (1971a); (D) Silberman LH (1971).

As a group, the Nevi'im appears to have been accepted as authoritative scripture within Pharisaic and Essenic Judaism at a date following that of the Torah's acceptance and preceding that of the Ketuvim. As the Torah was accepted by at least the early fourth century BCE, this places a firm upper limit on the time by which the Nevi'im was enjoying popular acceptance within Judaism by all but the Shamerin and Sadducees.[26] Further, the Nevi'im is mentioned as a distinct literary group of scriptural writings by the second century BCE, and this event establishes a firm lower limit on the time of the acceptance of the Nevi'im.[27]

With regard to the above dating, it is instructive to note that the Nevi'im is referred to as scripture in the second century BCE in the prologue to Ecclesiasticus, also known as The Wisdom of Jesus Ben-Sira and The Book of Sirach, and in the first century BCE in II Maccabees. Further, the combination of the Torah (the Law of Moses) and the Nevi'im (the prophets) is appealed to several times in the New Testament as being authoritative scripture, at least for the Pharisees and Essenes.

> Since many things and great have been delivered unto us through the Law and the Prophets and the others who followed after them—for which things' sake we must give Israel the praise of instruction and wisdom—and as not only must the readers themselves become adept, but also the lovers of learning must be able to profit them which are without both by speaking and writing; my grandfather Jesus, having given himself much to the reading of the Law and the Prophets and the other books of our fathers, and having acquired considerable familiarity therein, was

---

[26] (A) Silberman LH (1971); (B) Sundberg AC (1971); (C) Sarna NM (2003).
[27] McDonald LM (2005).

induced also himself to take a part in writing somewhat pertaining to instruction and wisdom, in order that those who are lovers of learning and instructed in these things might make so much the more progress by a manner of life (lived) in accordance with the Law. Ye are entreated, therefore, to make your perusal with favour and attention, and to be indulgent, if in any parts of what we have laboured to interpret we may seem to fail in some of the phrases. For things originally spoken in Hebrew have not the same force in them when they are translated into another tongue: and not only these, but the Law itself, and the Prophecies, and the rest of the books, have no small difference when they are spoken in their original form. (Prologue to Ecclesiasticus)[28]

…and comforting them out of the law and the prophets, as well as recalling the struggles they had endured, he made them more eager (for the fray). (II Maccabees 15:9)[29]

Think not that I am come to destroy the law, or the prophets: I am not come to destroy, but to fulfill. (Matthew 5:17, King James Version)

Therefore all things whatsoever ye would that men should do to you, do ye even so to them: for this is the law and the prophets. (Matthew 7:12, King James Version)

And beginning at Moses and all the prophets, he expounded unto them in all the scriptures the things concerning himself. (Luke 24:27, King James Version)

---

[28] Box GH, Oesterley WO (1971), p. 268-269.
[29] Moffatt J (1971), p. 153.

Philip findeth Nathanael, and saith unto him, We have found him, of whom Moses in the law, and the prophets, did write, Jesus of Nazareth, the son of Joseph. (John 1:45, King James Version)

For they that dwell at Jerusalem, and their rulers, because they knew him not, nor yet the voices of the prophets which are read every sabbath day, they have fulfilled them in condemning him. (Acts 13:27, King James Version)

And when they had appointed him a day, there came many to him into his lodging; to whom he expounded and testified the kingdom of God, persuading them concerning Jesus, both out of the law of Moses, and out of the prophets, from morning till evening. (Acts 28:23, King James Version)

Not withstanding the above discussion and the above quoted verses, it must be remembered that the official 24-book canon of scripture within Judaism was not established, and thus was not closed, until much later. As such, one is here talking about the Nevi'im being popularly accepted as scripture in a general way by the Pharisees and Essenes of Judaism by around 200 BCE. One is definitely not talking about the Nevi'im being included in an official, authorized canon of Jewish scripture, which would not happen until the establishment of that canon many centuries later.[30]

The synagogal collection of the Masoretic Text of the *Tanakh* includes 11 books in the Ketuvim. Utilizing titles found in the Protestant Old Testament, these 11 books include Psalms, Proverbs, Job, Song of Solomon, Ruth, Lamentations, Ecclesiastes, Esther, Daniel, Ezra-Nehemiah (corresponding

---

[30] McDonald LM (2005).

to the books of Ezra and Nehemiah in the Protestant Old Testament), and Chronicles (corresponding to the books of I and II Chronicles in the Protestant Old Testament). In the synagogal collection, all 11 books of the Ketuvim follow the books of the Nevi'im, which in turn follow the books of the Torah, and the 11 books of the Ketuvim are in the order presented immediately above. This ordering of books is, of course, quite different than that found in the Old Testament, where the various books of the Nevi'im and Ketuvim are interspersed, thus obscuring the three-fold division of the *Tanakh*.[31]

From various writings of the second century BCE, it can be determined that some of the books of the Ketuvim were beginning to gain popular acceptance within Pharisaic and Essenic Judaism by that time. For example, Jesus bin Sirach, the author of the book of Ecclesiasticus, which was written circa 180 BCE and is part of what Protestants consider to be the Old Testament Apocrypha, referred to some of the books of the Ketuvim, but appeared to have no knowledge of Ecclesiastes, Esther, and Daniel. Further, as the last two verses of Chronicles are repeated as the first three verses of Ezra, it appears that Chronicles and Ezra-Nehemiah were originally one book.[32]

In the above quoted verses from the Prologue to Ecclesiasticus, there is a rather ambiguous reference to the Ketuvim in the words "the others who followed after" the Law and the Prophets, "the Law and the Prophets and the other books of our fathers," and "the rest of the books." However, there is no clear definition of what comprised the Ketuvim. All that is demonstrated is that some books of the Ketuvim were becoming accepted as scripture by some segments of Judaism at the time the Prologue was written late in the

---

[31] Silberman LH (1971).
[32] Silberman LH (1971).

second century BCE. Likewise, in the following verse from the Gospel of Luke, the three-fold division of the *Tanakh* is again hinted at, but the only book from the Ketuvim that is listed is Psalms.

> And he said unto them, These are the words which I spake unto you, while I was yet with you, that all things must be fulfilled, which were written in the law of Moses, and in the prophets, and in the psalms, concerning me. (Luke 24:44, King James Version)

If the Torah and the Nevi'im had both been established by common acceptance as scripture by both the Pharisees and the Essenes by the time of Jesus in the first third of the first century CE, and if at least some books of the Ketuvim were commonly accepted by those same two groups by that same timeframe, then when were the final boundaries of the Ketuvim firmly established and the canon of the *Tanakh* finally solidified? Following the 19th-century work of Ryle,[33] the traditional view has been that the official canon of Jewish scripture was not established until late in the first century CE. More specifically, this tradition maintains that circa 90 CE, a rabbinical council convened at Jamnia, Palestine, which was about 12 miles south of modern Tel-Aviv/Jaffa. This council or synod reportedly established four primary criteria for the inclusion of a book into the official Jewish canon. These criteria were that the book in question had to: (1) conform to the teaching of the Torah, i.e., Genesis, Exodus, Leviticus, Numbers, and Deuteronomy; (2) be written no later than the time of Ezra, i.e., early in the fourth century BCE; (3) be written originally in Hebrew; and (4) be written originally in Palestine.[34]

If a final decision on the Jewish canon of scripture had been made at Jamnia,

---

[33] Ryle HE (1892).
[34] (A) Ryle HE (1892); (B) Hardon JA (1968). For a fuller discussion of these issues, see page 256 ff. in Hardon.

and if these four rules had been rigorously enforced, a lot fewer books would have found their way into the Jewish canon of scripture. For example, P was written in Babylonia, not Palestine.[35] On that basis alone, all five books of the Torah should have been excluded from the Jewish canon. In addition, none of the following books were written in their final form by the time of Ezra: Ezekiel,[36] Psalms,[37] Proverbs,[38] Song of Solomon,[39] Ecclesiastes,[40] Esther,[41] Daniel,[42] and possibly Job.[43] Thus, these books should also have been excluded. Further, the third criterion should have excluded two books: Job, which contains many Egyptian loan words;[44] and Daniel, chapters 2:4b-7:28 of which were written in Aramaic.[45] Finally, the fourth criterion should have excluded Isaiah, as chapters 40-66 of Isaiah appear to have been written in Babylonia.[46] Taken together, this represents 14 books that are in the official Jewish canon but that did not meet the criteria established at Jamnia for inclusion into the canon.

Given the above, it is not surprising that there were significant disputes recorded in the rabbinical writings that found their way into the *Babylonian Talmud* as to the inclusion of certain books in the Jewish canon of the *Tanakh*. Among the disputed books so mentioned, one finds references to Ezekiel, Ecclesiastes, Song of Solomon, and Esther.[47]

---

[35] Hyatt JP (1971).
[36] Brownlee WH (1971).
[37] Toombs LE (1971).
[38] Denton RC (1971a).
[39] Denton RC (1971b).
[40] Guthrie HH (1971b).
[41] Richardson HN (1971).
[42] (A) Knight GAF (1971); (B) McDonald LM (2005).
[43] Anderson H (1971).
[44] Anderson H (1971).
[45] Knight GAF (1971).
[46] Ackroyd PR (1971).
[47] Silberman LH (1971).

While Ryle's theory regarding the Council of Jamnia held sway in most scholarly circles for the better part of a century, it appears that the limits of the Ketuvim, and thus of the *Tanakh* as a whole, were not definitively established at Jamnia. A perusal of ancient Jewish literature, including the *Babylonian Talmud,* suggests that the rabbis continued to debate the exact nature and limits of their canon of scripture for another 200 to 400 years after the Council of Jamnia. In addition, several early Christian authors noted that the Jews of their day were using a 22-book canon of scripture, not the 24-book canon that was finally listed in the *Babylonian Talmud* and that exists in the *Tanakh* used by contemporary Jews. Among those Church Fathers attesting to the Jews having a 22-book canon of scripture, one can note Bishop Melito of Sardis (second century CE), Origen (circa 185-254 CE), and Saint Jerome (circa 347-420 CE). In short, the evidence suggests that there never was a definitive and formal decision by any council or synod of first-century rabbis at Jamnia regarding what was and was not to be part of the *Tanakh.* Rather, the decision was slowly made over several centuries by a process of common consensus and was finalized no later than the early sixth century CE and no earlier than the latter part of the second century CE. Thus, it appears that the official canon of the *Tanakh* was not finally and definitively determined until a date long after the early Christian church began to create its Old Testament.[48]

---

[48] McDonald LM (2005). Some, e.g., Beckwith R (1985), have tried to argue that the canon of the *Tanakh* was closed well before the Council of Jamnia in 90 CE. However, the above cited references by early Christian authors to the Jews maintaining a 22-book canon would seem to discount Beckwith's thesis. Further undermining that thesis is the fact that Josephus, the Jewish historian writing in the latter part of the first century CE, specifically stated that the Jews had 22 books of scripture, not yet 24. (Josephus, 1999)

THE SEPTUAGINT

By the third century BCE, those Jews living in the Diaspora outside of Palestine had begun to lose their ability to read and understand Hebrew and Aramaic. Greek had become their customary language. As such, the need arose for the Jews in the Diaspora, especially those in Egypt, to have a Greek translation of their Hebrew scriptures. This need was met when the Torah was translated from Hebrew into Greek, thus creating the Septuagint.[49]

According to the Letter of Aristeas, which was written late in the second century BCE by a Jew living in Alexandria, Egypt, a legendary and probably somewhat fictitious account of the origins of the Septuagint is provided. According to this source, Demetrius Phalerum, the chief librarian at Alexandria, formally petitioned the king, Ptolemy Philadelphus (ruled 284-247 BCE), to have a Greek translation of the Hebrew text of the Jewish scriptures made. Ptolemy Philadelphus concurred, and Eleazer, the Jewish high priest in Jerusalem, was asked to send a translation committee to Egypt. In response, Eleazer supposedly sent a team of 72 scholars, six men from each of the 12 tribes of Israel, to Egypt to complete the translation task, which allegedly took only 72 days to complete. This translation into Greek was known as the Septuagint from the Latin word "*septuaginta*," meaning 70. Why 70 instead of 72 is not known,[50] but it certainly is intriguing.

The original Septuagint would have only included the Torah.[51] However, as time went by, additional Jewish writings were translated into Greek and added to the Septuagint. Various books of the Nevi'im were most

---

[49] Smith TC (1997).
[50] Smith TC (1997).
[51] (A) McDonald LM (2005); (B) Smith TC (1997).

likely the next body of Jewish scripture to be translated and placed in the Septuagint. Finally, by around 130-150 BCE, the entirety of the Nevi'im and certain other Jewish writings, many of which would become part of the Ketuvim, were added to the Septuagint. However, not all the Jewish writings that were translated into Greek and placed in the Septuagint were later accepted into the *Tanakh*.[52]

Unfortunately, the original Septuagint manuscript no longer exists. However, later versions of the Septuagint were preserved by the early Christian churches, as the Septuagint served as the initial basis for the Christian Old Testament of the gentiles and of the Jewish Christians in the Diaspora. Further, these various copies of the Septuagint demonstrate that numerous revisions were being made in the text of the Septuagint during the first 1,000 years of its existence. Of note, all of these copies of the Septuagint differ in some important details from the Hebrew text of the Torah, and all these copies of the Septuagint differ among themselves to a greater or lesser extent.[53]

So what was included in the Septuagint that was later not included in the *Tanakh*? In part, the answer depends upon which copy of the Septuagint is being examined, as the different copies occasionally included somewhat different material. However, the following books are usually considered to be part of the Septuagint: Judith, Tobit, I and II Maccabees, Ecclesiasticus, Wisdom of Solomon, I Esdras, some additions to the Biblical book of Jeremiah (Baruch and the Epistle of Jeremiah), some additions to the *Tanakh's* book of Daniel (Bel and the Dragon, the Prayer of Azariah, and Susanna), and some additions to the *Tanakh's* book of Esther. In addition, some copies of the Septuagint also include Psalms chapter 151, the Prayer of

[52] (A) McDonald LM (2005); (B) Smith TC (1997); (C) Reumann J (1971).
[53] Reumann J (1971).

Manasseh, III and IV Maccabees, and the Psalms of Solomon, while others do not.[54]

THE OLD TESTAMENT IN EARLY CHRISTIANITY

When the early Christians that formed the Jerusalem church left Jerusalem in 62-66 CE following the murder of James the Just, the brother of Jesus, they moved across the Jordan River to Pella. At this point, the influence of Judaism on the early Christian church began to subside to a marked degree. As such, early Christianity was relatively unaffected by whatever debates went on about the limits of the *Tanakh* among the rabbis at the Council of Jamnia circa 90 CE and were even less concerned about the ongoing debates occurring in rabbinic Judaism about the canon of Jewish scriptures during the next few centuries. While not delineating the contents of the Old Testament canon of scripture, early Christianity had already decided to rely upon the Greek Septuagint as its version of Jewish scripture. However, some measure of uncertainty still existed within early Christianity regarding the books of the Septuagint, i.e., the Old Testament, as this body of work continued to evolve for a few centuries.[55]

The need to begin clarifying and defining the Old Testament canon started to become acute for early Christianity in reaction to the second-century Marcionite and Gnostic movements within Christianity, both of which called for a rejection of all Jewish religious literature prior to the time of Jesus.[56] While Christianity continued to use the Septuagint in its various forms, arriving at a definition of an Old Testament canon was a long, drawn out process, and no definitive decision was made by Christianity for many centuries thereafter.[57]

[54] (A) Smith TC (1997); (B) Mowry L (1971); (C) Marlowe M (---).
[55] McDonald LM (2005).
[56] (A) McDonald LM (2005); (B) Silberman LH (1971).
[57] (A) Hayes JH (1997); (B) Silberman LH (1971).

The state of uncertainty that existed within Christianity with regard to an Old Testament canon based on the Septuagint can be illustrated by several considerations. (1) Such early Church Fathers as Melito of Sardis (second century CE), Origen (circa 185-254 CE), Saint Cyril of Jerusalem (circa 315-386 CE), and Saint Jerome (circa 347-420 CE) either argued for an Old Testament canon identical with the *Tanakh* or at least expressed doubt about the authenticity of most of those books contained in the Septuagint that were not found in the *Tanakh*,[58] although it must be remembered that the *Tanakh* to which they were referring was a 22-book canon, not the 24-book canon that Judaism would later embrace. (2) Athanasius (circa 293-373 CE) published a list of accepted Old Testament books for the church in Egypt that conformed to the *Tanakh* with the exception that he accepted Baruch into his Old Testament canon, while omitting Esther from it.[59] (3) The three oldest codices of the *Bible* (the fourth-century Codex Vaticanus, the fourth-century Codex Sinaiticus, and the fifth-century Codex Alexandrinus) all differ among themselves as to which books are included in their versions of the Old Testament. For example, Codex Vaticanus contains none of the books of Maccabees,[60] while Codex Sinaiticus has I and IV Maccabees and Codex Alexandrinus has I, II, III, and IV Maccabees. (4) Early church councils also differed as to the contents of the Old Testament canon. For example, the Council of Laodicea circa 360-367 CE supported an Old Testament canon that added only Baruch to the books of the *Tanakh*.[61] However, subsequent church councils at Hippo in 393 and at Carthage in 397 and 419 supported a more inclusive Old Testament canon based on the Septuagint.[62] (5) The Old Testament used in Asia

---

[58] Hayes JH (1997).
[59] Marlowe M (---).
[60] Hayes JH (1997).
[61] Marlowe M (---).
[62] Hayes JH (1997).

Minor conformed to the *Tanakh*, with the single exception that Esther was omitted. In contrast, the Syrian churches used a much larger Old Testament based on the Septuagint, and it was this Old Testament that was confirmed by the African churches at the councils of Hippo and Carthage. In Palestine, the *Tanakh* minus Esther was the Old Testament in use at the time of Melito of Sardis' visit there in 170 CE, but in 348 CE Saint Cyril of Jerusalem indicated it consisted of the *Tanakh* plus Baruch and the Letter of Jeremiah.[63]

Given the ambiguity and disagreements that existed for centuries within the various early Christian churches about inclusions to and exclusions from the Old Testament, and given that various copies of the *Bible* also disagreed among themselves about what books were and were not included in the Old Testament, it is small wonder that contemporary Christianity continues to disagree about what books are to be included in the canon of the Old Testament. As will be shown in what follows, the Protestant, Roman Catholic, Greek Orthodox, Russian Orthodox, and Ethiopian Orthodox churches all disagree among themselves as to what constitutes the Old Testament.

THE PROTESTANT CHURCHES

Until the Protestant Reformation, the various churches of Christendom basically accepted a longer canon of books in their Old Testaments than was found in the Jewish *Tanakh*. However, the Wycliff translation of the *Bible* into English in 1382 included only the books found in the *Tanakh* in its Old Testament. This was also the case with the Catholic *Bible* published in Germany in 1527 and the Catholic *Bible* published in France in 1530. As the Protestant Reformation gained steam, Protestant

---

[63] Silberman LH (1971).

Reformers began to argue for an Old Testament content that was more or less consistent with the canon of the *Tanakh*, and this entailed rejection of those books that were found in the Septuagint that were not found in the *Tanakh*. As such, the Protestant Old Testament canon of 39 books was established, with these 39 books conforming to the 24-book canon of the *Tanakh* (refer back to Figure #1).[64]

The 39-book Old Testament canon was later confirmed by the Reformed churches in 1561 when they issued articles IV and V of the Belgica, which specifically excluded that material accepted by the Roman Catholic Church as being part of the Old Testament canon if it could not be found in the *Tanakh*. Likewise, in 1562 and 1571, the Church of England restricted its Old Testament canon to the 39-book canon of Protestantism in the sixth of its *Thirty-Nine Articles*, while acknowledging that the Old Testament Apocrypha could be read, but could not be used for establishing doctrine.[65]

> In the name of Holy Scripture we do understand those canonical books of the Old and New Testament, of whose authority was never any doubt in the Church...And the other books (as Jerome saith) the Church doth read for example of life and instruction of manners: but yet doth it not apply them to establish any doctrine. (Article #6, Articles of Religion of the Church of England)[66]

The Church of England was later to make an even stronger rejection of those books not found in the *Tanakh* but found in the Greek Septuagint or Latin Vulgate versions of the *Bible*. To illustrate this, consider the following statement from the Church of England's 1647 Westminster Confession:

---

[64] Hayes JH (1997).
[65] McDonald LM (2005).
[66] Marlowe M (---).

The books commonly called Apocrypha, not being of divine inspiration, are no part of the Canon of Scripture; and therefore are of no authority in the Church of God, nor to be any otherwise approved, or made use of, than other human writings. (Westminster Confession)[67]

So what do the Protestant churches do with those books that are part of the Old Testament canons of non-Protestant churches? They assign those books to one or another of two categories of religious literature, i.e., typically the Old Testament Apocrypha and occasionally the Old Testament Pseudepigrapha. The Old Testament Apocrypha is generally considered to consist of I Esdras, II Esdras (not found in the Septuagint, but added to the Apocrypha on the basis of its being in the Latin Vulgate version of the *Bible*), Tobit, Judith, Additions to Esther, Wisdom of Solomon, Ecclesiasticus, Baruch, Letter of Jeremiah, Prayer of Azariah and Song of the Three Young Men, Susanna, Bel and the Dragon, Prayer of Manasseh, and I and II Maccabees.[68]

Three brief addenda need to be made to this discussion of the Old Testament Apocrypha. (1) The term "apocrypha" is from the Greek and may be translated as "hidden." (2) Some of the books of the Apocrypha, e.g., II Esdras, continued to have later glosses and sections added to them until late in the first century CE, following the Roman conquest of Jerusalem and the destruction of the Second Temple in 70 CE. (3) The various books of the Apocrypha can be further classified and grouped according to their basic content material. In that regard, I Esdras and I and II Maccabees can be classified as history. Tobit, Judith, Additions to Esther, Susanna, and Bel and the Dragon may be counted as fiction.

---

[67] Marlowe M (---).
[68] Mowry L (1971).

Didactic books include Baruch, Letter of Jeremiah, Wisdom of Solomon, and Ecclesiasticus, with the last two belonging to that literary genre known as Wisdom Literature. Portions of II Esdras may be considered apocalyptic writing, and the Prayer of Manasseh is basically devotional writing.[69]

THE ROMAN CATHOLIC CHURCH

As noted previously, using the Septuagint as their yardstick, church councils at Hippo in 393 and at Carthage in 397 and 419, which were dominated by Western Church Fathers, supported a more inclusive Old Testament canon than was found in the *Tanakh*.[70] This was the position taken by the Roman Catholic Church, and it was to this canon of the Old Testament that the Protestant Reformers were objecting. However, it was not until the fourth session of the Council of Trent on April 8, 1546, that the canon of the Old Testament of the Roman Catholic Church became formally authorized.[71]

Based upon the decision reached at the Council of Trent, the Old Testament canon of the Roman Catholic Church includes a number of books and additions that are not to be found in the Protestant Old Testament. Included in this material not found in the Protestant Old Testament, one can list the following additions to books found in the Protestant Old Testament: 107 additional verses to Esther; and 174 additional verses to Daniel, including the Prayer of Azariah and the Song of the Three Young Men (68 verses inserted following 3:23), Susanna (64 verses), and Bel and the Dragon (42 verses).[72] Further, the Roman

---

[69] Mowry L (1971).
[70] Hayes JH (1997).
[71] (A) Hayes JH (1997); (B) McDonald LM (2005).
[72] Hayes JH (1997).

Catholic Old Testament canon includes the following books not found in the Protestant Old Testament: Tobit, Judith, Wisdom of Solomon (also known as the Book of Wisdom), Ecclesiasticus (also known as the Wisdom of Jesus bin Sirach), Baruch, and I and II Maccabees.[73] The Council of Trent's decision regarding the Old Testament canon of the Roman Catholic Church was later reaffirmed by the First Vatican Council (1869-70).[74] (See Figure # 3 below for a comparison of different Old Testament canons of various Christian denominations.)

THE GREEK ORTHODOX CHURCH

At the Synod of Jerusalem in March of 1672, the Greek Orthodox Church acknowledged the Wisdom of Solomon, Judith, Tobit, Bel and the Dragon, Susanna, Ecclesiasticus, and I, II, and III Maccabees as being part of the Old Testament canon.[75] However, this didn't totally settle the issue for the Greek Orthodox Church. Currently, the Old Testament canon of the Greek Orthodox Church is the same as that for the Roman Catholic Church, except that the Greek Orthodox Church also accepts I Esdras (also known as I Esdras A, Esdras B, II Esdras, III Esdras, Greek Ezra, Tertius Neemiae, and III Paraleipomenon[76]), a 151st psalm not found in the Protestant and Roman Catholic book of Psalms, and III Maccabees, with IV Maccabees placed in an appendix, as part of the Old Testament canon. This canon was affirmed in 1950 by the Holy Synod of the Greek Orthodox Church.[77] In addition, the Greek Orthodox Church adds the Prayer of Manasseh to its Old Testament book of II Chronicles.[78] (See Figure # 3 below for a comparison of different Old Testament canons of various Christian denominations.)

---

[73] (A) Hayes JH (1997); (B) McDonald LM (2005).
[74] McDonald LM (2005).
[75] Hayes JH (1997).
[76] Cook MA (1971).
[77] (A) Hayes JH (1997); (B) McDonald LM (2005).
[78] Marlowe M (---).

THE RUSSIAN ORTHODOX CHURCH

The Old Testament canon of the Russian Orthodox Church is the same as that of the Greek Orthodox Church, except that the Russian Orthodox Church does not recognize I Esdras and IV Maccabees.[79] (See Figure # 3 below for a comparison of different Old Testament canons of various Christian denominations.)

THE ETHIOPIAN ORTHODOX CHURCH

The Old Testament canon of the Ethiopian Orthodox Church has developed somewhat independently of the previously discussed churches, and there are a number of factors that make it difficult to be precise when it comes to discussing the Ethiopian Orthodox Old Testament canon. (1) The Old Testament canon of the Ethiopian Orthodox Church has historically been much more fluid and much more loosely defined than the canons of the other Christian churches.[80] (2) While it is agreed that the Ethiopian Orthodox Church's *Bible* contains a total of 81 books, there are two different canons for this *Bible*. There is a broader canon containing 46 books in its Old Testament and 35 books in its New Testament, and there is a narrower canon containing 54 books in its Old Testament and 27 books in its New Testament. Both canons are considered authoritative.[81] (3) The Ethiopian Orthodox Church sometimes uses different names for some Old Testament books, and it sometimes divides an Old Testament book into two books. For example, the Ethiopian Old Testament divides Proverbs into two separate books:

---

[79] McDonald LM (2005).
[80] Cowley RW (1974).
[81] (A) Cowley RW (1974); (B) Beckwith R (1985).

Messale (Proverbs, chapters 1-24), and Tagsas (Proverbs, chapters 25-31), the latter of which is also known as The Wisdom of Bagor. Further, it refers to I and II Chronicles as being I and II Paralipomenon. (4) It inserts the Prayer of Manasses into II Chronicles. (5) While the Ethiopian Orthodox Old Testament includes a I and II Maccabees, these are not the same books as the I and II Maccabees found in the Roman Catholic, Greek Orthodox, and Russian Orthodox Old Testaments.

(Please consult Figure #3 for a listing of books that are not found in the Protestant Old Testament and that have at one time or another, or in one canon or another, been listed as being part of the official Old Testament canon of the Ethiopian Orthodox Church.)

SUMMARY

As can be seen from the above discussion, Christianity has never agreed as to what does and does not constitute the Old Testament canon. Further, the disagreements to be found with regard to the Old Testament canon within Christianity would be enlarged beyond what has already been discussed if one were to consider the Old Testament canons of the Coptic, Eastern Syrian, and Armenian churches. However, it is believed that the present discussion suffices to demonstrate that Christianity never has agreed as to what constitutes its Old Testament. These disagreements are summarized below in Figure # 3.

Figure # 3

BOOKS AND ADDITIONS TO BOOKS FOUND IN OLD TESTAMENT
CANONS NOT FOUND IN THE PROTESTANT OLD TESTAMENT

ROMAN CATHOLIC CANON	GREEK ORTHODOX CANON	RUSSIAN ORTHODOX CANON	ETHIOPIAN ORTHODOX CANON [82]
Jeremiah additions	Jeremiah additions	Jeremiah additions	Jeremiah additions
	Psalms 151	Psalms 151	Psalms 151
Esther additions	Esther additions	Esther additions	Esther additions
Daniel additions	Daniel additions	Daniel additions	Daniel additions
	Prayer of Manasseh	Prayer of Manasseh	Prayer of Manasseh
Tobit	Tobit	Tobit	Tobit
Judith	Judith	Judith	Judith
I Maccabees	I Maccabees	I Maccabees	
II Maccabees	II Maccabees	II Maccabees	
	III Maccabees	III Maccabees	
	IV Maccabees		
Ecclesiasticus	Ecclesiasticus	Ecclesiasticus	Ecclesiasticus
Wisdom Solomon	Wisdom Solomon	Wisdom Solomon	Wisdom Solomon
Baruch	Baruch	Baruch	Baruch
	I Esdras		I Esdras
			Ezra Apocalypse[83]
			Pseudo-Josephus[84]
			Jubilees
			Ethiopian Enoch
			I Maccabees[85]
			II Maccabees[86]
			Ascension of Isaiah[87]

---

[82] The exact parameters of the Ethiopian Orthodox Church's Old Testament canon are difficult to delineate. This list given here is not meant to be seen as totally comprehensive and definitive. See Cowley RW (1974) and Beckwith R (1985) for a fuller discussion of the difficulties in determining the exact Old Testament canon of the Ethiopian Orthodox Church.

[83] Ezra Apocalypse is identical with chapters 3-14 of II Esdras, which is considered by Protestants to be part of the Old Testament Apocrypha.

[84] This is the same as Joseph ben Gorion's (Josippon's) medieval history of Jews and other nations. Beckwith R (1985).

[85] This is not the same book as the I Maccabees recognized by the Roman Catholic, Greek Orthodox, and Russian Orthodox Church.

[86] This is not the same book as the II Maccabees recognized by the Roman Catholic, Greek Orthodox, and Russian Orthodox Church.

[87] It may be that the Ascension of Isaiah is no longer considered canonical by the Ethiopian Orthodox Church, but it was certainly considered canonical in the past.

FORMATION OF THE NEW TESTAMENT CANON

INTRODUCTION

Although it certainly was not always the case, at the present time, most Christians adhere to a 27-book New Testament as shown in Figure # 4. Of these 27 books, one is an apocalypse,[88] one is an early church history,[89] 21 are epistles of one sort or another,[90] and four are labeled as being gospels.[91] Rather amazingly, almost all of those Christians who adhere to this 27-book canon of New Testament scripture believe that all of Christendom also accepts this same New Testament canon. While it is the case that Protestant, Roman Catholic, and Greek Orthodox Christians all share this same 27-book New Testament canon, several other Christian denominations have different New Testament canons.

Figure # 4

THE NEW TESTAMENT CANON OF PROTESTANT,
ROMAN CATHOLIC, AND GREEK ORTHODOX CHRISTIANS

Gospel of Matthew	Ephesians	Hebrews
Gospel of Mark	Philippians	James
Gospel of Luke	Colossians	I Peter
Gospel of John	I Thessalonians	II Peter
Acts of the Apostles	II Thessalonians	I John
Romans	I Timothy	II John
I Corinthians	II Timothy	III John
II Corinthians	Titus	Jude
Galatians	Philemon	Revelation

---

[88] Revelation.

[89] Acts of the Apostles.

[90] Romans, I and II Corinthians, Galatians, Ephesians, Philippians, Colossians, I and II Thessalonians, I and II Timothy, Titus, Philemon, Hebrews, James, I and II Peter, Jude, and I, II, and III John.

[91] Matthew, Mark, Luke, and John.

NEW TESTAMENT SCRIPTURE IN
THE EARLY WESTERN CHURCH

If the formation of the various Christian Old Testaments was a messy and drawn out affair, it was no less so for the formation of the various Christian New Testaments that exist today. At first, the early Christian churches scattered across Asia, Europe, and North Africa relied only on Jewish books as their sole set of written scriptures.[92] When Christian writings began to be considered as scripture early in the second century CE, each church, e.g., the church at Jerusalem, Antioch, Alexandria, Rome, etc., was independent of every other church. Each bishop of each church was free to define what was and was not considered Christian scripture for his own church. As a result, as is illustrated in the following presentation, there were sometimes wide variations among churches and among church leaders with regard to what was considered to be scripture.

(1) The Muratorian Canon was composed circa 170-200 CE[93] and offers a listing of books comprising the New Testament canon as the author knew it. The list includes two books not found in the 27-book New Testament canon revered by Protestant, Roman Catholic, and Greek Orthodox Christians. These two books are the Apocalypse of Peter and the Wisdom of Solomon, the latter being the same book that appears in the Roman Catholic, Greek Orthodox, Russian Orthodox, and Ethiopian Orthodox Old Testaments. Further, the list does not include five books currently in the 27-book New Testament canon. These five books are III John, James, Hebrews, and I and II Peter.[94]

---

[92] (A) Metzger BM (1997); (B) Sundberg AC (1971).

[93] While Sundberg AC (1973) and McDonald LM (2005), both date the Muratorian Canon to the fourth century CE, the vast majority of scholars, e.g., Metzger BM (1997), Kee HC (1997b), Ferguson E (1982), and Hinson EG (1997), place it in the latter fourth of the second century CE.

[94] (A) Hinson EG (1997); (B) Metzger BM (1997).

(2) Saint Irenaeus was born of Greek parents circa 120-140 CE in Asia Minor. As a child, he heard and saw Polycarp in Smyrna, Polycarp being the last living Christian to have had direct contact with the actual disciples of Jesus. Prior to 177 CE, Irenaeus served as a missionary in southern France. He was consecrated Bishop of Lyon (Lugdunum), a city that is located in southern France, in 177 CE. His principle written work is his *Adversus Omnes Haereses*, which was written circa 180 CE. Irenaeus died circa 200-203 CE, and his Western feast day is June 28th, while his Eastern feast day is August 23rd.[95]

In his *Adversus Omnes Haereses*, Irenaeus specifically cites the Shepherd of Hermas, a book generally considered to be New Testament Apocrypha, as being divine scripture.[96] Of further note, Irenaeus never once quoted from Jude, II Peter, James, Hebrews, III John, and Philemon, although he quoted from every other book that is currently included in the 27-book New Testament canon of most contemporary Christians. While his failure to quote from III John and Philemon may be secondary to the brevity of these two books, his failure to quote from the other four books may well indicate that he did not consider them to be scripture.[97]

(3) Tertullian, aka Quintus Eptimus Florens Tertullianus, was born circa 155-160 CE in Carthage, a city located in what is today the country of Tunisia in North Africa. He was educated at Carthage in grammar, rhetoric, literature, philosophy, and law. Subsequently, he journeyed to Rome for further study. When he returned to Carthage towards the end of the second century CE, he converted from paganism to Christianity.

---

[95] Wingren G (2003).
[96] (A) Sundberg AC (1971); (B) Hinson EG (1997); (C) Metzger BM (1997).
[97] Hinson EG (1997).

Tertullian quickly became one of the bright stars of North African Christianity and was apparently ordained into the priesthood. Dissatisfied with the laxity that he observed in Christianity, Tertullian converted to Montanism prior to 210 CE. His date of death is unknown.[98]

From Tertullian's voluminous writings as a Christian, one can determine that he recognized as scripture Matthew, Mark, Luke, John, the Acts of the Apostles, the 13 "Pauline" epistles, Hebrews, I John, I Peter, Jude, and Revelation. Further, at least early in his Christian career, he appeared to consider the Shepherd of Hermas as being scripture, although he subsequently changed his mind about this book. However, he never quoted from or referenced II Peter, James, and II and III John.[99]

(4) Saint Hippolytus of Rome was born circa 170 CE and died a martyr in 235 CE. Not much is known about his early life, although he apparently had been a pupil of Irenaeus. Circa 217-22 CE, Hippolytus came into conflict with Pope Callistus. He was then elected Bishop of Rome and became the first antipope. Hippolytus' writings indicate that he accepted only 22 books as being New Testament scripture, including Matthew, Mark, Luke, John, Acts, Romans, I and II Corinthians, Galatians, Ephesians, Philippians, Colossians, I and II Thessalonians, I and II Timothy, Titus, Philemon, I Peter, I and II John, and Revelation. Of note, he did not accept Hebrews, James, II Peter, III John, and Jude as inspired scripture. While he frequently quoted from Hebrews, it should be noted that he did not recognize it as scripture and that he also quoted from the Shepherd of Hermas, the Didache, the Epistle of Barnabas, the Apocalypse of Peter, the Acts of Peter, and the Acts of Paul.

---

[98] Wilkin RL (2003).
[99] Metzger BM (1997).

In short, Hippolytus recognized only a 22-book New Testament.[100]

(5) Origen, aka Oregenes Adamantius, was born circa 185 CE, probably in Alexandria, Egypt, and died circa 254 CE in Tyre, Phoenicia (now Lebanon). Origen's father Leonides was martyred in the persecution of Christians that took place in 202 CE under Emperor Septimus Severus of Rome. He became a pupil of Clement of Alexandria and later succeeded Clement as head of the catechetical school in Alexandria. A scholar of the first rank, Origen was a prolific writer, authoring a 32-book commentary on the Gospel of John, a commentary on the Gospel of Matthew that comprised at least 17 volumes, as well as a number of other commentaries on Old Testament and New Testament books. During a trip to Greece circa 229 CE, he was ordained a presbyter at Caesarea. He was imprisoned and tortured during the reign of Emperor Decius in 250 CE.[101]

Writing in the third century CE, Origen named several books as being of dubious authenticity or as having their status as scripture disputed. Among those books he classified in this manner were a number of books that eventually were accepted into the 27-book New Testament canon, including II Peter, II and III John, James, and Jude.[102] He also reported that several books that were eventually rejected from inclusion in the 27-book New Testament canon were regarded as scripture in some churches, while being rejected in others. Included in this group of books that were accepted as divine scripture in some Christian churches were the Epistle of Barnabas, the Shepherd of Hermas, and the Didache.[103] In addition, it is noted that Origen quoted from the Gospel of the Hebrews.[104]

---

[100] Metzger BM (1997).
[101] Chadwick H (2003).
[102] (A) Hinson EG (1997); (B) Metzger BM (1997).
[103] Hinson EG (1997).
[104] Metzger BM (1997).

(6) Cyprian of Carthage, aka Thascius Caecilius Cyprianus, was born circa 200-210 CE in Carthage. He received a good education and became a teacher of rhetoric and oratory. Circa 246 CE, he converted from paganism to Christianity. After only two years as a Christian, Cyprian was consecrated as the Bishop of Carthage, becoming the ecclesiastical head of all clergy in North Africa. As Bishop of Carthage, he authored numerous letters, treatises, and literary works, which give some indication of what books he considered to be New Testament scripture. These books included Matthew, Mark, Luke, John, the "Pauline" epistles minus Philemon and Hebrews, I Peter, I John, and Revelation. In contrast, he never once quoted or cited Hebrews, which he clearly considered to be non-canonical, Philemon, James, II Peter, II and III John, and Jude. He was martyred in 258.[105]

(7) Circa 300 CE, an anonymous author, perhaps a Catholic bishop writing in North Africa, penned *Adversus Aleatores* (Against Dice-Players). Of note, this text clearly cites the Shepherd of Hermas and the Didache as being "divine scripture."[106]

NEW TESTAMENT SCRIPTURE IN THE EARLY EASTERN CHURCH

(1) Tatian was born to pagan parents in Syria circa 120 CE. As a young man, he traveled from Syria to Rome where he converted to Christianity under the influence of Justin Martyr. While in Rome, he wrote the Greek Diatessaron, which was a harmonizing of the gospels of Matthew, Mark, Luke, and John. Circa 172, he returned to Syria where he founded, or at least became closely associated with, the Encraitites, an

---

[105] Metzger BM (1997).
[106] Metzger BM (1997).

extremely ascetic sect of Christianity that rejected matrimony, the eating of meat, and the drinking of wine. Thereafter, he translated his Diatessaron into Syriac, and it quickly became the only gospel accepted by the Syrian church. Thereafter, the Diatessaron continued to be the only authoritative gospel in the Syrian church for almost two centuries. Tatian died in April of 173 CE.[107]

With regard to the Diatessaron, it is instructive to note that the 14 "Pauline" epistles were added to the Diatessaron in the third century to create an early Syrian New Testament [108] and that the Doctrine of Addai, which was written circa 400 CE, provides a listing of the New Testament books that were authorized in the Syriac-speaking church. The following quotation refers to some Old Testament books, i.e., the Law and the Prophets, and refers to "the Gospel," i.e., the Diatessaron. In addition to the Diatessaron, the New Testament was to include the Pauline epistles and the Acts of the Apostles. As can be seen, at the minimum, this listing of the New Testament excluded James, I and II Peter, Jude, Revelation, I, II, and III John, and the gospels of Matthew, Mark, Luke, and John!

> The Law and the Prophets and the Gospel from which you read every day before the people, and the Epistles of Paul which Simon Cephas sent us from the city of Rome, and the Acts of the Twelve Apostles which John the son of Zebedee sent us from Ephesus—from these writings you shall read in the Churches of the Messiah, and besides them nothing else shall you read.[109]

---

[107] (A) Sundberg AC (1971); (B) Metzger BM (1997); (C) --- (2003o).
[108] Stendahl K, Sander ET (2003).
[109] Phillips G (1876), as quoted in Metzger BM (1997), p. 114.

(2) Clement of Alexandria, aka Titus Flavius Clement, converted from paganism to Christianity as an adult. Arriving in Egypt circa 180 CE, he became successively a student of Pantaenus, a presbyter (priest), and then about 190 CE the head of the catechetical school at Alexandria. In 202 CE, Clement was forced to flee Egypt because of the persecution of Christians going on under Emperor Septimus Severus. Clement died circa 215 CE.[110]

Clement quoted approvingly or referenced several books that later failed to be included in any New Testament canon. For example, he cited the Gospel of the Egyptians eight times, the Gospel of the Hebrews three times, and the Traditions of Matthias three times.[111] He also quoted from the Epistle of Barnabas, I Clement, the Shepherd of Hermas, the Didache, and the Preaching of Peter.[112] While being a book cited by Clement does not necessarily mean that Clement considered the book to be scripture, there are indications that Clement did consider several books that did not find their way into the 27-book New Testament canon favored by most modern Christians to be inspired scripture. For example, he once quoted a passage from the Gospel of the Hebrews by saying, "It is written," a verbal formula indicating that what is being quoted was considered scripture.[113] He referred to the Shepherd of Hermas as being "divinely spoken and by revelation."[114] Furthermore, he apparently considered I Clement, the Epistle of Barnabas, and the Apocalypse of Peter to be inspired scripture.[115] In contrast, not once in Clement's writings did he ever cite any passage from Philemon, James, II Peter, and II and III John.[116]

---

[110] Metzger BM (1997).
[111] (A) Metzger BM (1997); (B) McDonald LM (2005).
[112] McDonald LM (2005).
[113] Metzger BM (1997).
[114] Sundberg AC (1971), p. 1221.
[115] (A) Hinson EG (1997); (B) Metzger BM (1997); (C) Sundberg AC (1971).
[116] Metzger BM (1997).

(3) Saint Lucian of Antioch was born circa 240 CE in Samosata (now Samsat, Turkey). He was a noted Biblical scholar and became the Bishop of Antioch, i.e., one of the five patriarchs or princes of the church. He died on January 7, 312, in Nicomedia (now Izmit, Turkey), having been martyred by torture and starvation for refusing to eat meat that had been dedicated to the pagan gods of Rome.[117]

Lucian rejected a number of books that eventually found their way into the 27-book New Testament canon. Among those books so rejected by Lucian, one finds II Peter, II and III John, Jude, and Revelation. Thus, Lucian offered a 22-book New Testament that was accepted by the Syrian churches as their New Testament canon for over two centuries and that is still the official New Testament canon of the East Syrian Church.[118]

(4) Three great Cappadocian scholars emerged in the fourth century CE. One was Saint Gregory of Nazianzus, the son of Gregory, Bishop of Nazianzus in Cappadocia (now Turkey). Gregory was born circa 330 CE in Arianzus in Cappadocia (now in Turkey) and studied at Caesarea, Alexandria, and Athens (circa 351-356 CE). In 362 CE, Gregory was ordained into the priesthood and in 372 CE was consecrated as Bishop of Sasima, a position from which he quickly retired. From 379-381 CE, he served as Bishop and Patriarch of Constantinople, arguably the second highest position in all of Christendom, a position from which he voluntarily retired. He died in Arianzus circa 389 CE.[119]

The second was Saint Basil of Caesarea, the brother of Saint Gregory of Nyssa. Basil was born circa 329 CE, was baptized into the Christian faith

---

[117] --- (2003n).
[118] Hinson EG (1997).
[119] (A) Hardy ER (2003a); (B) Danielou J, Marrou H (1964).

circa 357, and then embraced the monastic life for a few years. He was ordained into the priesthood circa 365 and was later consecrated Bishop (Metropolitan) of Caesarea in 370 CE, from which position he fought tirelessly for the Trinitarian formulation of the godhead. He died on January 1, 379.[120]

The third Cappadocian scholar was Saint Gregory of Nyssa, aka Gregorius Nyssenus, the brother of Saint Basil of Caesarea. This Gregory was born in Caesarea (now Kayseri, Turkey) circa 335 CE. In his late 20s, after having worked as a teacher of rhetoric, he appears to have focused on religious studies. Circa 371, Gregory was consecrated as Bishop of Nyssa. Deposed from his episcopacy in 376, Gregory was later reinstated to his ecclesiastical post in 378. He died circa 394, having been a prolific writer for early Christianity.[121]

Saint Gregory of Nazianzus clearly rejected Revelation from his list of New Testament scriptures, resulting in a 26-book New Testament canon that otherwise conformed to the contemporary New Testament of Protestant, Roman Catholic, and Greek Orthodox Christians.[122] This 26-book canon was later ratified by the Trullan Synod in 692 CE![123] Further, it appears that both Saint Basil of Caesarea and Saint Gregory of Nyssa also rejected Revelation. As such, it appears that all three Cappadocian Fathers preferred a 26-book canon of the New Testament.[124]

---

[120] Danielou J, Marrou H (1964).
[121] (A) Hardy ER (2003b); (B) Danielou J, Marrou H (1964).
[122] (A) Hinson EG (1997); (B) Metzger BM (1997).
[123] Metzger BM (1997).
[124] Hinson EG (1997).

(5) Saint Epiphanius of Constantia (circa 315-403 CE) was born in Palestine, studied and practiced monasticism in Egypt, and then founded a monastery in Palestine. In 367, he became the Bishop of Constantia in Cyprus, and while in that post he wrote the *Panarian*, which was his major work.[125] In the 370s, Epiphanius included the Wisdom of Solomon in his list of New Testament books.[126] Ironically, this is the same book that is currently included in the Old Testament canons of the Roman Catholic, Greek Orthodox, Russian Orthodox, and Ethiopian Orthodox churches

(6) Theodore (circa 340-428 CE) was ordained a priest at Antioch and was later named Bishop of Mopsuestia, a position he held from 392 until 428 CE.[127] Theodore rejected a number of books that later were to be included in the 27-book New Testament canon. Included in Theodore's list of rejected books were James, Jude, I and II Peter, Revelation, and I, II, and III John, leaving Theodore with a 19-book New Testament.[128]

ATTEMPTING TO CLOSE THE NEW TESTAMENT CANON

As can be seen from the preceding discussion, there was no concept of an authorized and closed canon of New Testament scripture during the first three centuries of the so-called Christian era.[129] Various books were viewed as scriptural based either upon their self-stated claim to being inspired or upon their circulation and popularity among the various Christian churches.[130] As such, what was regarded as scripture in one

---

[125] --- (2003m).
[126] Fox RL (1992).
[127] Danielou J, Marrou H (1964).
[128] Hinson EG (1997).
[129] Fox RL (1992).
[130] Sundberg AC (1971).

locality was not regarded as scripture in another locality. However, in the fourth century CE, the situation slowly began to change as attempts began to define a closed canon of New Testament scripture, although different churches in the Roman Empire continued to uses different collections of scripture into the fifth century CE.[131]

(1) In the fifth-century CE Codex Claromontanus, there is a list of books comprising both the Old and New Testaments. While this list is written in Latin, it appears to have been originally written in Greek circa 300 CE, perhaps at Alexandria, Egypt. The New Testament list includes the following books: (A) the gospels of Matthew, Mark, Luke, and John; (B) 10 "Pauline" epistles, including Romans, I and II Corinthians, Galatians, Ephesians, I and II Timothy, Titus, Colossians, and Philemon; (C) I and II Peter; (D) James; (E) I, II, and III John; (F) Jude; (G) Revelation; and (H) the Acts of the Apostles. Thus, only 23 books of the 27-book New Testament canon accepted by most contemporary Christians can be found in this list. I and II Thessalonians, Hebrews, and Philippians are missing from this New Testament canon. However, of even greater interest, the list goes on to include the following books as being part of the New Testament: (A) the Epistle of Barnabas; (B) the Shepherd of Hermas; (C) the Acts of Paul, which is not to be confused with the Acts of the Apostles; and (D) the Revelation of Peter.[132]

The above listing of the books comprising the New Testament omits four books currently found in the 27-book New Testament canon. Further, it includes four books not currently found in the 27-book New Testament, although as will be seen later the Shepherd of Hermas may still be part of

---

[131] (A) Hinson EG (1997); (B) Sundberg AC (1971).
[132] (A) Metzger BM (1997); (B) Sundberg AC (1971).

the New Testament canon of the Ethiopian Orthodox Church. Clearly, this was a radically different New Testament than the one read by most contemporary Christians! Nonetheless, this was the New Testament of the author of this list circa 300 CE.

(2) In his *Ecclesiastical History*, Eusebius Pamphili (circa 260-339 CE), the fourth-century Bishop of Caesarea and prominent church historian, proposed a canon of New Testament scripture. Of significance, this proposed canon omitted many books currently found in the New Testament shared by Protestant, Roman Catholic, and Greek Orthodox Christians. For example, Eusebius rejected Revelation as being "not genuine," and he listed James, Jude, II Peter, and II and III John as being disputed.[133]

> At this point it may be appropriate to list the New Testament writings already referred to. The holy quartet of the Gospels are first, followed by the Acts of the Apostles. Next are Paul's epistles, I John, and I Peter...Those that are disputed yet known to most are the epistles called James, Jude, 2 Peter, and the so-named 2 and 3 John...Among the spurious books are the Acts of Paul, the Shepherd (of Hermas), the Revelation of Peter, the alleged epistle of Barnabas, the so-called Teachings of the Apostles (Didache), as well as the Revelation of John, if appropriate here.[134]

(3) Circa 360-367 CE, about 30 clergy gathered at the Synod of Laodicea, in what is today Turkey.[135] This council authorized a 26-book New Testament canon, all the books of which can be found in the contemporary Protestant,

---

[133] (A) Sundberg AC (1971); (B) Metzger BM (1997).
[134] Eusebius (1999), p. 115.
[135] Metzger BM (1997).

Roman Catholic, and Greek Orthodox New Testaments.[136] However, the council of clergy specifically rejected Revelation from the canon of New Testament scriptures,[137] thus demonstrating the continuing difficulty Revelation had in finding acceptance within Eastern Christianity.

(4) Saint Cyril of Jerusalem (circa 315-386 CE) was born in Jerusalem. In 350, having already been a senior presbyter in the church, Cyril was consecrated as Bishop of Jerusalem. In this position, he authored a collection of 23 catechetical lectures.[138] Included in these lectures is a definitive listing of Cyril's 26-book New Testament canon, which conformed exactly to the listing from the Synod of Laodicea. Of note, Cyril wrote of "a seal upon" these 26 books, indicating that in his mind the New Testament canon was now closed. Of note, once again, Revelation was omitted from the New Testament.[139]

(5) In 367 CE, Athanasius, the Bishop of Alexandria, circulated an Easter letter, which included the first listing of New Testament scripture to conform exactly to the New Testament currently shared by Protestant, Roman Catholic, and Greek Orthodox Christians,[140] although only a few years before he had still been championing the Shepherd of Hermas as being scripture, and although his Easter letter listed the Shepherd of Hermas and the Teaching of the Apostles, aka Didache, as books to be read by those receiving Christian education.[141] This canon of New Testament scripture was later ratified at the Council of Hippo in 393, the

---

[136] Some scholars, e.g., Metzger BM (1997), maintain that the list of New Testament books at the close of the Decrees of Laodicea was a later edition to the text.
[137] (A) Hinson EG (1997); (B) Jefford CN (1997).
[138] --- (2003p).
[139] Metzger BM (1997).
[140] (A) Hinson EG (1997); (B) Sundberg AC (1971).
[141] Sundberg AC (1971).

Synod of Carthage in 397, and the Carthaginian Council in 419.[142] However, there was not agreement with this proposed canon among most of the so-called Eastern churches until the sixth century CE, when the Syriac translation of circa 508 finally conformed to this canon.[143] However, even then, several Eastern churches continued to reject the 27-book New Testament canon as defined by Athanasius.

That Athanasius' proposed New Testament canon was not universally accepted can be readily seen by examining the earliest known copies of the New Testament. For example, the fourth-century CE Codex Sinaiticus adds the Letter of Barnabas and the Shepherd of Hermas to the 27-book New Testament canon. Codex Vaticanus, another fourth-century *Bible*, has a New Testament that lacks Philemon, Revelation, the Pastoral Epistles (Titus and I and II Timothy), and part of Hebrews. However, it may be that all these omissions are due to the manuscript simply being incomplete. Codex Alexandrinus is an early fifth-century CE manuscript of the *Bible*, and while it includes most of the 27-book New Testament canon, it also includes I and II Clement.[144]

It is rather amazing to consider that the three oldest *Bibles* that continue to exist in contemporary times have New Testaments that disagree with each other and that disagree with the 27-book New Testament of most modern Christians. At a minimum, these early *Bibles* suggest that the Letter of Barnabas, the Shepherd of Hermas, and I and II Clement were considered by many Christians of the fourth and fifth centuries CE to be legitimate books of the New Testament, despite attempts to close the

---

[142] (A) Hinson EG (1997); (B) Sundberg AC (1971); (C) Metzger BM (1997).
[143] Sundberg AC (1971).
[144] (A) Stendahl K, Sander ET (2003); (B) Reumann J (1971); (C) Bullard RA (1997).

New Testament canon by limiting it to the 27 books currently comprising the Protestant, Roman Catholic, and Greek Orthodox New Testaments!

Things were even more removed from Athanasius' proposed New Testament canon in the Syrian churches. For example, in 417 CE, Rabbula, the Bishop of Edessa, revised the New Testament previously used in the Syrian church. He deleted the Diatessaron and added James, I Peter, I John, and the gospels of Matthew, Mark, Luke, and John. This New Testament was called the *Peshitta* and had a total of 22 books. It continued to omit II Peter, II and III John, Jude, and Revelation from its New Testament canon. The *Peshitta* remained the New Testament of the Syrian church until around the seventh century CE.[145]

THE NEW TESTAMENT CANON TODAY

As can be seen from the above discussion, there were major disagreements within Christianity well into the fifth century about what did and did not constitute the New Testament. What most contemporary Christians probably don't know is that some of those disagreements continue to exist even until today. While the Protestant, Roman Catholic, and Greek Orthodox churches all eventually came to share the same 27-book New Testament canon, different New Testament canons developed independently for the East Syrian, Ethiopian Orthodox, and Coptic churches of Christianity. These differences continue to exist at present. The New Testament canons of these three branches of Christianity all differ from both the 27-book canon and from each other.

---

[145] (A) Hinson EG (1997); (B) Stendahl K, Sander ET (2003).

Figure # 5

BOOKS ADDED TO OR DELETED FROM
THE 27-BOOK NEW TESTAMENT CANON BY
THE EAST SYRIAN, ETHIOPIAN ORTHODOX,
AND COPTIC NEW TESTAMENTS*

EAST SYRIAN (NESTORIAN)	COPTIC	ETHIOPIAN ORTHODOX [146]
(II Peter)	I Clement	I Sinodos
(II John)	II Clement	II Sinodos
(III John)		III Sinodos
(Jude)		IV Sinodos
(Revelation)		I Book of the Covenant
		II Book of the Covenant
		Clement [147]
		Didascalia
		Shepherd of Hermas

* Books enclosed in parentheses are ones that
have been deleted from the 27-book canon.

---

[146] The exact parameters of the Ethiopian Orthodox Church's New Testament canon are difficult to delineate. This list given here is not meant to be seen as totally comprehensive and
definitive. See Cowley RW (1974) and Beckwith R (1985) for a fuller discussion of the difficulties in determining the exact New Testament canon of the Ethiopian Orthodox Church.
[147] Clement in the Ethiopian Orthodox New Testament is a totally different book than either
I or II Clement in the Coptic New Testament.

SUMMARY AND CONCLUSIONS

As should be clear by now, early Christianity had major disagreements as to what should and should not be included in its Old Testament and in its newly emerging New Testament. To a certain extent, these differences were especially apparent when comparing Eastern and Western Christianity, although in the earliest stages of Christianity, each church was an independent entity that decided its own scripture and doctrine. Over the centuries some consensus began to emerge among the churches, but complete agreement was never achieved with regard to the canons of both the Old and New Testaments. As a result, it is highly misleading to speak of the *Bible* as though there were only one *Bible*, when in fact there are current even today at least five different Old Testament canons and four different New Testament canons within contemporary Christianity.

CHAPTER 2

PAUL OF TARSUS AND
THE ORIGINS OF CHRISTIANITY

Paul was the…first corrupter of the doctrines of Jesus.
(Thomas Jefferson's 1820 letter to William Short)[148]

INTRODUCTION

THE ABOVE QUOTED WORDS FROM Thomas Jefferson are a
harsh and unflinching indictment of the Apostle Paul. What could have
possibly caused the third president of the United States to level such a
charge against the chief missionary of the nascent Christian community
to the gentiles? On what basis did he make his accusations against this
canonized saint of contemporary Christianity?

Before one casually dismisses Jefferson's assertion as the ravings of an
18th- and 19th-century Deist[149] who was intoxicated by the French
Enlightenment's emphasis on rationality, one should note that a number
of influential Christian thinkers and theologians have shared Jefferson's
sentiment. For example, consider the following words of Soren
Kierkegaard, the 19th-century theologian from Denmark.

> When Jesus Christ lived, he was indeed the prototype. The task
> of faith is…to imitate Christ, become a disciple…Now, through
> the Apostle Paul, comes a basic alteration…He draws attention
> away from imitation and fixes it decisively upon the death of

---

[148] Washington HA (1854).
[149] See chapter seven for a discussion of Jefferson's religious orientation.

Christ The Atoner...What Luther failed to realize is that the true situation is that the Apostle (Paul) has already degenerated by comparison with the Gospel...It becomes the disciple who decides what Christianity is, not the master, not Christ but Paul...(who) threw Christianity away completely, turning it upside down, getting it to be just the opposite of what it is in the (original) Christian proclamation.[150]

Protestantism is altogether untenable. It is a revolution brought on by proclaiming "the Apostle" (Paul) at the expense of the Master (Christ)...We confess that this teaching is a mitigation of Christianity which we humans have allowed ourselves, appealing to God to put up with it.[151]

Kierkegaard's words ring even more harshly in the ears of a contemporary Christian than do Jefferson's. For Kierkegaard, it was not just that Paul corrupted the teachings of Jesus but that Paul completely discarded them and, in fact, preached the opposite of what Christ had taught. Bear in mind that with Kierkegaard we are not dealing with an anti-Christian Deist like Jefferson, but with one of the most pre-eminent Christian theologians of the 19th century.

If Jefferson and Kierkegaard were not enough, one can easily locate additional anti-Pauline sentiments. For example, consider the following words of Ferdinand Christian Baur and Walter Bauer, two extremely qualified church historians. While Ferdinand Baur wrote his textbook of church history in the late 19th century, Walter Bauer wrote his *Orthodoxy and Heresy in Earliest Christianity* in the 20th century. In

---

[150] Kierkegaard S (---).
[151] Kierkegaard S (1996), p. 629.

addition, also consider the following statement of Howard Clark Kee, the Rufus Jones Professor of the History of Religion at Bryn Mawr College.

> The only question comes to be how the apostle Paul appears in his Epistles to be so indifferent to the historical facts of the life of Jesus. He seldom appeals to any traditions on the subject, though his apostolic activity, as well as that of the other apostles, would have been meaningless without them. He bears himself but little like a disciple who has received the doctrines and the principles which he preaches from the Master whose name he bears... A very personal question has now come to the front, a question which could not fail to be raised sooner or later, namely, the apostolic authority of Paul. What authority could he claim? In whatever way he had come to his present position, it certainly could not be said of him that he had become an apostle in the same way as the older apostles; was it not doubtful whether he could be regarded as a true and genuine apostle at all? [152]

> Thus, if one may be allowed to speak rather pointedly, the apostle Paul was the only heresiarch (Arch-Heretic) known to the apostolic age—the only one who was so considered in that period...With regard to...the authentic tradition of the life of Jesus,...we do know that Paul made little use of it in his preaching. [153]

We can postulate the existence of a formal and theological gap in the early church between the message of Paul and that of the gospel tradition...Other historians of early Christianity insist that a choice be made between Jesus and Paul. Some treat the

---

[152] Baur FC (1878), p. 50 & 61.
[153] Bauer W (1971), p. 236.

message of Paul as a regrettable development that has been super-imposed on the simple ethical message of Jesus…Others think that the message of Jesus…does not go beyond the categories of Judaism, and they consider Paul the source of the essential Christian message. [154]

What are we to make of this fusillade, fired broadside at Paul, by some of the most eminent Christian thinkers of the last few centuries? The answer lies in Paul's own works and writings. However, before beginning that journey, it is best to consider nascent Christianity at the time of Paul, just exactly what comprises the Pauline corpus of writings, and the life of Paul.

NASCENT CHRISTIANITY

Early Christianity was not a monolithic structure. Speaking in broad terms and at the risk of overly simplifying, first-century Christianity was characterized by three main groupings: Jewish Christianity, Gnostic Christianity, and Pauline Christianity.

Although not yet called Christianity, the earliest form of what would later be called Christianity was represented by the actual disciples of Jesus and by James the Just, the brother of Jesus and first Bishop of the Jerusalem Church. This brand of Christianity, often referred to as Jewish Christianity, restricted its message to the "children of Israel," continued to worship in the temple in Jerusalem, and did not even call themselves Christians, a term that first arose in the gentile church in Antioch, as witnessed by Acts 11:20-26. In fact, the early Christian Church of Jerusalem, led by the disciples and immediate followers of Jesus, was

---

[154] Kee HC (1977), p. 122-123.

proclaimed at the time to be authentically Jewish by no less a Jewish authority than Rabbi Gamaliel, the grandson of Rabbi Hillel, both of whom are recognized as being the preeminent Jewish scholars surrounding the time of Christ. [155]

Given the pronouncement by Rabbi Gamaliel that the Jerusalem Church was authentically Jewish, one can comfortably assert that the Jewish Christian movement, including the Jerusalem Church, Bishop James the Just, and the actual disciples of Jesus, did not ascribe divinity to Jesus and did not forsake the so-called Law of Moses. Furthermore, this Jewish-Christian tradition continued well after the destruction of the temple of Jerusalem in 70 CE. Such early Christian movements as the Ebionites, the Nazarenes (not to be confused with the modern Christian denomination), and the Elkasites appear to have represented this Jewish Christian tradition. With regard to the longevity of this Jewish Christian movement within early Christianity, one can point particularly to the Ebionites, who were apparently established shortly before the destruction of the temple in 70, whereupon they fled from the vicinity of Jerusalem and spread to what is today Jordan, Syria, Turkey, and Egypt. Of note, the Ebionites continued as a viable movement within greater Christianity throughout the second, third, and fourth centuries. Likewise, the Nazarenes were known to have existed in greater Syria at least as late as the fourth century, while the Elkasites also thrived from the second through fourth centuries. [156]

The second major movement within nascent Christianity was Gnostic Christianity. Not much was known with certainty about this movement prior to the discovery of early Gnostic Christian texts at Nag Hammadi,

---

[155] Armstrong K (1994), p. 79.
[156] (A) --- (2003s); (B) --- (2003t); (C) Koester H (1982), p. 198-207.

Egypt, in 1945. While there appear to have been many different Gnostic Christian sects, e.g., the Docetists, Marcionites, Basilideans, etc., there were some commonalities shared by most of them. Among those common beliefs shared by the Gnostic Christian sects, one can include the following: the god of creation and of the Old Testament was a demigod or demiurge who was not to be confused with the God of Jesus; the former was seen as being vain, angry, and demanding justice, while the latter was seen as goodness; a fundamental dualism existed between material creation (evil) and spirit (good); Jesus taught a secret knowledge (*gnosis*) that was the basis for redemption and that only the adepts were to be taught; Jesus did not have a corporeal body, but only a phantom body; and Jesus was not actually crucified, and a phantasm or substitute, e.g., Simon of Cyrene according to the Basilideans, was crucified in his place. Prominent early Gnostic Christians included Simon Magus, Theodotus the Gnostic, Marcion, Cerdo, Valentinus, Basilides, etc. [157]

It was against the backdrop of these two Christian movements that Paul introduced his own gospel, which was fundamentally opposed to Gnostic Christianity. With regards to Jewish Christianity, Paul's gospel shared some elements with it, but Pauline Christianity differed from Jewish Christianity in many others. Some of these differences between Pauline and Jewish Christianity will be discussed in some depth later in this chapter.

THE PAULINE CORPUS

At one time, it was widely held that Paul wrote 14 letters that were incorporated into the New Testament, as well as some letters that were lost. However, at present, almost all Biblical scholars reject Pauline authorship of Hebrews, and most also reject the concept that Paul wrote I and II

---

[157] (A) Jonas H (1967); (B) Pagels E (1979); (C) --- (2003u).

Timothy and Titus, while admitting that these latter three books represent Pauline thinking. In addition, many Biblical scholars see Ephesians, Colossians, and II Thessalonians as being authored by someone other than Paul, although again admitting that they reflect the Pauline approach to Christianity. The only undisputed Pauline works among modern Biblical scholars are Romans, I Corinthians, II Corinthians, Galatians, Philippians, I Thessalonians, and Philemon.[158]

Given the above, only seven books of the New Testament can be said to be primary source material on Paul, i.e., Romans, I Corinthians, II Corinthians, Galatians, Philippians, I Thessalonians, and Philemon. The remaining epistles that were once attributed to Paul, as well as the Biblical book of Acts, must be seen as secondary source material that stands at least one position removed from being firsthand evidence. In addition to these seven primary and seven secondary sources from the New Testament, there is another body of secondary source material having to do with Paul or falsely ascribed to Paul that is found in apocryphal Christian writings. This material includes the Acts of Paul and Thecla, the Clementine Homilies and Recognitions, the Letters of Paul and Seneca, the Acts of Paul, two different manuscripts entitled the Apocalypse of Paul, and the Prayer of the Apostle Paul.

In constructing an outline of Paul's life and teachings, the major emphasis will be on the seven Pauline epistles from the New Testament that can be reliably attributed to Paul. Secondary importance will be given to Acts and to the pseudo-Pauline epistles of the New Testament. Finally, the apocryphal Christian literature having to do with Paul will be utilized quite sparingly.

---

[158] (A) Drane JW (1993); (B) Soards ML (1997); (C) Robertson AT (2001); (D) Lindars B (2003).

A BRIEF *CURRICULUM VITAE*

In attempting to construct a brief survey of Paul's life, it must first of all be admitted that much of his life is shrouded in mystery and that little firm information exists concerning Paul's birth, childhood, early manhood, and eventual death[159] Further, even many of the dates and exact events of Paul's missionary efforts are in some dispute.[160] In fact, one might go so far as to maintain that the dating for every single event in the life of Paul is somewhat controversial, although the disagreements in dating some events have been narrowed down to a few years.[161] With such disclaimers in mind, the following brief outline of Paul's life is at least plausible.

Paul (Saul was his Hebrew name) was a Hellenized Jew who was born in Tarsus, a city in Cilicia (a part of what is today southern Turkey), probably in the first few years of the Common Era. [162] By his own report, he was a member of Israelite tribe of Benjamin,[163] but he was also born a Roman citizen.[164] As a Jewish child, Paul would have been educated in the Jewish faith at his local synagogue.[165] However, given Paul's residence in Tarsus, Paul's education would not have ended with his training at the local synagogue.

Situated on an alluvial plain next to the Tarsus River (aka Cydnus River), about 12 miles from the Mediterranean coast, Tarsus was a large metropolitan city that had been absorbed into the Roman province of Cilicia in 67 BCE.[166] While its economy was based primarily on agriculture and

---

[159] Soards ML (1997).
[160] For varying chronologies see the following: (A) Robertson AT (2001); (B) Soards ML (1997); (C) Duncan GB (1971a); (D) Peritz IJ (1929).
[161] Robertson AT (2001).
[162] Drane JW (1993).
[163] (A) Romans 11:1; (B) Philippians 3:5.
[164] Acts 16:37; 22:25-28.
[165] (A) Drane JW (1993); (B) Soards ML (1997).
[166] --- (2003q).

an important linen industry,[167] as well as being on the main trade route between East and West,[168] the real pride of Tarsus was its great university, which was known for its excellence in philosophy and educational literature.[169] In particular, the university at Tarsus was a center of Stoic thought,[170] a post-Aristotelian Greek philosophy founded by Zeno of Citium (Cyprus) that emphasized rationality, reason, and conduct marked by "tranquility of mind and certainty of moral worth."[171] As such, it is not surprising that some New Testament scholars see some Stoic influences in Paul's thought and writings, e.g., in I Corinthians 11:14, in I Corinthians 13, and in Paul's speech in Athens as reported in Acts 17.[172] Whether or not Paul was overtly influenced by Stoicism, he would certainly have been exposed to Stoic thought in Tarsus, as well as to the various mystery religions and myths of a dying-regenerating, redeemer god.[173]

At some point in his youth, Paul arrived in Jerusalem.[174] There, according to Acts 22:3, he received advanced studies in Judaism from the famous Rabbi Gamaliel, although some New Testament scholars doubt this assertion, as nowhere in Paul's own writings does he make this claim, even though he often tried to stress his Jewish credentials. In any case, Paul reportedly joined the Pharisaic sect of Judaism,[175] like his father before him.[176] In addition, some scholars have claimed that Paul became a rabbi

---

[167] --- (2003q).
[168] Lindars B (2003).
[169] (A) Robertson AT (2001); (B) --- (2003q).
[170] Robertson AT (2001).
[171] Saunders JL (2003).
[172] E.g., see Saunders JL (2003).
[173] (A) Saunders JL (2003); (B) Drane JW (1993); (C) Soards ML (1997).
[174] Acts 26:4.
[175] (A) Acts 23:6 & 26:5; (B) Philippians 3:5.
[176] Acts 23:6.

by age 30,[177] while other scholars find no evidence for this assertion.[178] Based upon their reading of Acts 26:10, some have even suggested that he became a member of the Jewish Sanhedrin,[179] which was the supreme Jewish legislative and judicial court in Palestine during the Roman occupation.[180] Regardless of whether or not Paul was a rabbi or even a member of the Sanhedrin, he would have had to support himself with a secular occupation, which in his case was that of a tentmaker.[181]

As a brief digression, it is noted that no physical description of Paul exists within the New Testament. However, the apocryphal Acts of Paul and Thecla 1:7 describes Paul as having been short, bald, bowlegged with crooked thighs, hollow-eyed and as having a crooked nose.[182] While lacking a physical description of Paul, the New Testament does suggest that Paul underwent numerous physical traumas after converting to his brand of Christianity, e.g., multiple imprisonments, being whipped with 39 stripes on five different occasions, beaten with rods on three occasions, stoned once, and shipwrecked three times.[183] These trauma apparently left Paul scarred with physical stigmata of some kind or another,[184] and they may have left him somewhat disfigured.[185]

Picking up the thread of Paul's life, we next meet him in Jerusalem around 34 CE at the stoning of Stephen, the first Christian martyr. As

---

[177] E.g., Robertson AT (2001).
[178] E.g., Soards ML (1997).
[179] (A) Drane JW (1993); (B) Robertson AT (2001).
[180] --- (2003zd).
[181] Acts 18:1-3.
[182] --- (1926).
[183] II Corinthians 11:23-26.
[184] Galatians 6:17.
[185] Robertson AT (2001).

portrayed in the Acts of the Apostles, Paul, at the very least, passively acquiesced to the murder of Stephen and may have been an active participant, helping to throw stones down on Stephen.

> When they heard these things, they were cut to the heart, and they gnashed on him with their teeth. But he (Stephen), being full of the Holy Ghost, looked up stedfastly into heaven, and saw the glory of God, and Jesus standing on the right hand of God. And said, Behold, I see the heavens opened, and the Son of man standing on the right hand of God. Then they cried out with a loud voice, and stopped their ears, and ran up on him with one accord, and cast him out of the city, and stoned him: and the witnesses laid down their clothes at a young man's feet, whose name was Saul (Paul). And they stoned Stephen, calling upon God, and saying, Lord Jesus, receive my spirit. And he kneeled down, and cried with a loud voice, Lord, lay not this sin to their charge. And when he had said this, he fell asleep. And Saul (Paul) was consenting unto his death. (Acts 7:54-8:1, King James Version)

Whether as a passive accomplice or as an active participant, Paul's involvement in the murder of Stephen was just the start of his brutal persecution of the nascent Christian community that was centered around the Jerusalem Church of James the Just, the brother of Jesus, and the actual disciples of Jesus. (As noted earlier in this chapter, this early form of Christianity as represented by the Jerusalem Church is best conceptualized as being Jewish Christian in nature.) Both Paul's own words and the secondary source material reported in Acts testify to Paul's attempt to exterminate the fledgling Jewish Christian community.

For I am the least of the apostles, that am not meet to be called an apostle, because I persecuted the church of God. (I Corinthians 15:9, King James Version)

For ye have heard of my conversation in time past in the Jews' religion, how that beyond measure I persecuted the church of God, and wasted it. (Galatians 1:13, King James Version)

And Saul, yet breathing out threatenings and slaughter against the disciples of the Lord, went unto the high priest, And desired of him letters to Damascus to the synagogues, that if he found any of this way, whether they were men or women, he might bring them bound into Jerusalem. (Acts 9:1-2, King James Version)

And I persecuted this way unto the death, binding and delivering into prisons both men and women. As also the high priest doth bear me witness, and all the estate of the elders from whom also I received letters unto the brethren, and went to Damascus to bring them which were there bound unto Jerusalem, for to be punished. (Acts 22:4-5, King James Version)

I verily thought with myself, that I ought to do many things contrary to the name of Jesus of Nazareth. Which thing I also did in Jerusalem: and many of the saints did I shut up in prison, having received authority from the chief priests; and when they were put to death, I gave my voice against them. (Acts 26:9-11, King James Version)

Having apparently secured the authorization of the Jewish authorities in Jerusalem, Paul proceeded to Damascus, probably his home city by that time,[186] in the company of a group of men. While on the road to Damascus, Paul supposedly underwent a miraculous conversion experience somewhere between the years 30-36 CE.[187] This event is described three times in Acts[188] and once in Galatians.[189] These four narratives of the conversion of Paul will be dealt with in some detail later in this chapter and will not be discussed now.

Reportedly converted, Paul spent a few days with the nascent Christian community in Damascus and then began his missionary activity by preaching at the Damascus synagogues. Arousing the anger of the Jews by his preaching, they plotted to kill him and lay in wait for him at the gates of the city. However, Paul escaped from Damascus by being lowered down from the wall of the city in a basket.[190]

What happened next is in some dispute. Acts 9:26-30 states that Paul's next move was to journey to Jerusalem, where he was initially rejected by the disciples of Jesus before they reportedly finally accepted him. Paul then spent a number of days in Jerusalem preaching in Jesus' name and arguing with the Hellenist Jews. At last, these Hellenist Jews plotted to kill Paul, and the disciples then sent Paul to Caesarea, from which he took a ship to Tarsus. In contrast to the above statement in Acts, Paul's own words state that he didn't immediately go to Jerusalem upon escaping from Damascus.

> Neither went I up to Jerusalem to them which were apostles before me; but I went into Arabia, and returned again unto Damascus. Then after three years I went up to Jerusalem to see Peter, and abode

---

[186] Soards ML (1997).

[187] (A) Soards ML (1997); (B) Robertson AT (2001); (C) Duncan G (1971a).

[188] Acts 9:3-19, 22:6-16, 26:12-18.

[189] Galatians 1:11-24.

[190] Acts 9:19-25.

with him fifteen days. But other of the apostles saw I none, save James the Lord's brother. (Galatians 1:17-19, King James Version)

According to Paul's own written record, it took him a full three years after his conversion to bother meeting with James the Just, Jesus' brother and head of the infant Christian community, and with Peter, one of the inner circle of Jesus' 12 disciples. Paul then spent only a little over two weeks with Peter, certainly not much time to familiarize himself with what the earthly Jesus had actually said and taught. Following that brief visit, Paul was hustled off to Caesarea, took a ship to Tarsus, and then engaged in missionary activity in Cilicia, Cyprus, South Galatia, and Syria.[191] After about 10 years in this mission field,[192] and after at some point having joined forces with Barnabas in Antioch,[193] Paul finally returns to Jerusalem to meet with James and the disciples,[194] at some point between 44 and 52 CE.[195]

This Jerusalem visit, frequently referred to as the Apostolic Council in Jerusalem, was a highly contentious meeting, which pitted Paul and his version of Christianity against the Jewish Christianity of James the Just, the disciples, and the Jerusalem Church. Paul briefly describes his version of this meeting in Galatians. One of the key issues of contention was Paul's abrogation of the Law of Moses regarding circumcision, dietary regulations, etc. For the Jewish Christians, the Law of Moses still held. The outcome of this conflict is investigated more fully later in this chapter.

As a slight digression, before proceeding to Paul's next missionary journey, it

---

[191] Galatians 1:21.
[192] Soards ML (1997).
[193] Lindars B (2003).
[194] (A) Soards ML (1997); (B) Lindars B (2003).
[195] (A) Soards ML (1997); (B) Duncan G (1971a); (C) Robertson AT (2001).

should be noted that Paul states that it was necessary for him to communicate "unto them that gospel which I preach…" This is a truly remarkable admission on Paul's part, suggesting that the Jerusalem Church, the actual headquarters of the earliest Christianity, had no idea what Paul was preaching and that what Paul was preaching was different from that taught by the Jerusalem Church.

> Then fourteen years after I went up again to Jerusalem with Barnabas, and took Titus with me also. And I went up by revelation, and communicated unto them that gospel which I preach among the Gentiles… (Galatians 2:1-2a, King James Version)

At some point between 46 and 52 CE, Paul began what is usually referred to as his second missionary journey.[196] On this journey, Paul was accompanied by Silas, having refused to take Barnabas because Barnabas insisted on taking Mark with them.[197] Traveling overland, Paul and Silas initially traveled through Syria and Cilicia, visiting the churches Paul had previously been at in his first missionary journey.[198] Stopping in Galatia,[199] Paul and Silas were joined by Timothy at the city of Lystra. Of note, Paul reportedly circumcised Timothy, who had not been previously circumcised because he had a Greek father, even though he had a Jewish mother.[200] This event is of some importance in evaluating Paul's mission, and its implications will be explored in more detail later.

From Galatia in southern Asia Minor, Paul traveled to Mysia (the northwestern corner of Asia Minor) and to the city of Troas on the Aegean coast.[201]

---

[196] (A) Robertson AT (2001); (B) Soards ML (1997); (C) Duncan G (1971a).
[197] Acts 15:36-40.
[198] Acts 15:41.
[199] Acts 16:6.
[200] Acts 16:1-3.
[201] Acts 16:7-8

From Troas, Paul moved to Macedonia and Greece, reportedly establishing churches in Philippi, Thessalonica, and Beroea, although running afoul of the Jews and magistrates in those areas.[202] Leaving Silas and Timothy behind in Thessalonica, Paul traveled to Athens[203] where he supposedly delivered his sermon on the "unknown god" that was being worshipped by some in Athens. Despite this sermon, Paul's efforts in Athens were generally unsuccessful, and no church was established there.[204]

From Athens, Paul moved to Corinth where he lived and worked with Aquila and Priscilla, fellow tentmakers.[205] In Corinth, Paul was again joined by Silas and Timothy,[206] and at Corinth Paul arguably had one of his most successful mission activities. He reportedly remained in Corinth for around two years.[207] (Note: Acts 18:14-17 identifies Gallio as being the proconsul in Corinth while Paul was there, and an inscription found at Delphi lists Gallio as having begun his year in office as proconsul in Corinth in 51 CE.)[208] From Corinth, Paul traveled with Aquila and Priscilla to Ephesus on the Aegean coast. Leaving Aquila and Priscilla in Ephesus, Paul then journeyed to Cenchreae where he shaved his head, then on to Caesarea, from where he continued on to Jerusalem, in order to keep a religious feast or festival in Jerusalem.[209]

Leaving Jerusalem, about which visit Paul never refers to in his own writings, he begins his third missionary journey by initially going to

---

[202] Acts 16:11-17:14.
[203] Acts 17:14-34.
[204] Lindars B (2003).
[205] Acts 18:1-3.
[206] Acts 18:5.
[207] Acts 18:11-18.
[208] Price JL (1971).
[209] Acts 18:19-21.

Antioch. Later, he moved to Ephesus, which was to be his base of operations for the next three years, and from which Paul apparently established churches at Colossae, Hierapolis, and Laodicea in the Lycus Valley. Towards the end of this three-year period, he moved again to Corinth. From Corinth, he then traveled to Jerusalem with a collection of money for the Christian community in Jerusalem (see Romans 15:25-27). At Jerusalem, Paul underwent the rites of a Nazirite (about which more later), was later arrested, and defended himself as best he could. When a plot to kill him became known, Paul was moved to Caesarea where he remained imprisoned for two years.[210]

Still a prisoner, Paul was sent by ship from Caesarea to Rome. The ship initially docked at Sidon and then continued past Cyprus before docking at Myra in Lycia. At Lycia, Paul was transferred to an Alexandrian ship sailing for Rome. This ship made poor progress before docking at Crete, as the wind was frequently against them. Leaving Crete, the ship was caught in a fierce storm and was shipwrecked at Malta. After spending three months at Malta, Paul was placed on another Alexandrian ship and was sent to Rome via Syracuse, Rhegium, and Puteoli. When he finally arrived at Rome, Paul was kept under house arrest for two years.[211]

Acts ends with Paul still under house arrest. Most New Testament scholars conclude that Paul was thereafter tried, found guilty, and put to death at Rome sometime during 61-67 CE, quite possibly during Nero's persecution of Christians.[212] As to Paul being martyred during Nero's reign, Bishop Eusebius of Caesarea (circa 260-339 CE), writing in his monumental *Ecclesiastical History*, noted the following.

---

[210] (A) Acts 18:22-26:32; (B) Lindars B (2003); (C) Soards ML (1997).

[211] (A) Acts 27:1-28:31.

[212] (A) Robertson AT (2001); (B) Soards ML (1997); (C) Lindars B (2003); (D) Duncan G (1971a).

> Once Nero's power was firmly established, he plunged into nefarious vices and took up arms against the God of the universe...It is related that in his reign Paul was beheaded in Rome itself...[213]

However, before immediately accepting that Paul's two years of house arrest resulted in his martyrdom, one should note that two alternative traditions exist within early Christianity concerning the fate of Paul. The first alternative is related by Bishop Eusebius of Caesarea, who claimed that Paul was able to defend himself successfully and was released from his Roman captivity. He then went on yet a fourth missionary journey before returning to Rome, where he was again arrested and then martyred.[214] If this fourth missionary journey actually happened, then Paul may have fulfilled his intention noted in Romans 15:24 and 28 to proselytize in Spain. Indeed, a letter attributed to Saint Clement of Rome (died either 97 or 101 CE, Bishop of Rome from 88-97 CE or from 92 to 101 CE)[215] suggests that Paul did travel to Spain on a fourth missionary journey before being beheaded in Rome.[216]

Still another early Christian tradition has Paul being released from Rome and undertaking a fourth missionary journey. This one also has Paul traveling to the West, presumably to Spain, before returning to the East. According to this tradition, Paul was martyred and entombed at Philippi, not at Rome. Indeed, a tomb reported to be that of Paul was a site of pilgrimage from at least the fourth through sixth centuries CE.[217]

---

[213] Eusebius (1999), p. 84-85.
[214] Eusebius (1999), p. 80.
[215] --- (2003r).
[216] Gardner JL (1983).
[217] Koester H (2007b).

PAUL VS. JESUS REGARDING THE LAW OF MOSES

Having briefly reviewed the two primary alternatives to Paul's gospel within early Christianity, i.e., Jewish Christianity and Gnostic Christianity, as well as Paul's life and what books of the New Testament can be properly attributed to him, it is time to consider Paul's actual teaching and how it differed from what Jesus reportedly taught. In doing so, it should first be noted that in the seven letters that Biblical scholars agree were actually written by Paul, i.e., Romans, I and II Corinthians, Galatians, Philippians, I Thessalonians, and Philemon, only once does Paul quote the Jesus of the gospels.[218] This can be easily verified by picking up a "red letter" edition of the New Testament and thumbing through the seven letters that can be reliably attributed to Paul. It's enough to make one think that perhaps Paul had little knowledge of Jesus' actual ministry and teaching. The only other conclusion would be that what the historical Jesus actually said and did had next to no bearing whatsoever on Paul's gospel. That one or the other of these two conclusions hits the mark can be seen by contrasting the reported teachings of Jesus and Paul on the Law of Moses, the path to salvation, and the mission field of early Christianity.

JESUS ON THE LAW OF MOSES

From the gospel accounts, it appears that Jesus reportedly modified and softened the Law of Moses in a couple of instances. For example, in Matthew 12:1-8 and Luke 6:1-5, Jesus is said to justify the action of his hungry disciples in picking a little grain on the Sabbath in order to have something

---

[218] Paul's quotation of the Jesus of the gospels is found in I Corinthians 11:24-25, which is nothing more than part of an early church liturgy for Holy Communion. While part of II Corinthians 12:9 appears in red letters, these words are not attributed to the earthly Jesus of the gospels but to Paul's claim of having received them from Jesus after the end of Christ's earthly ministry.

to eat. However, this is a compassionate understanding of the Law of Moses, not its abrogation. Likewise, in Matthew 5:38-42 and Luke 6:29-31, Jesus reportedly teaches that the *Lex Talionis*, i.e., an eye for an eye and a tooth for a tooth, should be modified with compassion and forgiveness. Finally, in Matthew 15:10-20 and Mark 7:14-23, Jesus reportedly taught that empty, ritualized following of the Mosaic Law was of no value if a person's spiritual life was not properly directed. These examples demonstrate that the Jesus of the gospels had a compassionate and caring interpretation of the Law of Moses. However, the statements attributed to Jesus in the gospels make it quite clear that he certainly was not abolishing the Law of Moses. The following quotations serve to drive that point home.

> Think not that I am come to destroy the law, or the prophets: I am not come to destroy but to fulfil. For verily I say unto you, Till heaven and earth pass, one jot or one tittle shall in no wise pass from the law, till all be fulfilled. Whosoever therefore shall break one of these least commandments, and shall teach men so, he shall be called the least in the kingdom of heaven: but whosoever shall do and teach them, the same shall be called great in the kingdom of heaven. (Matthew 5:17-19, King James Version)

> And, behold, one came and said unto him, Good Master, what good thing shall I do, that I may have eternal life? And he said unto him, Why callest thou me good? There is none good but one, that is, God: but if thou wilt enter into life, keep the commandments. (Matthew 19:16-17, King James Version)

> The law and the prophets were until John: since that time the kingdom of God is preached, and every man presseth into it. And it is easier for heaven and earth to pass, than for one tittle of the law to fail. (Luke 16:16-17, King James Version)

The gospels claim that Jesus offered a compassionate interpretation of some aspects of the Law of Moses and emphasized that ritualized observance without accompanying spirituality was worthless. However, as the above verses clearly indicate, there was no wholesale abrogation of the Mosaic Law by the Jesus of the gospels. Rather, the Jesus of the gospels taught that the Law of Moses was in effect and that one was to "keep the commandments."

PAUL ON THE LAW OF MOSES

In stark contrast, to the teachings of Jesus regarding the Law of Moses, Paul argued for the complete abrogation of the Mosaic Law in its entirety. Paul taught that the Law of Moses was nothing more than a curse and that all things were lawful. According to Paul, there was no reason to be circumcised, and there were no dietary restrictions that must be followed. Righteous living by adhering to the Law of Moses, even when done in all sincerity and with the correct spirituality, profited a person not one bit.

> We who are Jews by nature, and not sinners of the Gentiles,
> Knowing that a man is not justified by the works of the law, but
> by the faith of Jesus Christ, even we have believed in Jesus Christ,
> that we might be justified by the faith of Christ, and not by the
> works of the law: for by the works of the law shall no flesh be jus-
> tified. But if, while we seek to be justified by Christ, we ourselves
> also are found sinners, is therefore Christ the minister of sin?
> God forbid. For if I build again the things which I destroyed, I
> make myself a transgressor. For I through the law am dead to the
> law, that I might live unto God. I am crucified with Christ:
> nevertheless I live; yet not I, but Christ liveth in me: and the life
> which I now live in the flesh I live by the faith of the Son of God,
> who loved me, and gave himself for me. I do not frustrate the

grace of God: for if righteousness come by the law, then Christ is dead in vain. (Galatians 2:15-21, King James Version)

Paul's total rejection of the Mosaic Law is quite stark and absolute in the above passage. He clearly states that a person cannot be "justified by the works of the law" and that "by the works of the law shall no flesh be justified." In fact, one must be "dead to the law" in order that one "might live unto God." For Paul, the law has been totally abrogated, and justification comes only by believing "in Jesus Christ, that we might be justified by the faith of Christ, and not by the works of the law." If any other theological construct is true, then "Christ is dead in vain." Paul then continues his letter to the Galatians by claiming that those who rely on correct conduct and living the right life according to the Law of Moses are actually under a curse.

> For as many as are of the works of the law are under the curse: for it is written, Cursed is every one that continueth not in all things which are written in the book of the law to do them. But that no man is justified by the law in the sight of God, it is evident: for, The just shall live by faith. And the law is not of faith: but, The man that doeth them shall live in them. Christ hath redeemed us from the curse of the law, being made a curse for us: for it is written, Cursed is every one that hangeth on a tree… (Galatians 3:10-13, King James Version)

Paul quotes two passages from the Jewish scriptures in the above verses. The first is from Deuteronomy 27:26, which clearly states that the person who does not affirm and follow the Law of Moses is cursed.[219]

---

[219] Deuteronomy 27:26 reads as follows. "Cursed be he that confirmeth not all the words of this law to do them." (King James Version)

This contradicts Paul's claim that the Law of Moses need not be followed. The second passage is from Deuteronomy 21:22-23, and it claims that anyone who is hanged on a tree is accursed of God.[220] This passage represents a major stumbling block for Paul's belief that Jesus was both the "Son of God" and crucified, i.e., hung on a tree. How can Jesus be the "Son of God" and "accursed of God" at one and the same time? In an attempt to get out of this bind, Paul weakly argues that in being supposedly crucified, Jesus becomes a curse for mankind, thus removing from people any curse associated with their not following the Mosaic Law, so long as they have faith in Jesus Christ. This is clearly a doctrine that has no parallel in the teachings of Jesus as reported in the gospels. However, Paul is still not done in his diatribe against the Mosaic Law that the gospels say Jesus promoted.

> But now we are delivered from the law, that being dead wherein we were held; that we should serve in newness of spirit, and not in the oldness of the letter. (Romans 7:6, King James Version)

> All things are lawful for me, but all things are not expedient: all things are lawful for me, but all things edify not...Whatsoever is sold in the shambles, that eat, asking no question for conscience sake: For the earth is the Lord's and the fullness thereof. If any of them that believe not bid you to a feast, and ye be disposed to go; whatsoever is set before you, eat, asking no question for conscience sake. But if any man say unto you, This is offered in sacrifices unto idols, eat not for his sake that shewed it, and for conscience sake: for the earth is the Lord's, and the fullness there-

---

[220] Deuteronomy 21:22-23 reads as follows. "And if a man have committed a sin worthy of death, and he be to be put to death, and thou hang him on a tree: His body shall not remain all night upon the tree, but thou shalt in any wise bury him that day: (for he that is hanged is accursed of God:) that thy land be not defiled, which the Lord thy God giveth thee for an inheritance." (King James Version)

71

of: Conscience, I say, not thine own, but of the other: for why is my liberty judged of another man's conscience? (I Corinthians 10:23, 25-29, King James Version)

For circumcision verily profiteth, if thou keep the law: but if thou be a breaker of the law, thy circumcision is made uncircumcision. Therefore if the uncircumcision keep the righteousness of the law, shall not his uncircumcision be counted for circumcision?...But he is a Jew, which is one inwardly; and circumcision is that of the heart, in the spirit, and not in the letter; whose praise is not of men, but of God. (Romans 2:25-26, 29, King James Version)

For Christ is the end of the law for righteousness to every one that believeth. (Romans 10:4, King James Version)

As seen from the preceding quotations, after his conversion, Paul came to a new perspective on the Mosaic Law under which he had previously lived his whole life. He now claimed that the Law was merely an interim device or preparatory discipline to make people ready for the coming of Jesus. By contrasting the reported words of Jesus and Paul regarding the value of the Mosaic Law, we find two radically different perspectives emerging within Christianity during the middle of the first century CE. Jesus and the so-called Jewish Christians preached conformance to the Law, while Paul and the Pauline Church claimed that the Law had been abrogated in its totality.

PAUL VS. JESUS REGARDING SALVATION

JESUS ON SALVATION

Jesus' reported teaching regarding the path to salvation was clearly and concisely stated in the passage from Matthew 19:16-17, which was quoted earlier. Salvation comes through following the law and commandments. Nothing was said about salvation through faith or through vicarious atonement. Purely and simply, one was to "keep the commandments."

> And, behold, one came and said unto him, Good Master, what good thing shall I do, that I may have eternal life? And he said unto him, Why callest thou me good? There is none good but one, that is, God: but if thou wilt enter into life, keep the commandments. (Matthew 19:16-17, King James Version)

Furthermore, the New Testament explicitly states that Jesus taught that faith in him was not enough to secure salvation. Salvation comes from doing "the will of my Father which is in heaven." In other words, salvation comes from living a righteous life in conformance with the Mosaic Law.

> Not every one that saith unto me, Lord, Lord, shall enter into the kingdom of heaven; but he that doeth the will of my Father which is in heaven. Many will say to me in that day, Lord, Lord, have we not prophesied in thy name? and in thy name have cast out devils? and in thy name done many wonderful works? And then will I profess unto them, I never knew you: depart from me, ye that work iniquity. (Matthew 7:21-23, King James Version)

PAUL ON SALVATION

As seen previously and in marked contrast to Jesus' teachings, Paul claimed that the Law of Moses was abrogated in its entirely. Therefore, justification, and hence salvation, came not through living a righteous life in conformity to the Mosaic Law, but through faith, regardless of whether the Law of Moses was kept or not. In fact, Paul taught that those who believe in justification by the law have "fallen from grace" and that "Christ is become of no effect unto you." Paul's own writings emphasize this theological reformulation of the path to salvation, one that must be regarded as heretical when compared to what the historical Jesus taught.

Therefore we conclude that a man is justified by faith without the deeds of the law. (Romans 3:28, King James Version)

But before faith came, we were kept under the law, shut up unto the faith which should afterwards be revealed. Wherefore the law was our schoolmaster to bring us unto Christ, that we might be justified by faith. But after that faith is come, we are no longer under a schoolmaster. For ye are all the children of God by faith in Jesus Christ. (Galatians 3:23-26, King James Version)

We who are Jews by nature, and not sinners of the Gentiles, Knowing that a man is not justified by the works of the law, but by the faith of Jesus Christ, even we have believed in Jesus Christ, that we might be justified by the faith of Christ, and not by the works of the law: for by the works of the law shall no flesh be justified. (Galatians 2:15-16, King James Version)

Stand fast therefore in the liberty wherewith Christ hath made us free, and be not entangled again with the yoke of bondage. Behold, I Paul say unto you, that if ye be circumcised, Christ shall profit you nothing. For I testify again to every man that is circumcised, that he is a debtor to do the whole law. Christ is become of no effect unto you, whosoever of you are justified by the law; ye are fallen from grace. For we through the Spirit wait for the hope of righteousness by faith. For in Jesus Christ neither circumcision availeth any thing, nor uncircumcision; but faith which worketh by love. (Galatians 5:1-6, King James Version)

Paul's concept of salvation through faith is based upon Paul's idiosyncratic interpretation of the alleged crucifixion of Jesus. In fact, it is perhaps not going too far to maintain that Paul's entire gospel consists of his story of "The Cross." For Paul, "The Cross" assumes mythological proportions, as is illustrated in the following passages.

> For even Christ our Passover is sacrificed for us. (I Corinthians 5:7, King James Version)

> For Christ sent me not to baptize, but to preach the gospel: not with wisdom of words, lest the cross of Christ should be made of none effect. For the preaching of the cross is to them that perish foolishness; but unto us which are saved it is the power of God. (I Corinthians 1:17-18, King James Version)

> Moreover, brethren, I declare unto you the gospel which I preached unto you, which also ye have received, and wherein ye stand; By which also ye are saved, if ye keep in memory what I preached unto you, unless ye have believed in vain. For I delivered unto you first of all that which I also received, how that Christ died for our sins according to the scriptures; And that he was buried, and that he rose again the third day according to the scriptures… (I Corinthians 15:1-4, King James Version)

"Christ died for our sins…" This is the gospel of Paul, not the gospel of Jesus. This is Paul's theological formulation for salvation and the heart of his message. In contrast, Jesus reportedly taught that salvation came through keeping "the commandments," i.e., the Law of Moses. Despite Jesus' own message, Paul focused on "The Cross" and embodied in it three types of atonement for mankind: sacrificial,[221] vicarious,[222] and representative.[223]

---

[221] For example, see Philippians 2:8, Colossians 1:22 and 2:14, and Romans 3:25 and 5:9-10.
[222] For example, see Romans 5:8 and 3:25, Galatians 3:13 and 4:4-5, II Corinthians 5:14, 18-19, and 21, I Corinthians 1:23, 2:3, 6:20, 7:23, and 15:3, and I Thessalonians 5:10.
[223] For example, see Galatians 3:3 and II Corinthians 5:21.

In commenting on the last two quoted passages from I Corinthians, Helmut Koester, the John H. Morison Research Professor of Divinity and Winn Research Professor of Ecclesiastical History at Harvard Divinity School, noted the following.

> In Paul's writings, the words of Jesus play only a secondary role. In no way are they considered as capable of providing salvation. Rather, for Paul the proclamation of salvation is a story, namely the narrative of Jesus' suffering, cross, and resurrection, to which he points right at the beginning of his controversy with the Corinthians (I Cor 1:17-18) and which he quotes in I Corinthians 15 in a short formula as the "gospel."[224]

One might well ask where and how Paul derived his theological formulation of justification by faith and of salvation through vicarious atonement, since they were not what the New Testament gospels state that Jesus taught. One answer to this question focuses on Paul's childhood in Tarsus. As noted previously, in Tarsus Paul would have been exposed to Greek paganism and to various mystery religions, both of which were littered with stories of dying and regenerating redeemer gods.

Several dying and regenerating redeemer gods were worshipped as part of the Greek/Roman pantheon, all of whom were linked with fertility and the renewal of the seasons. For example, Adonis was said to undergo a death and resurrection each year, with his death conforming to the decay of winter and his resurrection being linked with rain and the revival of vegetation in the spring.[225] Dionysus, aka Bacchus and Liber, was another dying and regenerating fertility god in the Greek pantheon.[226]

---

[224] Koester H (2007a), p. 203.
[225] --- (2003w).
[226] --- (2003x).

Persephone, the daughter of Demeter, was also said to die and regenerate on a yearly basis.[227]

However, the idea of a dying and regenerating god was not limited to Greek mythology. Paul would have also been exposed to this concept by the various mystery religions in Tarsus. For example, Attis of Phrygia was a god of fertility and vegetation who was said have died and then been resurrected, with his death and resurrection explaining the seasons of the year and their impact on fruits and crops.[228] In Egyptian polytheism, Osiris was the dying and regenerating redeemer god, and rebirth in the next life was dependent upon following Osiris.[229] In the Mesopotamian pantheon, Tammuz was a fertility god, who was associated with both agriculture and pastoral life, and who underwent a yearly death and resurrection.[230]

In the Canaanite religion, Baal was the universal god of life and fertility, the storm god, the god of rain and dew, and the king of the gods. According to Canaanite belief, Baal was locked in mortal combat with Mot, the god of death and sterility. Two different stories existed concerning Baal's war with Mot. In the one, this mortal combat took place every seven years. If Mot won and killed Baal, then seven years of famine would follow before Baal would be resurrected to begin the combat with Mot yet once again. If Baal won the combat, then seven years of plenty would follow before the next combat with Mot. The second story maintained that the cycle of conflict between Baal and Mot took place on a yearly basis. In the yearly scenario, Mot would defeat Baal right before the start

---

[227] --- (2003z).
[228] --- (2003v).
[229] --- (2003y).
[230] --- (2003za).

of the barren dry season, and Baal would resurrect at the start of the rainy and fertile season. While originally a Canaanite dying and regenerating god, the cult of Baal found inroads among both the Egyptians and Aramaeans.[231]

Did Paul formulate his theology of salvation based upon his childhood exposure to dying and regenerating redeemer gods as preached in Greek mythology and many mystery religions? Certainly, many Biblical scholars maintain that this is exactly what happened.

> …(some) scholars argued…(s)ince Paul was thoroughly Hellenistic in heritage, this meant that he would interpret baptism and the Lord's Supper in relation to the practices of Hellenistic mystery religions, and he would have understood Christ in terms of a general, Hellenistic myth of a descending and ascending redeemer figure.[232]

SOME REFLECTIONS ON PAUL'S THEOLOGY

What happens when there is no law? What happens when there is no punishment for one's behavior, so long as that person has faith in Jesus and "The Cross?" Human nature being what it is, the answer is obvious. Without a moral, ethical, spiritual, and religious law to which one must adhere, one invites an "anything goes" moral licentiousness to match anything to be found in pagan societies. Why not rob, steal, murder, fornicate, rape, etc. if the law has been abrogated and if faith in Jesus and "The Cross" is all that is needed to insure eternal salvation?

The above scenario may seem somewhat farfetched to some, but Paul's own writings bear testimony that his abrogation of the Law of Moses and

---

[231] (A) Devries L (1997); (B) --- (2003zb).
[232] Soards ML (1997), p. 661.

his theology of salvation through a dying and regenerating redeemer god resulted in rampant immorality in the early church at Corinth. Sexual fornication, incest, and who knows what else became part and parcel of Corinthian Christianity.

> It is reported commonly that there is fornication among you, and such fornication as is not so much as named among the Gentiles, that one should have his father's wife...But now I have written unto you not to keep company, if any man that is called a brother be a fornicator, or covetous, or an idolater, or a railer, or a drunkard, or an extortioner; with such an one no not to eat.
> (I Corinthians 5:1 & 11, King James Version)

What was Paul's solution as to how to deal with fornicators, idolaters, drunks, and extortionists? He simply advised others not to eat with them. Here one sees the sad but inevitable moral decline that accompanies the abrogation of all religious law by total reliance on "The Cross."

Given the sum total of the above, one may well ask what drove Paul to such a complete rejection of the Law of Moses. One possible answer can be found in one of the attacks against Paul made by Jewish Christianity. As reported by Saint Epiphanius of Constantia (circa 315-403 CE), at least some Jewish Christians maintained that Paul had asked for the hand of the Jewish high priest's daughter and had been refused. As a result of this rejection, he began to rage against the Law of Moses. [233]

PAUL VS. JESUS REGARDING THE MISSION FIELD

JESUS ON THE MISSION FIELD

Jesus reportedly described his own mission field in the story of the

---

[233] Bauer W (1971), p. xxiv.

Canaanite woman who sought his help to heal her daughter from being possessed by a demon. When asked by the woman to perform this miracle, Jesus reportedly answered, "I am not sent but unto the lost sheep of the house of Israel."

> Then Jesus went thence, and departed into the coasts of Tyre and Sidon. And, behold, a woman of Canaan came out of the same coasts, and cried unto him, saying, Have mercy on me, O Lord, thou son of David; my daughter is grievously vexed with a devil. But he answered her not a word. And his disciples came and besought him, saying, Send her away; for she crieth after us. But he answered and said, I am not sent but unto the lost sheep of the house of Israel. Then came she and worshipped him, saying, Lord, help me. But he answered and said, It is not meet to take the children's bread, and to cast it to dogs. And she said, Truth, Lord: yet the dogs eat of the crumbs which fall from their masters' table. Then Jesus answered and said unto her, O woman, great is thy faith, be it unto thee even as thou wilt. And her daughter was made whole from that very hour. (Matthew 15: 21-28, King James Version)

That Jesus restricted the mission field to Jews is further illustrated by his commissioning of the 12 original disciples. In giving them their instructions, he reportedly forbade his disciples from preaching to either the Gentiles or the Samaritans, the latter of which was a Jewish sect of mixed ethnic heritage.

> These twelve Jesus sent forth, and commanded them, saying, Go not into the way of the Gentiles, and into any city of the Samaritans enter ye not. But go rather to the lost sheep of the house of Israel. (Matthew 10:5-6, King James Version)

Some might want to argue that the above commissioning of the 12 disciples was superceded by the so-called Great Commission allegedly given by Jesus after the crucifixion event. Four different versions of the Great Commission are given in the New Testament, one each in Matthew 28:18-20, Mark 16:14-18, Luke 24:46-47, and Acts 1:7-8. However, as will be seen in chapter five, the version recorded in Mark is actually a later addition to the original text of Mark. As such, one need only consider the versions recorded in Matthew, Luke, and Acts.

> And Jesus came and spake unto them, saying, All power is given unto me in heaven and in earth. Go ye therefore, and teach all nations, baptizing them in the name of the Father, and of the Son, and of the Holy Ghost: Teaching them to observe all things whatsoever I have commanded you: and, lo, I am with you always, even unto the end of the world. Amen. (Matthew 28:18-20, King James Version)

> And (Jesus) said unto them…And that repentance and remission of sins should be preached in his (Jesus') name among all nations, beginning at Jerusalem. (Luke 24:46-47, King James Version)

> And he (Jesus) said unto them…But ye shall receive power, after that the Holy Ghost is come upon you: and ye shall be witnesses unto me both in Jerusalem, and in all Judaea, and in Samaria, and unto the uttermost part of the earth. (Acts 1:7-8, King James Version)

There are several obvious problems with accepting the Great Commission as having actually been given by Jesus. The first is apparent as soon as one considers how the actual disciples of Jesus, as well as the immediate followers of those disciples, continued Jesus' ministry after the end of his earthly sojourn. The Biblical book of Acts preserves a statement indicating what the actual disciples of Jesus and their immediate followers did when it came to preaching the message of Jesus.

> Now they which were scattered abroad upon the persecution that arose about Stephen traveled as far as Phenice, and Cyprus, and Antioch, preaching the word to none but unto the Jews only. (Acts 11:19, King James Version)

The second drawback to accepting the Great Commission concerns the baptismal formula given in Matthew's version of the Great Commission. According to the passage in Matthew, Jesus instructed his disciples to baptize "in the name of the Father, and of the Son, and of the Holy Ghost." However, Acts 2:38 clearly states that Peter, one of the key disciples of Jesus, actually baptized using a different formula, i.e., "in the name of Jesus Christ." Further, Acts 10:48 has Peter baptizing "in the name of the Lord." There is no mention in any of these verses of being baptized "in the name of the Father, and of the Son, and of the Holy Ghost." It is hardly conceivable that Simon Peter would have so blatantly disobey a command from Jesus. Still further, Acts 19:4-5 states that Paul himself baptized only "in the name of the Lord Jesus." Given all these considerations, the Great Commission is again called into question.

The third problem with accepting the Great Commission is that the various New Testament passages proclaiming the Great Commission conflict with each other. For example, Matthew 28:16-20 has the Great Commission taking place on a mountain in Galilee, while both Acts 1: 4-8 and Luke 24:33-48 place it in Jerusalem. Why the discrepancy? Which version, if any, is to be believed?

PAUL ON THE MISSION FIELD

"(Jesus) answered and said, I am not sent but unto the lost sheep of the house of Israel...,"[234] and he instructed his disciples, "Go not into the way of the Gentiles, and into any city of the Samaritans enter ye not. But go rather to the lost sheep of the house of Israel."[235] Paul, with his mission to the gentiles, clearly ignored or refused to accept what Jesus had taught regarding his own mission and that of his actual disciples. That this is so can be clearly seen in the following passages from Acts.

> When therefore Paul and Barnabas...passed through Phenice and Samaria, declaring the conversion of the Gentiles... (Acts 15:2-3, King James Version)

> And when he (Paul) had saluted them, he declared particularly what things God had wrought among the Gentiles by his ministry. (Acts 21:19, King James Version)

> And when Silas and Timotheus were come from Macedonia, Paul was pressed in the spirit, and testified to the Jews that Jesus was Christ. And when they opposed themselves, and blasphemed, he shook his raiment, and said unto them, Your blood be upon your own heads; I am clean: from henceforth I will go unto the Gentiles. (Acts 18:5-6, King James Version)

Evidence of Paul's emphasis on missionary efforts to the gentiles is not confined to Acts. Paul's own writing in Galatians bears ample testimony to the fact that he was, first and foremost, taking his version of the gospel to the gentiles. In Paul's own mind, he had been specifically selected by God to preach to the gentiles.

---

[234] Matthew 15:24, King James Version.
[235] Matthew 10:5-6, King James Version.

But when it pleased God, who separated me from my mother's womb, and called me by his grace, To reveal his Son in me, that I might preach him among the heathen; immediately I conferred not with flesh and blood: Neither went I up to Jerusalem to them which were apostles before me; but I went into Arabia, and returned again unto Damascus. (Galatians 1:15-17, King James Version)

And I went up by revelation, and communicated unto them that gospel which I preach among the Gentiles, but privately to them which were of reputation, lest by any means I should run, or had run, in vain. (Galatians 2:2, King James Version)

(For he that wrought effectually in Peter to the apostleship of the circumcision, the same was mighty in me toward the Gentiles:) And when James, Cephas, and John, who seemed to be pillars, perceived the grace that was given unto me, they gave to me and Barnabas the right hands of fellowship; that we should go unto the heathen, and they unto the circumcision. Only they would that we should remember the poor; the same which I also was forward to do. (Galatians 2:8-10, King James Version)

Now I would not have you ignorant, brethren, that oftentimes I purposed to come unto you, (but was let hitherto,) that I might have some fruit among you also, even as among other Gentiles. (Romans 1:13, King James Version)

For I speak to you Gentiles, inasmuch as I am the apostle of the Gentiles, I magnify mine office... (Romans 11:13, King James Version)

Nevertheless, brethren, I have written the more boldly unto you in some sort, as putting you in mind, because of the grace that is given to me of God, That I should be the minister of Jesus Christ to the Gentiles, ministering to the gospel of God, that the offering up of the Gentiles might be acceptable, being sanctified by the Holy Ghost. (Romans 15:15-16, King James Version)

Just as Paul abrogated the Law of Moses, he also abrogated Jesus' teaching as to the appropriate mission field. Why did Paul once again go his own way? Why did he focus so exclusively on the gentiles? Probably because Paul's version of the gospel, one that abrogated the Law of Moses and taught salvation through faith and the atonement of "The Cross," instead of through righteous living in conformance with the Law of Moses, was bound to be rejected by Jews and by Jewish Christians. That this is so can be seen in the following passages from Acts, in which Jews and presumably Jewish Christians flatly rejected Paul's message. Having been totally rejected by the Jews and Jewish Christians, Paul then turned to the gentiles.

But when the Jews saw the multitudes, they were filled with envy, and spake against those things which were spoken by Paul, contradicting and blaspheming. Then Paul and Barnabas waxed bold, and said, It was necessary that the word of God should first have been spoken to you: but seeing ye put it from you, and judge yourselves unworthy of everlasting life, lo, we turn to the Gentiles. (Acts 13:45-46, King James Version)

And there came thither certain Jews from Antioch and Iconium, who persuaded the people, and having stoned Paul, drew him out of the city, supposing he had been dead. (Acts 15:19, King James Version)

And certain men which came down from Judaea taught the brethren and said, Except ye be circumcised after the manner of Moses, ye cannot be saved. When therefore Paul and Barnabas had no small dissension and disputation with them, they determined that Paul and Barnabas, and certain other of them, should go up to Jerusalem unto the apostles and elders about this question. (Acts 15:1-2, King James Version)

And when Silas and Timotheus were come from Macedonia, Paul was pressed in the spirit, and testified to the Jews that Jesus was Christ. And when they opposed themselves, and blasphemed, he shook his raiment, and said unto them, Your blood be upon your own heads; I am clean: from henceforth I will go unto the Gentiles. (Acts 18:5-6, King James Version)

PAUL VS. THE JERUSALEM CHURCH AND JEWISH CHRISTIANITY

PAUL'S PERSECUTION OF THE JERUSALEM CHURCH

Paul's persecution of nascent Christianity was previously documented by recourse to several Biblical passages, i.e., I Corinthians 15:9, Galatians 1:13, and Acts 7:54-8:1, 9:1-2, 22:4-5, and 26:9-11. However, there is yet another account of Paul persecuting the early church. This narrative, found in the Clementine Recognitions, is specific to Paul attacking the Jerusalem Church and the very person of James the Just, the brother of Jesus and the first Bishop of the Jerusalem Church.

The Clementine Recognitions, aka the Pseudo-Clementine Recognitions, is Jewish Christian in origin, was penned by a pseudonymous author, and was then attributed to Saint Clement of Rome (died either 97 or 101 CE).

Copies of the Clementine Recognitions exist in both Latin and Syriac, although it is assumed that both are translations from a Greek original. In its present form, it dates to the fourth century CE. However, it is likely that its source goes back the second-century Circuits of Peter, a book that was mentioned by both Bishop Eusebius of Caesarea (circa 260-339 CE) and Origen (circa 185-254 CE).[236]

In terms of understanding Paul's relationship to the Jerusalem Church and to Jewish Christianity, the Clementine Recognitions is truly remarkable, for it gives us what is perhaps the only Jewish Christian writing to deal with Paul. Not only does it accuse Paul of being the initiator of the persecution of early Christianity, but it also claims that Paul was guilty of the attempted murder of James the Just, brother of Jesus and the first Bishop of the Jerusalem Church. This alleged attempt to murder James reportedly happened towards the end of a theological debate, which lasted seven days, and which James was having at the Jerusalem Temple. When it became clear that James was winning the debate, Paul reportedly interrupted. The following account of that incident from the Clementine Recognitions is supposed to be Clement's recording of what he was told by Simon Peter, the disciple of Jesus. It is found in Book I, Chapters 70-71, of the Clementine Recognitions.

> But when he (James) had spoken some things also concerning baptism, through seven successive days he persuaded all the people and the high priest that they should hasten straightway to receive baptism. And when matters were at that point that they should come and be baptized, some one of our enemies, entering the temple with a few men, began to cry out, and to say, "What

---

[236] (A) Koch G (1997); (B) Jones FS (1995); (C) Smith T (1880); (D) Eisenman R (1997); (E) Eisenman R (2006); (F) --- (2003zc).

mean ye, O men of Israel?" While he was thus speaking, and adding more to the same effect, and while James the bishop was refuting him, he began to excite the people and to raise a tumult, so that the people might not be able to hear what was said. Therefore he began to drive all into confusion with shouting, and to undo what had been arranged with much labour, and at the same time to reproach the priests, and to enrage them with revilings and abuse, and, like a madman, to excite every one to murder, saying "What do ye? Why do ye hesitate? Oh, sluggish and inert, why do we not lay hands upon them, and pull all these fellows to pieces?" When he had said this, he first, seizing a strong brand from the altar, set the example of smiting. Then others also, seeing him, were carried away with like madness. Then ensued a tumult on either side, of the beating and the beaten. Much blood is shed; there is a confused flight, in the midst of which that enemy attacked James, and threw him headlong from the top of the steps; and supposing him to be dead, he cared not to inflict further violence upon him…Then after three days one of the brethren came to us from Gamaliel, whom we mentioned before, bringing to us secret tidings that the enemy had received a commission from Caiaphas, the chief priest, that he should arrest all who believed in Jesus, and should go to Damascus with his letters, and that there also, employing the help of the unbelievers, he should make havoc among the faithful; and that he was hastening to Damascus chiefly on this account, because he believed that Peter had fled thither.[237]

There are several points that need to be made with regard to the above

---

[237] Smith T (1880), p. 188-189.

narrative. (1) Adjoining material to the above quoted passage makes it clear that James was not killed but that he merely appeared to be dead. He survived and was carried away to safety. (2) The ending of the quoted material makes it clear that the "Enemy" who assaulted James was Paul, for this same "Enemy" then proceeded to secure a commission and letters from the chief priest authorizing him to attack the early Christians in Damascus. This closely parallels the statement about Paul recorded in Acts 9:1-2, [238] and it identifies Paul as the "Enemy" of Jewish Christianity and as the attempted murderer of James the Just. (3) If the identification of the "Enemy" with Paul is not already strong enough, it should be noted that a marginal note in one of the extant copies of the Clementine Recognitions specifically states that the "Enemy" was Paul.[239]

A parallel account of James being thrown from the Temple steps is found in Bishop Eusebius of Caesarea's (circa 260-339 CE) fourth-century *Ecclesiastical History*, in which he quotes from the second-century Memoirs of Hegesippus. This account differs in two key ways from that found in the Clementine Recognitions: (A) in Eusebius' account, James is killed in this encounter, first by being pushed down from the temple parapet and then by stoning and by being hit in the head with a club, and (B) Paul is not mentioned as being the perpetrator of this crime.

> So the scribes and Pharisees made James stand on the temple parapet …Many were convinced and rejoiced at James's testimony, crying "Hosanna to the Son of David." Then the scribes and Pharisees said to each other, "We made a bad mistake

---

[238] Acts 9:1-2 reads as follows. "And Saul, yet breathing out threatenings and slaughter against the disciples of the Lord, went unto the high priest, And desired of him letters to Damascus to the synagogues, that if he found any of this way, whether they were men or women, he might bring them bound unto Jerusalem." (King James Version)

[239] (A) Smith T (1880); (B) Eisenman R (1997); (C) Eisenman R (2006).

in providing such testimony to Jesus, but let us go up and throw him down so that they will be afraid and not believe him."...So they went up and threw down the righteous one. Then they said to each other, "Let us stone James the Just," and they began to stone him, since the fall had not killed him...Then one of them, a laundryman, took the club that he used to beat out clothes and hit the Just on the head. Such was his martyrdom. [240]

Flavius Josephus, the first-century Jewish historian, also records that James the Just was martyred by stoning circa 61 CE. However, Josephus presents the martyrdom of James as being the result of a formal trial before the Jewish Sanhedrin, not as a mob action following James being pushed from the Temple parapet.

...Ananus (the high priest)...assembled the Sanhedrin of judges, and brought before them the brother of Jesus, who was called Christ, whose name was James, and some others...and when he had formed an accusation against them as breakers of the law, he delivered them to be stoned... [241]

Which of the three accounts of the martyrdom of James the Just reported above is accurate, if any, is really irrelevant to establishing Paul's relationship with Jewish Christianity. It is sufficient that a known Jewish Christian document, i.e., the Clementine Recognitions, refers to Paul as the "Enemy" and accuses him of the attempted murder of James. Whether or not Paul actually did throw James down the Temple steps, obviously Paul was reviled enough by Jewish Christianity that it was willing to attribute that crime to him. Quite clearly, Paul was the "Enemy" as far as Jewish Christianity was concerned.

[240] Eusebius (1999), p. 82-83.
[241] Josephus F (1999), p. 656.

THE APOSTOLIC COUNCIL

The so-called Apostolic Council of Jerusalem was a contentious meeting between Paul and the Jerusalem Church, in which Paul was called upon to defend his decision to abrogate the Law of Moses for gentile converts to his gospel. Paul described his version of the confrontation at the Apostolic Council in Galatians 2:1-10, and a second version may be found in Acts 15. In Paul's version, he carries the day, and the Jerusalem Church assigns him the responsibility of missionary activity to the gentiles and assigns to itself missionary activity to the Jews.[242] While Acts also maintains that Paul won his point about the Law of Moses not pertaining to gentile converts to Christianity, Acts portrays this as a partial victory for Paul at best. In Acts, James the Just supposedly settles the dispute between Paul and the Jewish Christians by writing a letter to the gentile Christians that absolves them from some, but not all of the Law of Moses.

> Then all the multitude kept silence, and gave audience to Barnabas and Paul, declaring what miracles and wonders God had wrought among the Gentiles by them. And after they had held their peace, James answered, saying Men and brethren hearken unto me...Wherefore my sentence is, that we trouble not them, which from among the Gentiles are turned to God: But that we write unto them, that they abstain from pollutions of idols and from fornication, and from things strangled, and from blood...Then pleased it the apostles and elders, with the whole church, to send chosen men of their own company to Antioch with Paul and Barnabas; namely, Judas surnamed Barsabas, and Silas, chief men among the brethren: And they wrote letters by them after this manner; The apostles and elders

---

[242] Galatians 2:9.

and brethren send greeting unto the brethren which are of the Gentiles in Antioch and Syria and Cilicia: Forasmuch as we have heard, that certain which went out from us have troubled you with words, subverting your souls, saying, Ye must be circumcised, and keep the law: to whom we gave no such commandment: It seemed good unto us, being assembled with one accord, to send chosen men unto you with our beloved Barnabas and Paul, Men that have hazarded their lives for the name of our Lord Jesus Christ. We have sent therefore Judas and Silas, who shall also tell you the same things by mouth. For it seemed good to the Holy Ghost, and to us, to lay upon you no greater burden than these necessary things; That ye abstain from meats offered to idols, and from blood, and from things strangled, and from fornication: from which if ye keep yourselves, ye shall do well. Fare ye well. (Acts 15:12-13, 19-20, 22-29, King James Version)

Taken at face value, the above passage from Acts would indicate that Paul was supported by the leadership of the Jerusalem Church with regard to gentile converts not having to be circumcised, although certain other aspects of the Mosaic Law still had to be fulfilled by gentile converts. However, one must remember that Acts is basically a Pauline apologetic. Therefore, one has to look carefully at the text to try to decipher what exactly what was going on. In doing so, it becomes immediately apparent that James and the Jerusalem Church were unwilling to allow Paul to give his own version of the Apostolic Council's decision to the gentiles. James insisted on writing a letter to the gentiles detailing the Council's decision and, in addition, sent two Jewish Christians to accompany Paul to give verbal confirmation of what had been decided. It was to Judas Barsabas and Silas that James entrusted this letter, not to Paul.

Clearly, this does not sound like Paul carried the day, and it raises the question of whether the Jerusalem Church really did declare that gentile converts need not be circumcised. This question appears to be answered at the start of Acts 16.

> Then came he (Paul) to Derbe and Lystra: and, behold, a certain disciple was there, named Timotheus, the son of a certain woman, which was a Jewess, and believed; but his father was a Greek: Which was well reported of by the brethren that were at Lystra and Iconium. Him would Paul have to go forth with him; and took and circumcised him because of the Jews which were in those quarters: for they knew all that his father was a Greek. (Acts 16:1-3, King James Version)

If James the Just, the first Bishop of the Jerusalem Church, the de facto head of all Christianity at the time, and the brother of Jesus, had actually ruled that gentiles need not be circumcised, it seems inconceivable that Paul would have circumcised Timothy simply because of Jewish and Jewish Christian pressures to fulfill the Law of Moses regarding circumcision. After all, Paul would have had James' permission not to circumcise the gentiles, and that would certainly have been a strong enough argument to satisfy Jews and Jewish Christians. The conclusion, therefore, seems obvious, i.e., Paul was never given permission by the Jerusalem Church to forego circumcision for gentile converts. As such, one wonders if gentile converts were exempted from any of the Mosaic Laws by the Apostolic Council held in Jerusalem.

MORE CONFLICT WITH THE JERUSALEM CHURCH

Several New Testament passages, e.g., Acts 15:1-5, Acts 21:17-26, and Galatians 2:1-9, dramatically illustrate that Paul, with his insistence on preaching to the gentiles and on abrogating the Law of Moses, was in frequent conflict with the Jerusalem Church. With regard to these three passages, it is instructive to note both Acts and Galatians are Pauline documents and do not reflect the teachings of the Jerusalem Church and of the actual disciples of Jesus. As an illustration of this Pauline bias, one can profitably examine Acts 21:17-26, where the Pauline writer of this text attempts to show that the Jerusalem Church supported Paul in the end.

> And when we were come to Jerusalem, the brethren received us gladly. And the day following Paul went in with us unto James; and all the elders were present. And when he had saluted them, he declared particularly what things God had wrought among the Gentiles by his ministry. And when they heard it, they glorified the Lord, and said unto him, Thou seest, brother, how many thousands of Jews there are which believe; and they are all zealous of the law: And they are informed of thee, that thou teachest all the Jews which are among the Gentiles to forsake Moses, saying that they ought not to circumcise their children, neither to walk after the customs. What is it therefore? the multitude must needs come together: for they will hear that thou art come. Do therefore this that we say to thee: We have four men which have a vow on them; Them take, and purify thyself with them, and be at charges with them, that they may shave their heads: and all may know that those things, whereof they were informed concerning thee, are nothing; but that thou thyself also walkest orderly, and keepest the law. As touching the Gentiles which believe, we have written and concluded that they observe no such thing, save only that they keep themselves from things offered to idols, and from blood, and from strangled, and from

fornication. Then Paul took the men, and the next day purifying himself with them entered into the temple, to signify the accomplishment of the days of purification, until that an offering should be offered for every one of them. (Acts 21:17-26, King James Version)

Once again, it is important to analyze this Pauline apologetic to uncover what was actually going on. When doing so, several points emerge. (1) Clearly, Paul was reporting to James as any underling would report to his superior. (2) The Jewish Christians, i.e., "Jews there are which believe," were once again up in arms about Paul's message and activities. (3) By this time, Paul was not only abrogating the Law of Moses for gentile converts, but also for Jews and for Jewish Christians. This can be readily seen in the statement that "thou teachest all the Jews which are among the Gentiles to forsake Moses, saying that they ought not to circumcise their children, neither to walk after the customs." In this, Paul was far exceeding any possible dispensation from the Law of Moses that he might have previously received from James for gentile converts, although as previously noted one wonders if Paul ever received any such dispensation from James. (4) To purify himself, to pay penance for what he had been doing, and to reaffirm Paul's devotion to the Law of Moses, i.e., "walkest orderly, and keepest the law," James and the elders of the Jerusalem Church ordered Paul to undergo the temporary rites of being a Nazirite,[243] as indicated by the statements regarding the shaving of heads and the making of vows.

---

[243] To be a Nazirite, one shaved one's head and then took a vow to abstain from all alcoholic drink, grape products, cutting of one's hair, and contact with the dead (Lee JW, 1997). When the days of the vow were fulfilled, a sacrificial sin offering was made, and one's head was again shaven. For a fuller description of what it meant to be a Nazirite, see Numbers 6:1-21.

Paul was made to pay penance, to purify himself, and to show his devotion to the Law of Moses by undergoing the temporary rites of being a Nazirite. Clearly, Paul was once again on the outs with the leadership of the Jerusalem Church. Apparently, however, this wasn't the only time Paul underwent the Nazirite rites in relation to his visiting the Jerusalem Church, as illustrated in the following passage in the reference to Paul shaving his head and having taken a vow.[244]

> And Paul after this tarried there yet a good while, and then took his leave of the brethren, and sailed thence into Syria, and with him Priscilla and Aquila; having shorn his head in Cenchrea: for he had a vow. And he came to Ephesus, and left them there: but he himself entered into the synagogue, and reasoned with the Jews. When they desired him to tarry longer time with them, he consented not; But bade them farewell, saying, I must by all means keep this feast that cometh in Jerusalem... (Acts 18:18-21, King James Version)

PAUL AND THE COLLECTION FOR THE JERUSALEM CHURCH

Twice in Paul's letters he refers to what many people understand to be a collection of money that he was making for the Jewish Christians of the Jerusalem Church. In the first such instance, i.e., that found in Galatians, Paul never actually mentions a collection of money. What he does say is that James directed him to "remember the poor." The other passage, i.e., the one found in Romans, does specifically mention that Paul was taking up a collection of money to take to "the poor saints which are at Jerusalem."

---

[244] Baird W (1971b).

And when James, Cephas, and John, who seemed to be pillars, perceived the grace that was given unto me, they gave to me and Barnabas, the right hands of fellowship; that we should go unto the heathen, and they unto the circumcision. Only they would that we should remember the poor: the same which I also was forward to do. (Galatians 2:9-10, King James Version)

But now I go unto Jerusalem to minister unto the saints. For it hath pleased them of Macedonia and Achaia to make a certain contribution for the poor saints which are at Jerusalem. It hath pleased them verily; and their debtors they are. For if the Gentiles have been made partakers of their spiritual things, their duty is also to minister unto them in carnal things. (Romans 15:25-27, King James Version)

The latter passage clearly states that Paul has with him a sum of money to be given to the "poor saints" of the Jerusalem Church. However, in describing this visit to Jerusalem, Acts never once mentions this collection of money. Why not? The answer may well be that the Jerusalem Church interpreted Paul's collection as a bribe to buy their approval for his gospel and missionary activities. Whether or not the Jerusalem Church so interpreted Paul's collection, it appears likely that the collection was summarily rejected.

At the end of the letter (Romans 15:30-32) Paul expressed his fear of danger from the Jews in Jerusalem and even hinted that the church there might not feel able to accept the collection. It seems that both these fears were realized. Acts tells that Paul was accompanied by delegates from the Gentile churches but does not mention the collection. This omission is best explained on the assumption that Luke did not wish to say that the church in Jerusalem did not dare to accept it. If so, Paul's hope that it would symbolize the gathering of the Gentiles into the one family of God was disappointed.[245]

PAUL AND THE EBIONITES

In the above passage from Galatians 2:9-10, Paul claims that James directed him to "remember the poor." Likewise, Romans 15:25-27 has Paul referencing a collection of money for the "poor saints which are at Jerusalem." Most readers of these passages probably interpret these verses in terms of there being impoverished Christians in Jerusalem, possibly due to persecution or to famine. However, there is another possible meaning, one that is highly instructive.

The Greek word that is translated as "poor" in both of the above passages derives from *ptochos*. However, James would not have been speaking to Paul in Greek; he would have been speaking in Hebrew or Aramaic. If we search for the Hebrew or Aramaic word that has been rendered in Greek as *ptochos*, the word is *'ebyon* in the singular form and *'ebyonim* or *ebionim* in the plural form (*ebiona* in the emphatic form in Aramaic[246]), which words denote the poor or righteous ones, and it is from these Semitic words that the word "Ebionites" is derived.[247]

With the above etymology in mind, one can now construct a radically different understanding of James' reported directive to Paul. James was rebuking Paul and was directing him to remember the Ebionites, i.e., to conform to Ebionite belief and practices. In other words, James, as Bishop of the Jerusalem Church and as titular head of early Christianity,

---

[245] Lindars B (2003).
[246] Thomson JEH (2001).
[247] (A) *Strong's Old Testament Dictionary*, in --- (2001); (B) *Vine's Old Testament Dictionary.* In --- (2001); (C) Thomson JEH (2001); (D) Eisenman R (1997); (E) Eusebius (1999); (F) --- (2003s).

was commanding Paul to cease his preaching of his own gospel and to accept the Ebionite way, which, as noted previously in this chapter, was one of the main branches of early Jewish Christianity.

To fully understand James' directive to Paul, one must gain some better appreciation of Ebionite belief and practices. Unfortunately, this is no easy task, as most of the information that currently exists about the Ebionites is drawn from their enemies, i.e., from those who followed the Pauline form of Christianity. Nonetheless, some worthwhile information can be gleaned from those sources, as shown in the following quotation from Bishop Eusebius' (circa 260-339 CE) fourth-century *Ecclesiastical History*.

> They (the Ebionites) regarded him [Christ] as a plain, ordinary man, born of intercourse between a man and Mary, who gained righteousness through character growth. They observed every detail of the Law and did not think that they would be saved by faith in Christ alone and a corresponding life.

> Others, however, had the same name but escaped the absurd folly of the aforementioned. They did not deny that the Lord was born of a virgin and the Holy Spirit but nevertheless shared their failure to confess his preexistence as God the Word and Wisdom. Thus equally impious, they too were zealous in observing the Law literally and thought that the letters of the apostle [Paul] ought to be rejected totally, calling him an apostate from the Law. They used only the so-called Gospel of the Hebrews and accorded the others little respect. Like the former, they observed the Sabbath and the whole Jewish ceremonial, but on the Lord's Days they celebrated rites like ours in commemoration of the Savior's resurrection. [248]

---

[248] Eusebius (1999), p. 116-117.

As the above quotation illustrates, some Ebionites believed in the virgin birth of Jesus, and others apparently did not. However, as a group, the Ebionites denied the divinity of Jesus, emphasized obedience to the Law of Moses, denied that salvation was merely a matter of having faith in Jesus, and viewed Paul as little more than a heretic. Quite obviously, the Ebionites strongly condemned Paul and his message. Further, it should be noted that an essentially similar picture of the Ebionites emerges in the writings of: Bishop Irenaeus (130-200 or 140-210 CE) in his *Adversus Omnes Haereses*, a book that was written circa 180 CE; Tertullian (circa 155-post 220 CE); Hippolytus (170-235 CE); Origen (circa 185-254 CE); Saint Jerome (circa 347-420 CE); and Saint Epiphanius (circa 315-403 CE).[249] For example, Origen noted that the Ebionites kept Jewish religious observances, rejected Paul and his writings, and denied the divinity of Jesus.[250] Finally, it should be noted that the Ebionites rejected the canonical gospels and had their own gospel, variously known as the Gospel According to the Hebrews and the Gospel According to the Ebionites.[251]

If "remember the poor" means "remember the Ebionites," then James was instructing Paul to be like the Ebionites in preaching and practicing conformance to the Law of Moses, including circumcision, all Jewish dietary restrictions, etc. It also would have meant that James commanded Paul to cease his message of salvation through faith in Jesus and in "The Cross" of Jesus. Further, it would have meant that Paul was to cease any rhetoric that might be taken to mean that Jesus was somehow divine.

---

[249] Thomson JEH (2001).
[250] Strecker G (1971).
[251] Thomson JEH (2001). Note: in the present author's opinion, one cannot be sure whether the Gospel According to the Hebrews and the Gospel According to the Ebionites were two names for the same gospel or two different gospels.

In closing this section on the Ebionites, one cannot help but ask whether the followers of Jesus were known as Ebionites during Jesus' own earthly ministry, and whether Jesus didn't refer to them specifically when he talked about who would inherit the kingdom of heaven. A simple substitution of "Ebionites" for "poor" in the following verse would seem to indicate that he might have.

Blessed are the poor in spirit: for theirs is the kingdom of heaven. (Matthew 5:3, King James Version)

PAUL IN THE CLEMENTINE HOMILIES

Like the Clementine Recognitions, the Clementine Homilies represents Jewish Christian literature. In a letter prefixed to the Homilies, Simon Peter, the disciple of Jesus and, according to the Gospel of Matthew 16:18, the rock upon whom the church was to be built, writes to James the Just, the brother of Jesus and the first Bishop of the Jerusalem Church. In this letter, Peter reportedly asks James not to distribute Peter's sermons to the gentiles, but to share them only with those "who adhere firmly to the doctrine of the unity of God, after the mysterious manner of delivery which Moses had followed with regard to the seventy who afterwards sat in his seat..."[252] Peter then reportedly gives his reasons as follows, referring to "the enemy" and those who "tell such lies against me."

If this is not done, our doctrine of truth will be divided into a multitude of opinions. I know this not only as a prophet, but because I already see the beginning of the evil. For some of the Gentiles have rejected the lawful preaching which was delivered by me, and have received the lawless and worthless doctrine of the enemy. And even in my lifetime some have attempted to pervert my words by cunning interpretations to the abolition of

---

[252] Baur FC (1878), p. 90.

the law, as if I myself held such opinions, and did not teach sincerely or honestly; which be far from me. To do this is nothing else than to act against the law of God, which was given by Moses, and attested by our Lord when he said of its permanent duration: "Heaven and earth shall pass away, but one jot or one tittle shall not pass away from the law." But those who profess to set forth, I know not how, my thoughts, and think they can interpret the meaning of the discourses they have heard instructed by me, that my doctrine and opinion is so and so, a thing which never entered into my mind. If they venture to tell such lies against me while I am still living, how much more will they do so when I am gone? [253]

Who was this enemy who was telling lies about the gospel that Peter was preaching? In commenting on the above quotation from the letter prefixed to the Clementine Homilies, Ferdinand Baur gives his answer in a markedly pointed question. "Who can this enemy have been, whose lawless doctrine is being accepted among the heathen, but the apostle Paul?" [254]

PAUL'S LACK OF AUTHORITY

Within nascent Christianity, who had the authority to preach the gospel? How was such authority transmitted, and how was it maintained? The Clementine Recognitions answers those questions directly and unequivocally. Authority to preach Jesus' gospel came only from James, the first Bishop of the Jerusalem Church, the titular leader of early Christianity, and the brother of Jesus. Only those who had a written letter or testimonial from James that authorized them to preach the gospel were to

---

[253] Baur FC (1878), p. 90-91.
[254] Baur FC (1878), p. 91.

be received and welcomed by the early Christian communities. The following passage is from Book IV, Chapter 35, of the Clementine Recognitions.

> Wherefore observe the greatest caution, that you believe no teacher, unless he bring from Jerusalem the testimonial of James the Lord's brother, or of whosoever may come after him. For no one, unless he has gone up thither, and there has been approved as a fit and faithful teacher for preaching the word of Christ,— unless, I say, he brings a testimonial thence, is by any means to be received. But let neither prophet nor apostle be looked for by you at this time, besides us. For there is one true Prophet, whose words we twelve apostles preach; for He is the accepted year of God, having us apostles as His twelve months.[255]

What about Paul? Did he have any such written testimonial from James authorizing him to preach? As seen in the previously quoted passage from Acts 15:12-13, 19-20, and 22-29, at the close of the Apostolic Council in Jerusalem, James did not entrust his letter to the gentiles to Paul. Instead, he gave it to Judas Barsabas and Silas. It was Judas and Silas who received James' testimonial letter, but no letter of attestation was given to Paul.

Indeed, Paul appears to be attempting to confront his own lack of credentials from James and the Jerusalem Church in a passage found in II Corinthians. In typical Pauline fashion, he attempts to turn a weakness into a strength by downplaying the importance of having such a letter, and he suggests that having such a letter is actually a drawback and flaw,

---

[255] Smith T (1880), p. 301. Note: reflecting Jewish Christian belief, Jesus is referred to as being a prophet, not as being divine.

i.e., "for the letter killeth." Lest some should think that the "letter" referred to in the following passage from II Corinthians 3:1-3, 5-6 is a letter of the alphabet, as opposed to an epistle, it should be noted that the Greek word being translated as "letter" in the above passage is *gramma* and that *gramma* may be variously translated as letter, note, epistle, book, and something written.[256]

> Do we begin again to commend ourselves? or need we, as some others, epistles of commendation to you, or letters of commendation from you? Ye are our epistle written in our hearts, known and read of all men: Forasmuch as ye are manifestly declared to be the epistle of Christ ministered by us, written not with ink, but with the Spirit of the living God; not in tables of stone, but in fleshy tables of the heart...Not that we are sufficient of ourselves to think any thing as of ourselves; but our sufficiency is of God; Who also hath made us able ministers of the new testament; not of the letter, but of the spirit: for the letter killeth, but the spirit giveth life. (II Corinthians 3:1-3, 5-6, King James Version)

Paul's claim to legitimacy is based solely on his own self-report of having been entrusted with the task of preaching to the gentiles by his vision of the "risen Jesus." As such, he discounts and mocks the authority of the Jerusalem Church, of the actual disciples of Jesus, and of James, the titular head of the church. In fact, Paul goes so far as to claim that anyone, human or angel, who preaches anything other than Paul's own message is cursed. In other words, Paul has placed himself above all human and angelic authority and is, in essence, claiming the divine attribute of infallibility for himself.

---

[256] (A) *Strong's New Testament Dictionary*, in --- (2001); (B) *Vine's New Testament Dictionary*, in --- (2001).

But though we, or an angel from heaven, preach any other gospel unto you than that which we have preached unto you, let him be accursed. As we said before, so say I now again, If any man preach any other gospel unto you than that ye have received, let him be accursed. (Galatians 1:8-9, King James Version)

Again, Paul tries to make a virtue of the fact that he has received no authority or legitimacy from James and the Jerusalem Church. He emphasizes that he learned his gospel from no man, including the actual disciples and James, the brother of Jesus. For Paul, whatever claim he has to religious authority is based in his self-report of having received a vision of the "risen Jesus."

Paul, an apostle, (not of men, neither by man, but by Jesus Christ, and God the Father, who raised him from the dead;)...But I certify you, brethren, that the gospel which was preached of me is not after man. For I neither received it of man, neither was I taught it, but by the revelation of Jesus Christ...But when it pleased God, who separated me from my mother's womb, and called me by his grace, To reveal his Son in me, that I might preach him among the heathen; immediately I conferred not with flesh and blood: Neither went I up to Jerusalem to them which were apostles before me; but I went into Arabia, and returned again unto Damascus. Then after three years I went up to Jerusalem to see Peter, and abode with him fifteen days. But other of the apostles saw I none, save James the Lord's brother. (Galatians 1:1, 11-12, 15-19, King James Version)

The preceding passage makes it abundantly clear that Paul did not learn his gospel message from the actual disciples of Jesus. Moreover, according to Paul's own statement, it took him three years after his so-called conversion experience before he even bothered to seek out Peter and James. Even then, whatever they could have taught him was of no merit to Paul. Moreover, as has been previously seen in this chapter, what Jesus actually said and did during his earthly life must have been of no value to Paul. As Rudolph Bultmann, the great 20th-century theologian, has noted:

> ...it is clear that Paul is not dependent on Jesus. Jesus' teaching is—to all intents and purposes—irrelevant for Paul.[257]

SUMMARY STATEMENT

In closing this section on Paul's relationship to the Jerusalem Church, it is instructive to consider the words of Ian Wilson and of Hugh J. Schonfield, the latter a prominent Jewish critic of Christianity. In making their remarks, both authors focus on Paul's relationship with Jewish Christianity and the Jerusalem Church.

> We seem to be faced with a straight, first-century clash of theologies, Paul's on the one hand, James' on the other, and despite the authority which should be due to the latter, Paul's is all that has been allowed to come down to us. Or, in fairness, almost all.[258]

> For this Apostolic Church much that Paul taught was grievous error and not at all in accord with the mind and message of the Messiah. The original Apostles could urge that the truth was known only to them. Paul had never companied with Jesus or heard what he said day after day...[259]

> It was not only the teaching and activities of Paul which made him obnoxious to the Christian leaders; but their awareness that he set

---

[257] Bultmann R (1969), p. 223.
[258] Wilson I (1985), p. 127.
[259] Schonfield HJ (1968), p. 60.

his revelations above their authority and claimed an intimacy with the mind of Jesus greater than that of those who had companied with him on earth and had been chosen by him. To them he was a presumptuous upstart. It was an abomination, especially as his ideas were so contrary to what they knew of Jesus, that he should pose as the embodiment of Messiah's will and dare to instruct them as if he were Jesus himself...Paul, was seen as the demon-driven enemy of the new David (Jesus)...Paul was a dangerous and disruptive influence, bent on enlisting a large following from among the Gentiles in order to provide himself with a numerical superiority with the support of which he could set at defiance the Elders at Jerusalem. Paul had been the enemy from the beginning, and because he had failed in his former open hostility he had craftily insinuated himself into the fold to destroy it from within.[260]

PAUL VS. PAUL

In previous sections of this chapter, it has been demonstrated that Paul's gospel was frequently in conflict with that of Jesus and with that of the Jerusalem Church. The present section examines Paul's own lack of consistency with himself. This is done with regard to his conversion experience, the Apostolic Council in Jerusalem, and the Mosaic Law.

PAUL'S CONVERSION

As noted previously, accounts of Paul's conversion experience and its immediate aftermath are recorded in one passage in Galatians and in three passages in Acts. Of note, significant differences emerge in those accounts when they are closely examined. This can be readily seen by examining the four passages in question.

---

[260] Schonfield HJ (1968), p. 66-67.

And as he journeyed, he came near Damascus: and suddenly there shined round about him a light from heaven: And he fell to the earth, and heard a voice saying unto him, Saul, Saul, why persecutest thou me? And he said, Who art thou, Lord? And the Lord said, I am Jesus whom thou persecutest: it is hard for thee to kick against the pricks. And he trembling and astonished said, Lord, what wilt thou have me to do? And the Lord said unto him, Arise, and go into the city, and it shall be told thee what thou must do. And the men which journeyed with him stood speechless, hearing a voice, but seeing no man. And Saul arose from the earth; and when his eyes were opened, he saw no man: but they led him by the hand, and brought him into Damascus. And he was three days without sight, and neither did eat nor drink...And Ananias went his way, and entered into the house; and putting his hands on him said, Brother Saul, the Lord, even Jesus, that appeared unto thee in the way as thou camest, hath sent me, that thou mightest receive thy sight, and be filled with the Holy Ghost. And immediately there fell from his eyes as it had been scales: and he received sight forthwith, and arose, and was baptized. And when he had received meat, he was strengthened. Then was Saul certain days with the disciples which were at Damascus...And after that many days were fulfilled, the Jews took counsel to kill him: But their laying await was known of Saul. And they watched the gates day and night to kill him. Then the disciples took him by night, and let him down by the wall in a basket. And when Saul was come to Jerusalem, he assayed to join himself to the disciples: but they were all afraid of him, and believed not that he was a disciple. But Barnabas took him, and brought him to the apostles, and declared unto them how he had seen the Lord in the way, and that he had spoken to him, and how he had preached boldly at Damascus in the name of Jesus. And he was with them coming in and going out at Jerusalem. (Acts 9:3-9, 17-19, 23-28, King James Version)

There are several points in the above passage that need to be highlighted in order to compare them with what is stated in other Biblical accounts of Paul's conversion. (1) In the above account, Paul's traveling companions heard the voice, but they didn't see anything out of the ordinary (Acts 9:7). (2) In contrast, Paul reportedly heard the voice (Acts 9:4-6) and saw the supposedly risen Jesus (Acts 9:27). (3) Although a light is mentioned, it is not described as being blinding (Acts 9:3), and Paul continues to see the supposedly risen Jesus (Acts 9:27). (4) Having been led into Damascus, Ananias visits Paul and lays his hands on him. With this laying on of hands, Paul's vision is immediately restored (Acts 9:17-18). (5) After spending a few days preaching in Damascus, Paul then journeys to Jerusalem to spend what appears to be several days with the actual disciples of Jesus (Acts 9:26-27). This above scenario can now be compared to the report found in Acts 22.

And it came to pass, that, as I made my journey, and was come nigh unto Damascus about noon, suddenly there shone from heaven a great light round about me. And I fell unto the ground, and heard a voice saying unto me, Saul, Saul, why persecutest thou me? And I answered, Who art thou, Lord? And he said unto me, I am Jesus of Nazareth, whom thou persecutest. And they that were with me saw indeed the light, and were afraid; but they heard not the voice of him that spake to me. And I said, What shall I do, Lord? And the Lord said unto me, Arise, and go into Damascus, and there it shall be told thee of all things which are appointed for thee to do. And when I could not see for the glory of the light, being led by the hand of them that were with me, I came into Damascus. And one Ananias, a devout man according to the law, having a good report of all the Jews which dwelt there, Came unto me, and stood, and said unto me, Brother Saul, receive thy sight. And the same hour I looked up upon him…And it came to pass, that, when I was come again to Jerusalem, even while I prayed in the temple, I was in a trance; And saw him saying unto me, Make haste, and get thee quickly out of Jerusalem: for they will not receive thy testimony concerning me…And he said unto me, Depart: for I will send thee far hence unto the Gentiles. (Acts 22:6-13, 17-18, 21, King James Version)

Referring back to the points made with regard to the conversion story in Acts 9, the following is noted. (1) In the immediately preceding passage, Paul's companions see a light, but they hear no voice (Acts 22:9). This is just the opposite of what was previously reported in Acts 9:7. (2) In Acts 9, Paul reportedly hears the voice and sees Jesus. In contrast, in the above passage, Paul hears the voice and sees a blinding light (Acts 22:6-11). (3) In Acts 9, as soon as Ananias lays his hands upon Paul, Paul's vision is immediately restored. However, in the above passage, there is no laying on of hands, and the restoration of sight occurs not immediately, but within an hour (Acts 22:12-13). (4) Finally, as in Acts 9, the above passage has Paul journeying from Damascus to Jerusalem. However, unlike the account in Acts 9, the preceding passage does not have Paul meeting with the actual disciples of Jesus. With these discrepancies in mind, consider the much abbreviated account to be found in Acts 26.

At midday, O king, I saw in the way a light from heaven, above the brightness of the sun, shining round about me and them which journeyed with me. And when we were all fallen to the earth, I heard a voice speaking unto me, and saying in the Hebrew tongue, Saul, Saul, why persecutest thou me? it is hard for thee to kick against the pricks. And I said, Who art thou, Lord? And he said, I am Jesus whom thou persecutest. But rise, and stand upon thy feet: for I have appeared unto thee for this purpose, to make thee a minister and a witness both of these things which thou hast seen, and of those things in the which I will appear unto thee...Whereupon, O king Agrippa, I was not disobedient unto the heavenly vision: But shewed first unto them of Damascus, and at Jerusalem, and throughout all the coasts of Judaea, and then to the Gentiles... (Acts 26:13-16, 19-20, King James Version)

Each of the three above accounts of Paul's conversion experience and its immediate aftermath comes from Acts. In all fairness, it must be remembered that Acts was not written by Paul, even though it was written from within the Pauline school of thought, presumably by Luke. As such, the above passages represent secondary source material, even though in places Paul is supposedly being quoted. However, when one turns to the account in Galatians of Paul's conversion, one is dealing with what Paul himself actually wrote.

But when it pleased God, who separated me from my mother's womb, and called me by his grace, To reveal his Son in me, that I might preach him among the heathen; immediately I conferred not with flesh and blood: Neither went I up to Jerusalem to them which were apostles before me; but I went into Arabia, and returned again unto Damascus. Then after three years I went up to Jerusalem to see Peter, and abode with him fifteen days. But other of the apostles saw I none, save James the Lord's brother. (Galatians 1:15-19, King James Version)

The discrepancies to be found regarding Paul's conversion experience in the four above quoted passages are briefly summarized in Figure #6 below.

Figure # 6

PAUL'S CONVERSION

	ACTS 9	ACTS 22	ACTS 26	GAL. 1
Paul's companions heard	a voice	nothing	???	???
Paul's companions saw	nothing	a light	a light	???
Paul heard	a voice	a voice	a voice	???
Paul saw	Jesus	a light	a light	???
Paul is blinded	yes	yes	???	???
Paul's blindness healed	immediately	within an hr.	???	???
Paul goes to	Jerusalem	Jerusalem	Jerusalem	Arabia
Paul with the disciples	yes	no	???	not for 3 years

??? = Nothing is said with regard to the item in question.

PAUL AND THE APOSTOLIC COUNCIL

Just as there are discrepancies to be found in the Biblical scriptures regarding Paul's conversion experience and its immediate aftermath, there is also a major contradiction to be found with regard to Paul's participation in the so-called Apostolic Council in Jerusalem. The first version is found in a passage from Galatians 2, which is quoted immediately below, while the second is in Acts 15, which is quoted thereafter.

> Then fourteen years after I went up again to Jerusalem with Barnabas, and took Titus with me also. And I went up by revelation, and communicated unto them that gospel which I preach among the Gentiles... (Galatians 2:1-2a, King James Version)

> And certain men which came down from Judaea taught the brethren and said, Except ye be circumcised after the manner of Moses, ye cannot be saved. When therefore Paul and Barnabas had no small dissension and disputation with them, they determined that Paul and Barnabas, and certain other of them, should go up to Jerusalem unto the apostles and elders about this question. (Acts 15:1-2, King James Version)

In the passage from Galatians, Paul claimed that divine revelation called him to go to Jerusalem for the Apostolic Council. However, in Acts, Paul and Barnabas were basically ordered by representatives of the Jerusalem Church to go with them to Jerusalem to defend themselves for preaching a deviant gospel. How one might possibly account for such a discrepancy is an issue that will be addressed subsequently.

PAUL AND THE LAW

In numerous passages written by Paul and quoted previously in this chapter, Paul preached the total abrogation of the Law of Moses. Those passages need not be needlessly repeated at this time. However, in what would appear to be a blatant contradiction with such a gospel message, Acts 18:18-21 and 21:18-26 both appear to show that Paul himself twice underwent the temporary rites of being a Nazirite. This is indicated by Paul shaving his head in the first instance and by the reported statement of James in the second instance. Both of these episodes were in relation to a trip to Jerusalem, and both were in conformance to the Mosaic Law as stipulated in Numbers 6:1-21. In the incident reported in Acts 21:18-26, it is specifically stated that Paul undergoes this rite to "purify thyself with them" and to show "that thou thyself also walkest orderly, and keepest the law" (Acts 21:24).

How is it that Paul can preach the total abrogation of the Law of Moses, but then turn around and undergo the ascetic rites of being a Nazirite in conformance to the Law of Moses? How is it that Paul can claim that those who conform to the Mosaic Law are "under the curse,"[261] but still practice those same laws in twice undergoing the rites of being a temporary Nazirite? What does this say about Paul's character and beliefs?

One aspect of the Mosaic Law that Paul specifically abrogated was male circumcision. Paul made this argument in two previously quoted passages from his letters. The one is from Romans, and the other is from Galatians.

> For circumcision verily profiteth, if thou keep the law: but if thou be a breaker of the law, thy circumcision is made uncircumcision. Therefore if the uncircumcision keep the righteousness of the law, shall not his uncircumcision be counted for circumcision?...But he is a Jew, which is one inwardly; and circumcision is that of the heart, in the spirit, and not in the letter; whose praise is not of men, but of God. (Romans 2:25-26, 29, King James Version)

---

[261] Galatians 3:10. If they are counting on conformance to the Law of Moses to save them, then they must conform to all aspects of the Mosaic Law without any exception, or they are cursed. (Deuteronomy 27:26).

Stand fast therefore in the liberty wherewith Christ hath made us free, and be not entangled again with the yoke of bondage. Behold, I Paul say unto you, that if ye be circumcised, Christ shall profit you nothing. For I testify again to every man that is circumcised, that he is a debtor to do the whole law. Christ is become of no effect unto you, whosoever of you are justified by the law; ye are fallen from grace. For we through the Spirit wait for the hope of righteousness by faith. For in Jesus Christ neither circumcision availeth any thing, nor uncircumcision; but faith which worketh by love. (Galatians 5:1-6, King James Version)

Further, in Galatians, Paul bolstered his argument that circumcision had been abrogated, at least for the gentiles, by claiming that the Jerusalem Church did not insist on Titus, a Greek convert to Christianity, undergoing circumcision. If it is a truthful report, and the truthfulness of the report can be questioned, the following passage would appear to confirm what Paul said about circumcision being abrogated, at least for gentile converts to Christianity.

Then fourteen years after I went up again to Jerusalem with Barnabas, and took Titus with me also…But neither Titus, who was with me, being a Greek, was compelled to be circumcised…" (Galatians 2:1, 3, King James Version)

However, against this backdrop of Paul abrogating the law of male circumcision, in a passage from Acts quoted previously, Paul circumcised Timothy, another convert to Christianity.

Then came he (Paul) to Derbe and Lystra: and, behold, a certain disciple was there, named Timotheus, the son of a certain woman, which was a Jewess, and believed; but his father was a

Greek: Which was well reported of by the brethren that were at Lystra and Iconium. Him would Paul have to go forth with him; and took and circumcised him because of the Jews which were in those quarters: for they knew all that his father was a Greek. (Acts 16:1-3, King James Version)

If the Mosaic Law of male circumcision has been abrogated as Paul claims, then why did he make Timothy undergo the needless pain of adult circumcision? Why did Paul take knife in hand and circumcise his friend and companion if there were no religious need?

SUMMARY AND CONCLUSIONS

What does one make of a man whose conversion story has so many embedded discrepancies from one telling to another? How does one account for there being two different accounts of why Paul attended the Apostolic Council at Jerusalem? Why does a man simultaneously deny the legitimacy of the Law of Moses and yet twice undergo the Nazirite rites of purification to show that he "walkest orderly, and keepest the law" (Acts 21:24)? How can this self same man deny the legitimacy of male circumcision and then turn around and circumcise Timothy, merely "because of the Jews which were in those quarters" (Acts 16:3)? The answer may be found in the following passages written by Paul himself.

For if the truth of God hath more abounded through my lie unto his glory; why yet am I also judged as a sinner? (Romans 3:7, King James Version)

For though I be free from all men, yet have I made myself servant unto all, that I might gain the more. And unto the Jews I became as a Jew, that I might gain the Jews; to them that are under the law, as under the law that I might gain them that are under the law; To them that are without law, as without law, (being not without law to God, but under the law to Christ,) that I might gain them that are without law. To the weak became I as weak, that I might gain the weak: I am made all things to all men, that I might by all means save some. And this I do for the gospel's sake, that I might be partaker thereof with you. (I Corinthians 9:19-23, King James Version)

There is a word that describes a person who lies to achieve a goal, however admirable he may believe that goal may be. There is a word that describes a person who attempts to be all things to all people, conforming his actions and statements to what is wanted from him, in order to lead those people to one's own version of the gospel. There is a word that describes a person who denies the Mosaic Law, yet attempts by the rites of being a Nazirite to confirm his zealousness for the Law of Moses. There is a word that describes a person who denies the religious requirement of male circumcision and then turns around and circumcises someone because of pressure from others. That word is not "saint," and it is not "apostle." The correct word is "hypocrite."

CHAPTER 3

HOLY WAR AND GENOCIDE

INTRODUCTION

THE CONCEPT OF HOLY WAR has dominated the news media of the first decade of the 21st century. Whether the news' spotlight focuses on the Middle East, the Indian subcontinent, or the islands of the Far East, Holy War seems to be the hot topic of conversation. Typically, the concept of Holy War is presented as something quite foreign to the Judaeo-Christian tradition, as something that is only associated with other religions that are far removed from the self-perceived higher ethical and spiritual values of Judaism and Christianity. However, such a view is more than a little myopic, for the concept of Holy War and the history of engaging in Holy War are central to Biblical history, especially when it comes to the Israelite invasion of Canaan, i.e., what is today called Palestine.

The narrative of the Israelite invasion and conquest of Canaan is told in graphic detail in the Biblical book of Joshua, although aside from a sanitized rendition of the walls of Jericho "come tumbling down," this is a story that receives relatively little attention in Sunday school classes. It is a story of Holy War and mass genocide carried out strictly in the name of the Israelite religion. As Joshua tells it, this is mass extinction carried out in the name of and under the explicit orders of God. This is not something far removed from or foreign to the Judaeo-Christian tradition. This is a series of atrocities that lie at the very heart of Biblical history. In what follows, the Holy War and mass genocide recorded in the Biblical books of Numbers, Deuteronomy, and Joshua are reviewed, both in terms of the immediately preceding events before entering Palestine and in terms of the invasion and conquest of Canaan.

HOLY WAR AGAINST MIDIAN

Numbers 25:1-5 tells a story about Moses and the Israelites in the Transjordan. Reportedly, Israelite men were taking Moabite women as their wives or lovers, and these Moabite women were influencing the Israelite men into worshipping Baalpeor, the local Moabite deity. In reaction, God reportedly tells Moses that those Israelite men who have started to worship Baalpeor are to be killed, and Moses then passes along that command to the judges of Israel. It is in this context that an Israelite named Zimri took Cozbi, a Midianite woman, as his wife.[262] (See chapter four for a fuller discussion of this latter event.) In response to the Israelite men now taking wives from the Midianites, God reportedly commands that the Midianites be exterminated in order to remove temptation from the Israelite men.

> And the Lord spake unto Moses, saying, Vex the Midianites, and smite them: For they vex you with their wiles, wherewith they have beguiled you in the matter of Peor, and in the matter of Cozbi, the daughter of a prince of Midian... (Numbers 25:16-18, King James Version)

> And the Lord spake unto Moses, saying, Avenge the children of Israel of the Midianites: afterward shalt thou be gathered unto thy people. And Moses spake unto the people, saying, Arm some of yourselves unto the war, and let them go against the Midianites, and avenge the Lord of Midian. (Numbers 31:1-3, King James Version)

---

[262] (A) Guthrie HH (1971); (B) Eisenman R (1997).

After relaying these alleged instructions from God and allowing the Israelite men time to gird themselves for war, Moses selected 12,000 soldiers from the Israelites, one thousand from each of the 12 tribes of Israel. [263] This army of 12,000 Israelites was then sent out with "the holy instruments"[264] to wage a first-strike war of extinction against the Midianites, a people that had not attacked the Israelites but had only begun to intermarry with them. The carnage that followed, reportedly at the direct command of God, represented nothing less than mass genocide.

> And they warred against the Midianites, as the Lord command-
> ed Moses; and they slew all the males. And they slew the kings of
> Midian, beside the rest of them that were slain; namely, Evi,
> and Rekem, and Zur, and Hur, and Reba, five kings of Midian:
> Balaam also the son of Beor they slew with the sword. And the
> children of Israel took all the women of Midian captives, and
> their little ones, and took the spoil of all their cattle, and all their
> flocks, and all their goods. And they burnt all their cities where-
> in they dwelt, and all their goodly castles, with fire. (Numbers
> 31:7-11, King James Version)

The above description is more than graphic in its details. Every last adult man of Midian was killed! The Midianite women and children were taken captive as slaves. The Midianite livestock was appropriated as spoils of war, and the Midianite towns were burned to the ground. However, the carnage and atrocities of this Holy War did not stop at that point. Incredibly, there was still more to come.

> And they brought the captives, and the prey, and the spoil, unto
> Moses, and Eleazar the priest, and unto the congregation of the

---

[263] Numbers 31:4-5.
[264] Numbers 31:6.

children of Israel, unto the camp at the plains of Moab, which are by Jordan near Jericho...And Moses said unto them, Have ye saved all the women alive? Behold, these caused the children of Israel, through the counsel of Balaam, to commit trespass against the Lord in the matter of Peor, and there was a plague among the congregation of the Lord. Now therefore kill every male among the little ones, and kill every woman that hath known man by lying with him. But all the women children, that have not known a man by lying with him, keep alive for yourselves. (Numbers 31:12, 15-18, King James Version)

As can be seen from the above quoted passage, it was not enough to kill every adult Midianite man and to enslave the rest of the Midianite population. After taking the Midianite women and children captive, these defenseless ones were subject to yet more genocidal Holy War at the hands of the Israelites. Every male child of the Midianites was summarily slain, no matter how young he might be. Further, every Midianite female who had already experienced sexual relations was also killed. The only ones who were allowed to live from the Midianites were female children who had never had sexual relations, and these were to be kept as slaves and concubines for the Israelites.

To just what extent did the above atrocities extend? According to Numbers 31:35, the total number of Midianite girls who were enslaved was 32,000! If that Biblical figure is accepted as being accurate, it provides a useful yardstick for estimating the total number of Midianites killed. Assuming that half the Midianite children were boys, one would estimate that 32,000 male children were killed. The number of adults killed, including both men and women, should have been at least equal to the total number of Midianite children, i.e., 64,000. Thus, the Biblical indication is that somewhere in the vicinity of at least 100,000 Midianites, including thousands upon thousands of women and children, were killed in a first-strike, Holy War of extermination and genocide. It is little wonder that this Biblical lesson is never taught in modern Sunday schools!

GOD'S COMMANDS FOR HOLY WAR

As Israel prepared to enter the Promised Land, i.e., Biblical Palestine, God supposedly gave the Israelites two sets of commands for how the Israelites were to deal with other people. The first set of instructions had to do with how the Israelites were to interact with the people whose land the Israelites had to cross in order to reach Palestine. According to these commandments, Israel was first to offer peace to the inhabitants of that area. If the offer of peace was accepted, then those people were to become Israelite tributaries, i.e., people who serve the Israelites at forced labor. [265] If the offer of peace was not accepted, then every adult male of the other people was to be killed, and their wives and children were to become enslaved spoils of war.

> When thou comest nigh unto a city to fight against it, then pro-
> claim peace unto it. And it shall be, if it make thee answer of
> peace, and open unto thee, then it shall be, that all the people
> that is found therein shall be tributaries unto thee, and they shall
> serve thee. And if it will make no peace with thee, but will make

---

[265] In Deuteronomy 20:11, the King James Version euphemistically says "tributaries unto thee, and they shall serve thee," when the actual meaning is closer to "enslaved, forced labor." Using Roman letters, the actual Hebrew of this verse reads *"lamac wa'abaduwka."* *"Lamac"* is from *"mac,"* which has the meaning of "a burden" or "a tax in the form of forced labor." *"Wa'abaduwka"* is from *"'abad,"* which has the meaning of "to work," "to serve," or "to enslave." *Strong's Old Testament Dictionary,* in --- (2001).

war against thee, then thou shalt besiege it: And when the Lord thy God hath delivered it into thine hands, thou shalt smite every male thereof with the edge of the sword: But the women, and the little ones, and the cattle, and all that is in the city, even all the spoil thereof, shalt thou take unto thyself; and thou shalt eat the spoil of thine enemies, which the Lord thy God hath given thee. Thus shalt thou do unto all the cities which are very far off from thee, which are not of the cities of these nations. (Deuteronomy 20:10-15, King James Version)

The above commands for dealing with the people living in areas that the Israelites had to traverse in order to reach Palestine are striking and add some additional flavor to the Israelite and Biblical concept of Holy War. Merely because a people lived in the path the Israelites were taking to Palestine, they were given a choice between two totally unacceptable alternatives: either submit peacefully to serving the Israelites as forced labor or engage in a war in which all their men would be killed and their women and children totally enslaved. However, the situation was even worse for the inhabitants of Palestine, i.e., the land that God supposedly gave to the Israelites "for an inheritance."

But of the cities of these people, which the Lord thy God doth give thee for an inheritance, thou shalt save alive nothing that breatheth: But thou shalt utterly destroy them; namely, the Hittites, and the Amorites, the Canaanites, and the Perizzites, the Hivites, and the Jebusites; as the Lord thy God hath command- ed thee: That they teach you not to do after all their abomina- tions, which they have done unto their gods; so should ye sin against the Lord your God. (Deuteronomy 20:16-18, King James Version)

In Palestine, there was to be no peaceful co-existence. There wasn't even to be an offer of submitting peacefully to the Israelites and thus becoming their forced labor. There was to be no alternative given except total, genocidal annihilation of the indigenous inhabitants of Palestine. All men, all women, and all children were to be put to the sword. No one was to be left alive. This was the Holy War that the Israelites were to bring to Palestine, supposedly at the direct command of God. This was the Holy War of the conquest of Canaan.

HOLY WAR IN TRANSJORDAN

HOLY WAR AGAINST HESHBON

As reported in both Deuteronomy and Joshua, the first of the two commands reported above was carried out in full. The first concrete example of this has to do with the Amorite people of Heshbon, a city in Transjordan about 23 miles east and slightly south of Jericho.[266] What happened was that the Israelites demanded the right to cross the land of Heshbon to journey towards Jericho, and the Israelites also demanded that the people of Heshbon sell meat and water to them as they crossed the land of Heshbon.[267] (One can only wonder at the response of any modern country to a demand from thousands upon thousands of people that the country allows them to march through it in order that they can attack its neighbor. What would the United States do in response to a similar demand from a people wanting to march through the United States in order to attack Canada?) Not surprisingly, the king of Heshbon denied the Israelite demands.

> But Sihon king of Heshbon would not let us pass by him:
> for the Lord thy God hardened his spirit, and made his heart

---

[266] --- (1971).
[267] Deuteronomy 2:26-28.

obstinate, that he might deliver him into thy hand, as appeareth this day. And the Lord said unto me, Behold, I have begun to give Sihon and his land before thee: begin to possess, that thou mayest inherit his land. Then Sihon came out against us, he and all his people, to fight at Jahaz. And the Lord our God delivered him before us; and we smote him, and his sons, and all his people. And we took all his cities at that time, and utterly destroyed the men, and the women, and the little ones, of every city, we left none to remain. Only the cattle we took for a prey unto ourselves, and the spoil of the cities which we took. (Deuteronomy 2:30-35, King James Version)

As can be seen by the above account, the Israelites carried their Holy War even beyond the command supposedly given to them by God. The command, as reported in Deuteronomy 20:10-15, was to kill all the men and enslave the women and children. However, the Israelites in their zest for Holy War went even further. Not only did they kill all the Amorite men of Heshbon, but in furtherance of genocide they also killed all the women and children. Once again, this is an example of Biblically-based Holy War that receives little attention in contemporary Sunday school classes.

HOLY WAR AGAINST BASHAN

Having exterminated the Amorites of Heshbon down to every last man, woman, and child, the Israelites next turned their attention to Bashan, an Amorite kingdom due east of the Sea of Galilee.[268] Once again, the Israelite's Holy War consisted of mass extermination of every living Amorite in Bashan, down to and including every child and infant.

---

[268] --- (1971).

So the Lord our God delivered into our hands Og also, the king of Bashan, and all his people: and we smote him until none was left to him remaining. And we took all his cities at that time, there was not a city which we took not from them, threescore cities, all the region of Argob, the kingdom of Og in Bashan. All these cities were fenced with high walls, gates, and bars; beside unwalled towns a great many. And we utterly destroyed them, as we did unto Sihon king of Heshbon, utterly destroying the men, women, and children, of every city. (Deuteronomy 3:3-6, King James Version)

SUMMARY

The Israelite campaigns of Holy War against the Amorite kingdoms of Heshbon and Bashan are summarized in the following passage from Joshua. The passage gives one a better area of the Israelites swath of destruction. Using the landmarks listed in the passage, one can determine that the Israelites' Holy War of extermination extended as far north as Mount Hermon (approximately 40 miles north of the northernmost tip of the Sea of Galilee) and as far south as the River Arnon (approximately halfway down the Dead Sea).[269]

Now these are the kings of the land, which the children of Israel smote, and possessed their land on the other side Jordan toward the rising of the sun, from the river Arnon unto mount Hermon, and all the plain on the east: Sihon king of the Amorites, who dwelt in Heshbon, and ruled from Aroer, which is upon the bank of the river Arnon, and from the middle of the river, and from half Gilead, even unto the river Jabbok, which is the border of the children of Ammon; and from the plain to the sea of Chinneroth on the east, and unto the sea of the plain, even

---

[269] --- (1971).

the salt sea on the east, the way to Bethjeshimoth; and from the south, under Ashdothpisgah: And the coast of Og king of Bashan, which was of the remnant of the giants, that dwelt at Ashtaroth and at Edrei, and reigned in mount Hermon, and in Salcah, and in all Bashan, unto the border of the Geshurites, and the Maachathites, and half Gilead, the border of Sihon king of Heshbon. Them did Moses the servant of the Lord and the children of Israel smite: and Moses the servant of the Lord gave it for a possession unto the Reubenites, and the Gadites, and the half tribe of Manasseh. (Joshua 12:1-6, King James Version)

HOLY WAR AGAINST JERICHO AND AI

INTRODUCTION

The Israelites' reported genocide of the Amorites in Transjordan was unfortunately just the prelude to the atrocities committed by the Israelites once they began the invasion of Palestine. As the Israelites began their military conquest of Palestine, they were under the command of Joshua, who had assumed leadership of the Israelites following the death of Moses. However, before beginning a review of the Holy Wars carried out by the Israelites in Palestine, it may be helpful to review once more what they believed was the command of God concerning their conduct in these Holy Wars.

But of the cities of these people, which the Lord thy God doth give thee for an inheritance, thou shalt save alive nothing that breatheth: But thou shalt utterly destroy them; namely, the Hittites, and the Amorites, the Canaanites, and the Perizzites, the Hivites, and the Jebusites; as the Lord thy God hath command-ed thee: That they teach you not to do after all their abominations, which they have done unto their gods; so should ye sin against the Lord your God. (Deuteronomy 20:16-18, King James Version)

THE CONQUEST OF JERICHO

Prior to the Israelites crossing westward over the River Jordan, Joshua sent two spies to scout the city-state of Jericho, a city about seven to eight miles north of the northern tip of the Dead Sea and about five miles west of the River Jordan. [270] Upon entering Jericho, these Israelite spies were given shelter and hidden by a prostitute named Rahab. However, Rahab had an ulterior motive for helping the two Israelite spies. She had heard of the Israelite conquests in Transjordan and was fearful for her life and the lives of her parents and siblings. As such, her hiding the two Israelites came with a price: she and her parents and siblings were to be spared from the ensuing Israelite slaughter of the inhabitants of Jericho. To this, the two Israelite spies acquiesced. [271]

Upon the two spies returning to the Israelite camp in Transjordan, Joshua readied the Israelites to invade Palestine. The Ark of the Covenant was carried in front of the Israelites, and the waters of the River Jordan were miraculously stopped from flowing so that the Israelites could cross over into Palestine on dry land. Having arrived in Palestine near Jericho, the Israelites then reportedly circumcised all the Israelite males who had been born in the wilderness during the time since the Israelites left Egypt. As the Israelites then recovered from this mass circumcision ceremony, they celebrated Passover. [272]

---

[270] --- (1971).
[271] Joshua 2:1-24.
[272] Joshua 3:1-5:15.

With the Passover rites completed, God reportedly told Joshua that the Israelites were to engage in the following ritual around the walled city of Jericho. (1) For six consecutive days, seven priests were to carry trumpets before the Ark of the Covenant, and all of Israel were to circumambulate around Jericho once each day. (2) On the seventh day, seven circumambulations were to be performed. (3) At the close of the seventh circumambulation on the seventh day, the priests were to blow on their trumpets, and the people were to give out a great shout. At that moment, the walls of the city of Jericho would miraculously fall down.[273]

Joshua so instructed the Israelites, and the ritual was performed as instructed, but not before Joshua warned the Israelites to preserve Rahab and her parents and siblings from destruction. The Israelites then did as they were commanded, and the following verses indicate what happened next.

> So the people shouted when the priests blew with the trumpets: and it came to pass, when the people heard the sound of the trumpet, and the people shouted with a great shout, that the wall fell down flat, so that the people went up into the city, every man straight before him, and they took the city. And they utterly destroyed all that was in the city, both man and woman, young and old, and ox, and sheep, and ass, with the edge of the sword. But Joshua had said unto the two men that had spied out the country, Go into the harlot's house, and bring out thence the woman, and all that she hath, as ye sware unto her. And the young men that were spies went in, and brought out Rahab, and her father, and her mother, and her brethren, and all that she had; and they brought out all her kindred, and left them without the camp of Israel. And they burnt the city with fire, and all that was

---

[273] Joshua 6:1-5.

therein: only the silver, and the gold, and the vessels of brass and of iron, they put into the treasury of the house of the Lord. And Joshua saved Rahab the harlot alive, and her father's household, and all that she had; and she dwelleth in Israel even unto this day; because she hid the messengers, which Joshua sent to spy out Jericho. (Joshua 6:20-25, King James Version)

In the Transjordan, the Israelite Holy War resulted in the death of every man, woman, and child in the conquered kingdoms. In Palestine, the destruction was even greater. As seen in the foregoing passage, aside from Rahab and her family, not only were every man, woman, and child of Jericho put to the sword, but even every animal was slain. With the single exception of Rahab and her family, every man, every woman, every child, every infant, every ox, every sheep, and even every donkey in the city of Jericho were ruthlessly exterminated. Not one living thing was left. Such was the manner in which the Israelites followed what they believed was the command of God regarding how they were to wage Holy War.

THE CONQUEST OF AI

After annihilating Jericho, the Israelites turned their attention to Ai, a city about 11 miles northwest of Jericho.[274] An Israelite scouting party reported back that Ai was relatively weak and wouldn't require more than about 3,000 men to level the city. However, an Israelite force of 3,000 men was repulsed, and 36 Israelites were killed in the battle. When Joshua bewailed this loss, God reportedly informed him that the Israelites had suffered this defeat because they had sinned in that an Israelite had stolen from the war booty taken at Jericho. Through an elaborate sorting out process, this Israelite was identified as being Achan of the tribe of

---

[274] --- (1971).

Judah. Once identified, Achan confessed that he had withheld a garment, two hundred shekels of silver, and a piece of gold weighing 50 shekels (about 20 ounces[275]). In punishment, Achan and all his animals and children, some of whom were presumably innocent, were stoned to death, and their bodies were burned. Having thus punished the transgressor among them, the Israelites reportedly received a message from God through Joshua.[276]

> And the Lord said unto Joshua, Fear not, neither be thou dismayed: take all the people of war with thee, and arise, go up to Ai: see, I have given into thy hand the king of Ai, and his people, and his city, and his land: and thou shalt do to Ai and her king as thou didst unto Jericho and her king: only the spoil thereof, and the cattle thereof, shall ye take for a prey unto yourselves: lay thee an ambush for the city behind it. (Joshua 8:1-2, King James Version)

Joshua then sent a force of 30,000 Israelites to lie hidden in wait to the west of the city of Ai. Once that was done, Joshua and the rest of the Israelite army, apparently a much smaller force than the 30,000 men in hiding, marched to Ai, approaching it from the north. This smaller force then camped for the night out of sight of Ai, and Joshua dispatched another group of 5,000 Israelites to serve as a second ambush group. The following morning, the remaining Israelites with Joshua showed themselves in full view of the city. Seeing the small Israelite force advancing on them, the inhabitants of Ai threw open the gates to their city and rushed out to attack the numerically smaller Israelite force. The Israelites then began to retreat into the wilderness, and the inhabitants of Ai followed

---

[275] Duncan GB (1971b).
[276] Joshua 7:1-8:1.

them, leaving not a single man in the city. In pursuing the Israelites, the people of Ai were then apparently joined by the people of Bethel (a city only about two miles northwest of Ai [277]). Once the people of Ai and Bethel had been drawn away from their walled cities, the Israelites waiting in ambush stormed into the unprotected city of Ai, set Ai on fire, and then attacked the people of Ai and Bethel from their rear.[278]

> And when Joshua and all Israel saw that the ambush had taken the city, and that the smoke of the city ascended, then they turned again, and slew the men of Ai. And the other issued out of the city against them; so they were in the midst of Israel, some on this side, and some on that side: and they smote them, so that they let none of them remain or escape. And the king of Ai they took alive, and brought him to Joshua. And it came to pass, when Israel had made an end of slaying all the inhabitants of Ai in the field, in the wilderness wherein they chased them, and when they were all fallen on the edge of the sword, until they were consumed, that all the Israelites returned to Ai, and smote it with the edge of the sword. And so it was, that all that fell that day, both of men and women, were twelve thousand, even all the men of Ai. For Joshua drew not his hand back, wherewith he stretched out the spear, until he had utterly destroyed all the inhabitants of Ai. Only the cattle and the spoil of that city Israel took for a prey unto themselves, according unto the word of the Lord which he commanded Joshua. And Joshua burnt Ai, and made it an heap for ever, even a desolation unto this day. And the king of Ai he hanged on a tree until eventide: and as soon as the sun was down, Joshua commanded that they should take his

---

[277] --- (1971).
[278] Joshua 8:3-22.

carcase down from the tree, and cast it at the entering of the gate of the city, and raise thereon a great heap of stones, that remaineth unto this day. (Joshua 8:21-29, King James Version)

Once again, reportedly at the direct command of God, the Israelites practiced Holy War and total genocide against another city-state. According to the text cited above, only the animals of Ai were allowed to live. Every man, woman, and child of Ai were put to death, and the total killed was around 12,000 people. Once again, an entire people had been exterminated in a Biblically-mandated and Biblically-justified act of Holy War.

HOLY WAR IN SOUTHERN PALESTINE
THE DEFEAT OF THE FIVE KINGS

Having totally annihilated the men, women, and children of both Jericho and Ai, the Israelites were poised to continue their murderous assault on the citizens of the various kingdoms within Palestine. However, at this point in the sequence of Holy Wars, the Israelites were tricked into entering into a peace deal with the inhabitants of Gibeon (a city about six miles northwest of Jerusalem[279]). A delegation of Gibeonites approached the Israelites, pretending to be emissaries from a distant people who were seeking a peaceful affiliation with the Israelites. Thinking that these Gibeonites were not inhabitants of Palestine, the Israelites entered into a peace covenant with the Gibeonites. However, once the Israelites discovered the true nature of the affair, they honored their covenant of peace by letting the Gibeonites continue to live, but at the cost of becoming the forced labor pool of the Israelites.[280]

---

[279] --- (1971).
[280] Joshua 9:1-27.

Hearing that Gibeon had made peace with the Israelites, Adonizedec, the king of Jerusalem, organized a confederation of the kings of southern Palestine. Included in this confederation were four different kings besides Adonizedec: Hoham, the king of Hebron (a city about 17 miles southwest of Jerusalem[281]); Piram, the king of Jarmuth (a city about 18 miles west southwest of Jerusalem); Japhia, the king of Lachish (a city about 29 miles southwest of Jerusalem [282]); and Debir, the king of Eglon (a city about 35 miles southwest of Jerusalem[283]). These five Amorite kings then gathered their military forces together and attacked Gibeon for betraying them by entering into a peace treaty with the Israelites. The Gibeonites responded by beseeching the Israelites, who were then camped at Gilgal, for military help.[284]

> So Joshua ascended from Gilgal, he, and all the people of war with him, and all the mighty men of valour. And the Lord said unto Joshua, Fear them not: for I have delivered them into thine hand; there shall not a man of them stand before thee. Joshua therefore came unto them suddenly, and went up from Gilgal all night. And the Lord discomfited them before Israel, and slew them with a great slaughter at Gibeon, and chased them along the way that goeth up to Bethhoron, and smote them to Azekah, and unto Makkedah. (Joshua 10:7-10, King James Version)

As if the above carnage weren't enough, two miraculous events then reportedly happened to further the annihilation of the Amorite armies of the five kings. (1) As the Amorite warriors fled from the battle, giant hailstones fell from the sky, striking the Amorites and killing even more

---

[281] --- (1971).
[282] -- (1971).
[283] --- (1971).
[284] Joshua 10:1-6.

of them than did the Israelites. (2) To further allow the Israelites to slay the Amorites by the sword, the sun and moon reportedly stood still in the sky, lengthening the daylight hours so that the Israelites could continue their slaughter unto the last man of the Amorite armies.[285]

The five Amorite kings, seeing their armies completely vanquished, fled and hid in a cave near Makkedah (a city about 17 miles west southwest of Jerusalem and only about two to three miles northwest of Jarmuth[286]). Unfortunately for the five kings, their presence was discovered by the Israelites who initially barricaded the entrance to the cave while the Israelites continued their extermination of the Amorite armies. When the last of the Amorite soldiers were killed, the cave was reopened, and the five kings were humiliated by having each Israelite soldier put his foot on the kings' necks. After this degrading spectacle had been completed, the five Amorite kings were slaughtered, and their bodies were hung up on trees for public viewing for the rest of the day. As evening then approached, the bodies of the five kings were taken down from the trees and thrown into the cave, which was then barricaded once again.[287]

THE CONQUEST OF MAKKEDAH

Having disposed of the five Amorite kings, the Israelites turned their attention to the city of Makkedah. Here again, the Israelites were victorious, and every resident of Makkedah was summarily killed, regardless of whether that resident was male or female, young or old, child or adult. Thus, the string of Israelite genocides extended to yet a third city-state in Palestine.

---

[285] Joshua 10:11-14.
[286] --- (1971).
[287] Joshua 10:16-27.

And that day Joshua took Makkedah, and smote it with the edge of the sword, and the king thereof he utterly destroyed, them, and all the souls that were therein; he let none remain: and he did to the king of Makkedah as he did unto the king of Jericho. (Joshua 10:28, King James Version)

THE CONQUEST OF LIBNAH

Having now utterly exterminated every person of Jericho, Ai, and Makkedah, as well as the armies of the five Amorite kings of southern Palestine, the Israelites turned their attention to the city of Libnah, which by this time had a new king. Once again, the Israelites achieved a military victory, resulting in the mass genocide of the residents of Libnah.

Then Joshua passed from Makkedah, and all Israel with him, unto Libnah, and fought against Libnah: and the Lord delivered it also, and the king thereof, into the hand of Israel; and he smote it with the edge of the sword, and all the souls that were therein; he let none remain in it; but did unto the king thereof as he did unto the king of Jericho. (Joshua 10:29-30, King James Version)

THE CONQUEST OF LACHISH

Lachish was the next city-state on the Israelites' list of Holy War victims. It reportedly fell to the Israelites on only the second day of battle, and all of its citizens were put to death. Thus, Lachish became the fifth city-state in Palestine to be subjected to the Israelites' Holy War of genocidal extermination.

And Joshua passed from Libnah, and all Israel with him, unto Lachish, and encamped against it, and fought against it: and the Lord delivered Lachish into the hand of Israel, which took it on the second day, and smote it with the edge of the sword, and all the souls that were therein, according to all that he had done to Libnah. (Joshua 10:31-32, King James Version)

THE CONQUEST OF GEZER

Seeing the ever growing reign of terror and genocide being practiced by the Israelites, Horam, the king of Gezer (a city about 21 miles west north-west of Jerusalem [288]), rallied his army to help the embattled people of Lachish before that city fell. However, the army of Gezer was unable to turn the tide of battle against the Israelites and was vanquished to the point of their being "none remaining."

> Then Horam king of Gezer came up to help Lachish; and Joshua smote him and his people, until he had left him none remaining. (Joshua 10:33, King James Version)

THE CONQUEST OF EGLON

Six city-states had now fallen to the Israelites in Palestine. In each case, the entire population of those city-states had been put to death. Eglon was to become the seventh city-state to be annihilated by the Israelites in their ongoing and genocidal Holy War.

> And from Lachish Joshua passed unto Eglon, and all Israel with him; and they encamped against it, and fought against it: and they took it on that day, and smote it with the edge of the sword, and all the souls that were therein he utterly destroyed that day, according to all that he had done to Lachish. (Joshua 10:34-35, King James Version)

THE CONQUEST OF HEBRON

Following the fall of Eglon, Hebron was the next target on the list of

---

[288] --- (1971).

Israelite aggression, becoming the eighth city-state to fall under the Israelite sword of Holy War. As was the Israelite pattern of conduct in their prior Holy Wars in Palestine, a pattern of conduct they justified by claiming that they were merely following God's command to them, the Israelites killed every man, woman, and child of Hebron and of the surrounding villages that Hebron controlled.

> And Joshua went up from Eglon, and all Israel with him, unto Hebron; and they fought against it: and they took it, and smote it with the edge of the sword, and the king thereof, and all the cities thereof, and all the souls that were therein; he left none remaining, according to all that he had done to Eglon; but destroyed it utterly, and all the souls that were therein. (Joshua 10:36-37, King James Version)

THE CONQUEST OF DEBIR

Debir was a city-state about 32 miles southwest of Jerusalem and about 13 miles southwest of Hebron.[289] Following the Israelite annihilation of Hebron, Debir became the ninth city-state of Palestine to fall before the Israelite advance.

> And Joshua returned, and all Israel with him, to Debir; and fought against it: and he took it, and the king thereof, and all the cities thereof; and they smote them with the edge of the sword, and utterly destroyed all the souls that were therein; he left none remaining: as he had done to Hebron, so he did to Debir, and to the king thereof; as he had done also to Libnah, and to her king. (Joshua 10:38-39, King James Version)

---

[289] --- (1971).

THE FINAL CONQUEST OF SOUTHERN PALESTINE

The author of Joshua ends his story of Israelite Holy War in southern Palestine in a summary statement that groups together numerous city-states and kingdoms as being the victims of Israelite military aggression. While details are lacking about these conquests, one can safely assume that the same mass genocide that the Israelites practiced elsewhere in Palestine was also the order of the day with regard to these additional conquests.

> So Joshua smote all the country of the hills, and of the south, and of the vale, and of the springs, and all their kings: he left none remaining, but utterly destroyed all that breathed, as the Lord God of Israel commanded. And Joshua smote them from Kadeshbarnea even unto Gaza, and all the country of Goshen, even unto Gibeon. And all these kings and their land did Joshua take at one time, because the Lord God of Israel fought for Israel. And Joshua returned, and all Israel with him, unto the camp to Gilgal. (Joshua 10:40-43, King James Version)

HOLY WAR IN NORTHERN PALESTINE

The Israelites had now conquered and exterminated the inhabitants of Jericho, Ai, and southern Palestine. Seeing this, the kings of northern Palestine grouped their forces together in an attempt to stand against the genocidal Holy War of the Israelites at the waters of Merom. Gathered together at that spot were King Jabin of Hazor and King Jobab of Madon, as well as the king of Shimron, the king of Achshaph, and many other kings of northern Palestine. These kings and their armies grouped together at Merom in a desperate, last ditch attempt to stave off the genocide approaching them.[290]

---

[290] Joshua 11:1-5.

So Joshua came, and all the people of war with him, against them by the waters of Merom suddenly; and they fell upon them. And the Lord delivered them into the hand of Israel, who smote them, and chased them unto great Zidon, and unto Misrephothmaim, and unto the valley of Mizpeh eastward; and they smote them, until they left them none remaining. And Joshua did unto them as the Lord bade him: he houghed their horses, and burnt their chariots with fire. And Joshua at that time turned back, and took Hazor, and smote the king thereof with the sword: for Hazor beforetime was the head of all those kingdoms. And they smote all the souls that were therein with the edge of the sword, utterly destroying them: there was not any left to breathe: and he burnt Hazor with fire. And all the cities of those kings, and all the kings of them, did Joshua take, and smote them with the edge of the sword, and he utterly destroyed them, as Moses the servant of the Lord commanded. But as for the cities that stood still in their strength, Israel burned none of them, save Hazor only; that did Joshua burn. And all the spoil of these cities, and the cattle, the children of Israel took for a prey unto themselves; but every man they smote with the edge of the sword, until they had destroyed them, neither left they any to breathe. (Joshua 11:7-14, King James Version)

Northern Palestine had now fallen in a massive bloodbath. As each city had fallen, the Israelites made sure that "every man they smote with the edge of the sword" and that "neither left they any to breathe." This they did according to their understanding of God's directive to them. What else can this be called besides a Holy War of genocidal annihilation?

140

SUMMARY OF THE ISRAELITES' CONQUESTS

Two different passages summarize the Israelites' conquests in Palestine. Both are worth quoting in order to appreciate fully the magnitude of what happened in the Israelite's Holy War in Palestine.

So Joshua took all the land, the hills, and all the south country, and all the land of Goshen, and the valley, and the plain, and the mountain of Israel, and the valley of the same: even from the mount Halak, that goeth up to Seir, even unto Baalgad in the valley of Lebanon under mount Hermon: and all their kings he took, and smote them, and slew them. Joshua made war a long time with all those kings. There was not a city that made peace with the children of Israel, save the Hivites the inhabitants of Gibeon: all other they took in battle. For it was of the Lord to harden their hearts, that they should come against Israel in battle, that he might destroy them utterly, and that they might have no favour, but that he might destroy them, as the Lord commanded Moses. And at that time, came Joshua, and cut off the Anakims from the mountains, from Hebron, from Debir, from Anab, and from all the mountains of Judah, and from all the mountains of Israel: Joshua destroyed them utterly with their cities. There was none of the Anakims left in the land of the children of Israel: only in Gaza, in Gath, and in Ashdod, there remained. So Joshua took the whole land, according to all that the Lord said unto Moses; and Joshua gave it for an inheritance unto Israel according to their divisions by their tribes. And the land rested from war. (Joshua 11:16-23, King James Version)

And these are the kings of the country which Joshua and the children of Israel smote on this side Jordan on the west, from

Baalgad in the valley of Lebanon even unto the mount Halak, that goeth up to Seir; which Joshua gave unto the tribes of Israel for a possession according to their divisions; in the mountains, and in the valleys, and in the plains, and in the springs, and in the wilderness, and in the south country: the Hittites, the Amorites, and the Canaanites, the Perizzites, the Hivites, and the Jebusites: the king of Jericho, one; the king of Ai, which is beside Bethel, one; the king of Jerusalem, one; the king of Hebron, one; the king of Jarmuth, one; the king of Lachish, one; the king of Eglon, one; the king of Gezer, one; the king of Debir, one; the king of Geder, one; the king of Hormah, one; the king of Arad, one; the king of Libnah, one; the king of Adullam, one; the king of Makkedah, one; the king of Bethel, one; the king of Tappuah, one; the king of Hepher, one; the king of Aphek, one; the king of Lasharon, one; the king of Madon, one; the king of Hazor, one; the king of Shimron-meron, one; the king of Achshaph, one; the king of Taanach, one; the king of Megiddo, one; the king of Kedesh, one; the king of Jokneam of Carmel, one; the king of Dor in the coast of Dor, one; the king of the nations of Gilgal, one; the king of Tirzah, one: all the kings thirty and one. (Joshua 12:7-24, King James Version)

The second passage quoted above lists 31 kings and city-states that were totally destroyed. In each case, according to the Israelites' understanding of God's directive to them, they killed every human being they encountered in those nations. Seldom has history witnessed a more complete and thorough genocide!

CONCLUSIONS

How many grandfathers and grandmothers, how many fathers and mothers, how many young men in the prime of their lives, how many young women pregnant with child, how many teens awaiting marriage, how many children before the age of reason who otherwise would have been frolicking in play, and how many nursing babies were thrust through or hacked to pieces with the Israelite sword of aggression so that the Israelites could occupy the land that they claimed that God had given to them? At what point do a god and a religion become too bloodthirsty for its adherents to justify? How does one continue to walk through city after city, thrusting one's sword into living flesh, one man, woman, and child after another? At what point is the bloodlust satisfied?

The answers to the above questions will probably never be known with any certainty. What is known, however, is that the concept of Holy War is firmly embedded in the Biblical tradition, even if that aspect of Biblical history is seldom taught in modern Sunday schools. Whether or not the Biblical tradition reported above is, as some scholars maintain,[291] grossly exaggerated is not relevant. The point is that the above tradition from Joshua is the Biblically-based tradition of Holy War.

Lest some think that this Biblical tradition of Holy War is strictly Old Testament teaching that has nothing whatsoever to do with the Christian thinking that evolved in the centuries after Jesus Christ, consider the words of Pope Urban II at the Council of Clermont in 1095 as he launched the First Crusade against Muslims in the Holy Land. It was at this church council that Pope Urban II sanctified the Christian concept of Holy War when he urged his soon-to-be Crusaders to "exterminate this vile race (i.e., Muslims) from our lands," a charge that he justified by claiming "God wills it."[292]

---

[291] For example: (A) Smith RH (1971); (B) Noth M (1960).
[292] Armstrong K (2001), p. 3.

CHAPTER 4:

SOME BIBLICAL CURIOSITIES

INTRODUCTION

THE FOLLOWING REPRESENTS A BRIEF selection from a series of topics to which the average parishioner is likely never to have been exposed in either Sunday school or church. Some of the items may be considered little more than Biblical trivia. Others, however, have important implications for Christian belief.

THE NON-ISRAELITE ISRAELITES

INTRODUCTION

Who were the Israelites? Supposedly, they were the descendants of Jacob, the son of Isaac, the son of Abraham. When Jacob's name was changed to Israel,[293] he became the eponymous ancestor of the Israelite people, who took their name from his new name.

ORIGINS OF THE TRIBE OF JUDAH

The ancient Israelite tribe of Judah reportedly descended from Judah, the son of Jacob, and had a maternal lineage tracing to one Canaanite, i.e., the daughter of Shua,[294] and to Tamar. Who was Tamar, and what was her ethnic identity? Either she was a Canaanite, which is the conclusion of most *Bible* scholars,[295] or she was a descendant of Aram, which is what is recorded in Jubilees 41:1.[296] With regard to the latter possibility,

---

[293] Genesis 32:28.
[294] Genesis 38:1-5.
[295] (A) Marks JH (1971); (B) May HG (1971b); (C) Fritsch CT (1971); (D) Robinson TH (1929).
[296] Charles RH (1969).

Genesis 10:22 lists Aram as being the son of Shem and the brother of Arpachshad. As Aram was a distant ancestor of Jacob, it can be seen that even this attribution of ethnic identity to Tamar leaves her as a non-Israelite, i.e., someone who did not descend from Jacob.

However, this is just the tip of the genealogical and ethnic iceberg of the tribe of Judah. Quite frankly, there is substantial Biblical evidence to suggest that the Israelite tribe of Judah included whole segments within it that were of 100% non-Israelite origin! To appreciate this startling revelation, one only has to turn to the first chapter of Judges.

JUDAH AND THE KENITES

Contained in the first 20 verses of the first chapter of Judges, one finds a concise history of how the tribe of Judah took its land in Palestine from the Canaanites. In that passage, one is informed that the tribe of Judah acted in concert with the Kenite clan of the Midianite tribe,[297] who were the descendants of Midian, the son of Abraham and Keturah,[298] and who were the people of Zipporah, the wife of Moses.[299] Clearly, the Kenite clan of the Midianites was allied with, if not actually amalgamated into, the tribe of Judah.

THE CASE OF CALEB

When the Israelites were wandering in the wilderness, Moses sent out a total of 12 spies to scout out the area of Palestine, one spy representing each tribe of Israel. After forty days, the spies reported back to Moses, and 10 of the 12 said that the inhabitants of Palestine were much too

---

[297] Judges 1:16.
[298] Genesis 25:1-2.
[299] (A) Exodus 2:15-22; 3:1; 4:18; 18:1-12; (B) Numbers 10:29; (C) Judges 1:16.

strong for the Israelites to conquer them, that some of them were giants, and that they represented too many diverse peoples of great strength. However, two of the spies relied on God and urged the Israelites to enter Palestine despite the formidable nature of the indigenous population. Unfortunately, the Israelites rejected the testimony of these two faithful men. [300]

Who were the two stalwart Israelites who relied on God? One of them represented the tribe of Ephraim, one of the subtribes of Joseph. This was Oshea, the son of Nun, whom Moses renamed Jehoshua (Joshua). This was the Joshua who would assume the leadership of the Israelites after the death of Moses many years later, and who would then lead the Israelites into Palestine. [301]

The second stalwart Israelite was Caleb, who represented the tribe of Judah. [302] It was Caleb who first urged the Israelites to trust in God and enter Palestine. The Israelites, however, rejected Caleb's advice, which is quoted immediately below, and only Joshua supported his position.

> And Caleb stilled the people before Moses, and said, Let us go up at once, and possess it; for we are well able to overcome it. (Numbers 13:30, King James Version)

> And Joshua the son of Nun, and Caleb the son of Jephunneh, which were of them that searched the land, rent their clothes: And they spake unto all the company of the children of Israel, saying, The land, which we passed through to search it, is an exceeding good land. If the Lord delight in us, then he will bring

---

[300] Numbers 13:1-14:10.
[301] Numbers 13:8 & 16; 14:6-9.
[302] Numbers 13:6.

us into this land, and give it us; a land which floweth with milk and honey. Only rebel not ye against the Lord, neither fear ye the people of the land; for they are bread for us: their defense is departed from them, and the Lord is with us: fear them not. But all the congregation bade stone them with stones. (Numbers 14:6-10a, King James Version)

Because of the faithlessness of the Israelite people, they were barred from entering Palestine and were made to continue wandering in the wilderness for 40 years, i.e., until the faithless of Israel had died off. [303] However, special exception was made for Joshua and Caleb.

And the Lord said, I have pardoned according to thy word: But as truly as I live, all the earth shall be filled with the glory of the Lord. Because all those men which have seen my glory, and my miracles, which I did in Egypt and in the wilderness, and have tempted me now these ten times, and have not hearkened to my voice; Surely they shall not see the land which I sware unto their fathers, neither shall any of them that provoked me see it: But my servant Caleb, because he had another spirit with him, and hath followed me fully, him will I bring into the land whereinto he went; and his seed shall possess it…I the Lord have said, I will surely do it unto all this evil congregation, that are gathered together against me: in this wilderness they shall be consumed, and there they shall die. And the men, which Moses sent to search the land, who returned, and made all the congregation to murmur against him, by bringing up a slander upon the land, Even those men that did bring up the evil report upon the land, died by the plague before the Lord. But Joshua the son of Nun,

---

[303] Numbers 14:20-38

and Caleb the son of Jephunneh, which were of the men that went to search the land, lived still. (Numbers 14:20-24, 35-38, King James Version)

Not only did Caleb live to enter Palestine, but the city of Hebron was given over to Caleb, the Kenizzite.[304] Further, the Kenizzites conquered additional territory for the tribe of Judah.[305] Interestingly, in the account given in Judges, Caleb is identified only as being the older brother of "Othniel son of Kenaz." [306] However, in Joshua, Caleb is identified as being "son of Jephunneh the Kenizzite."[307] Given both verses, one can see that "son of Kenaz" is just another way of saying "the Kenizzite." However, the real clincher is to be found in Numbers 13:6, where it is stated that Caleb was "from the tribe of Judah, Caleb son of Jephunneh." To summarize from across these various Biblical passages: (1) Caleb was the son of Jephunneh, (2) Caleb was a Kenizzite, and (3) Caleb was considered to be a member of the tribe of Judah.

Aside from the few passages from Joshua and Numbers noted in the above paragraph, the word "Kenizzite" or "Kenizzites" appears only one other place in the entire *Bible*.[308] In Genesis 15:19-21, one finds the word "Kenizzites" in the midst of a list of non-Israelite people! The Kenizzites were not even Israelites; yet, Caleb the Kenizzite, his brother Othniel, and their descendants and families were considered to be members of the tribe of Judah. One cannot help wondering if it wasn't the case that the Kenizzite people as a whole had been incorporated into the Israelite tribe of Judah, even though they were not Israelites.

[304] Judges 1:20.
[305] Judges 1:11-15.
[306] Judges 1:13.
[307] Joshua 14:6,14.
[308] Kohlenberger III JR (1991).

Certainly, the text from the first chapter of Judges appears to indicate that such a process had occurred.

By this time, given the sum total of the above, the reader may well be wondering just who were the Kenizzites. The answer can be found by the simple expedient of looking for an eponymous ancestor. As suggested in Judges 1:13, the Kenizzites were none other than the sons and descendants of Kenaz. Who was Kenaz? Kenaz is consistently identified in the *Bible* as being the son of Eliphaz, the firstborn son of Esau, the older twin brother of Jacob.[309] In short, the Kenizzites were Edomites; they were not Israelites. Nonetheless, the Kenizzites had become affiliated with the Israelite tribe of Judah and were counted as members of the tribe of Judah in the Israelite census.[310] Given this finding, one strongly suspects that the Kenite clan of the Midianites had also been incorporated into the Israelite tribe of Judah.

THE CASE OF OTHNIEL

Not only had the Kenizzite clan of the Edomites become incorporated into the Israelite tribe of Judah, but a Kenizzite actually rose to such prominence and attained such spirituality that he ruled over the entire tribe of Judah in the days before the monarchy.

> And the children of Israel did evil in the sight of the Lord, and forgat the Lord their God, and served Baalim and the groves. Therefore the anger of the Lord was hot against Israel, and he sold them into the hand of Chushanrishathaim king of Mesopotamia: and the children of Israel served Chushanrishathaim eight years. And when the children of Israel

---

[309] (A) Genesis 36:9-11,15-16,40-43; (B) I Chronicles 1:34-37,51-54.
[310] I Chronicles 4:1-23.

149

cried unto the Lord, the Lord raised up a deliverer to the children of Israel, who delivered them, even Othniel the son of Kenaz, Caleb's younger brother. The Spirit of the Lord came upon him, and he judged Israel, and went out to war: and the Lord delivered Chushanrishathaim king of Mesopotamia into his hand; and his hand prevailed against Chushanrishathaim. And the land had rest forty years. And Othniel son of Kenaz died. (Judges 3: 7-11, King James Version)

Edomites of the clan of the Kenizzites had become incorporated into the Israelite tribe of Judah and were included in their census.[311] Moreover, Othniel, a member of the Kenizzite clan of the Edomites, actually became the religious and temporal ruler of the tribe of Judah. It was Othniel, the Kenizzite, who saved the tribe of Judah from idolatry and false worship. It was Othniel, the Kenizzite, who saved the tribe of Judah from foreign bondage.

THE LOCATION OF MT. SINAI

In approximately 1,446 BCE, after repeated confrontations with the reigning pharaoh of Egypt and after repeated plagues had been inflicted upon the Egyptians by God, Moses led the captive Israelites out of the land of Egypt and toward the "promised land" of Palestine. However, this trek from Egypt to Palestine was not a direct or short journey. In order to purge the Israelites of their idolatrous ways and of their lack of faith, the Israelites were directed to wander in the wilderness for 40 years. During the course of this wandering, Moses reportedly received a covenant from God at a location that is variously identified as being Mt. Sinai (J and P strands of the Torah) or Mt. Horeb (E and D strands of the Torah). Of note, the *Bible* provides no geographic location for either Mt. Sinai or Mt. Horeb (hereinafter, these two

---

[311] Numbers 13:6.

mountains are referred to merely as Mt. Sinai), other than to note that it was in the wilderness. Contrary to popular opinion, there is no solid Biblical evidence locating Mt. Sinai at the site of the mountain currently known as Mt. Sinai, nor is there solid Biblical support for locating the covenant mountain anywhere in the Sinai Peninsula.

It is an interesting Biblical puzzle to consider the information presented by the Torah (the first five books of the Old Testament) regarding the covenant mountain and to list the pros and cons attached to various possible locations. With regard to identifying information, the Torah states or implies that the covenant mountain was: (1) known as Mt. Horeb;[312] (2) known as Mt. Sinai;[313] (3) located in the geographic area inhabited by the Midianites,[314] the descendants of Midian, the son of Abraham and Keturah; (4) volcanic;[315] and (5) on a route that the Israelites took out from Egypt, which consisted of the sequential stopping points of Rameses (northern Egypt, also known as Zoan, Tanis, and Avaris), Succoth (northern Egypt), Etham, Pihahiroth (northern Egypt), Marah, Elim, the Sea of Reeds (now part of the Suez Canal) or the Red Sea, the Wilderness of Sin (unknown,[316] and not to be confused with the Wilderness of Zin), Dophkah (unknown, and mentioned nowhere else in the Torah), Alush (unknown, and mentioned nowhere else in the Torah), Rephidim (near Mt. Sinai, and apparently in the geographic area of the

---

[312] (A) Exodus 3:1; 17:5-6; 33:6; (B) Deuteronomy 1:1-2, 6,& 19; 4:9-15; 5:2; 9:8-17; 18:16; 29:1.

[313] (A) Exodus 19:11-12, 18, & 20-23; 34:2-4; (B) Exodus 24:16; 31:18a; 34:29-32; (C) Leviticus 7:37-38; 25:1; 26:46; 27:34; (D) Numbers 3:1; 28:6.

[314] (A) Exodus 3:1; 18:1 & 5; (B) Numbers 10:29, in context.

[315] (A) Exodus 13:21; 19:18; (B) Exodus 19:16; (C) Deuteronomy 4:9-15; 18:16; (D) Exodus 24:16-17.

[316] It is interesting to note that the name "Sin" was associated with the Akkadian moon god, and one might speculate about an ancient Akkadian influence on this otherwise unknown wilderness area. --- (2003e)

Amalekites[317]), the Wilderness of Sinai (presumably the site of Mt. Sinai), Kibrothhattaavah (presumably close to Massah,[318] which was quite close to Mt. Sinai [319]), Hazeroth, Rithmah (unknown, and mentioned nowhere else in the Torah), Rimmonperez (unknown, and mentioned nowhere else in the Torah), Libnah (unknown, and mentioned nowhere else in the Torah), Rissah (unknown, and mentioned nowhere else in the Torah), Kehelathah (unknown, and mentioned nowhere else in the Torah), Mount Shepher (unknown, and mentioned nowhere else in the Torah), Haradah (unknown, and mentioned nowhere else in the Torah), Makheloth (unknown, and mentioned nowhere else in the Torah), Tahath (unknown, and mentioned nowhere else in the Torah), Terah (unknown, and mentioned nowhere else in the Torah), Mithkah (unknown, and mentioned nowhere else in the Torah), Hashmonah (unknown, and mentioned nowhere else in the Torah), Moseroth, Bencjaakan, Horhaggidgad, Jotbathah, Abronah (unknown, and mentioned nowhere else in the Torah), Eziongeber (Aqaba, Jordan), Kadesh (about 65 miles south of Gaza), Mount Hor (near Petra, Jordan), Zalmonah (unknown, and mentioned nowhere else in the Torah), Punon (unknown, and mentioned nowhere else in the Torah), Oboth, Iyeabarim, Dibongad, Almondiblathaim, Mount Nebo (near Madaba, Jordan), and the Plains of Moab on the east side of the Jordan River.[320] Given the sum total of the above information, one can begin to analyze the possible sites of Mt. Sinai, looking at each of the five types of information in order.

The place name of Mt. Horeb offers no identifying information in and of itself. However, there is a hint as to its location found in the opening passage of Deuteronomy. According to this passage, Mt. Horeb was

---

[317] Exodus 17:1b-2, 4-6, & 8-16.
[318] Deuteronomy 9:22.
[319] Exodus 17:7, taken in context with Exodus 17:4-6.
[320] Numbers 33:1-49.

located 11 days away from Kadeshbarnea, by way of Mt. Seir.[321] In this regard, it should be noted that Kadeshbarnea or Kadesh was located about 65 miles south of Gaza and about 40 miles west of the Great Rift Valley, which runs from the southern tip of the Dead Sea to Aqaba, while Mt. Seir was located well east of the Great Rift Valley in the land of the Edomites, i.e., the descendants of Esau, the son of Isaac, in the vicinity of Petra, Jordan.[322] Such a route would tend to exclude the modern Sinai Peninsula as being the site of Mt. Horeb. Why would the route be to travel northeast from the Sinai Peninsula to Mt. Seir and then to double back due west to Kadeshbarnea? Clearly, such a route makes little sense. Instead, the route listed in Deuteronomy would suggest a site somewhere in southern or southeastern Jordan or in northwestern Saudi Arabia, i.e., the northern Hijaz region.

It is tempting to use the place name of Mt. Sinai to locate the covenant mountain in the Sinai Peninsula. However, in reality, this would be circular reasoning. The Sinai Peninsula derives its name precisely from the frequent assumption that it is the geographic location of Mt. Sinai. As such, one can hardly affirm a thought process which consists of the following logic: (1) because the Sinai Peninsula is often assumed to be the site of Mt. Sinai, it is called Sinai; and (2) because Mt. Sinai and the Sinai Peninsula have a common name, Mt. Sinai must be located in the Sinai Peninsula.

As noted above, Mt. Sinai appears to have been located in the geographical area inhabited by the Midianite tribe. Of note, the Midianite tribe's area of nomadic activity was primarily east of the Gulf of Aqaba.[323] While one cannot totally exclude the possibility that some Midianite

---

[321] Deuteronomy 1:2.
[322] --- (1971).
[323] (A) Noth M (1960); (B) --- (1971); C) Beegle DM (2003).

clans may have migrated into the area west of the Gulf of Aqaba, the sum total of the Midianite consideration suggests a location for the covenant mountain in the northern Hijaz of contemporary Saudi Arabia.

Given that Mt. Sinai appears to have been volcanic, it must be noted that the available geological information contraindicates a site in the Sinai Peninsula. Simply stated, geological considerations appear to negate the possibility of an active volcano in the Sinai Peninsula during the second millennium BCE. In contrast, geological science does suggest the presence of active volcanic activity in the northern Hijaz during the time in question. More specifically, such volcanic activity can be documented as having occurred in the area southeast of Tabuk (a city about 125 miles southeast of Aqaba), along the caravan route linking southern Arabia with the Fertile Crescent. As such, once again, the probabilistic conclusion would be that Mt. Sinai was located in the northern Hijaz area of contemporary Saudi Arabia.[324]

Finally, one turns to the route of the Israelite Exodus from Egypt, as reported in Numbers. There are several features of this route that deserve consideration. Firstly, as one considers the place names of those sites near to Mt. Sinai, one is struck by the fact that so many of these names cannot be identified and that they appear nowhere else in the Torah. This is the case with two of the three stopping points (Dophkah and Alush) immediately prior to Mt. Sinai and with several stopping points (Rithmah, Rimmonperez, Libnah, Rissah, Kehelathah, Mt. Shepher, Haradah, Makheloth, Tahath, Terah, Mithkah, Hashmonah, and Abronah) that reportedly were between Mt. Sinai and Eziongeber (Aqaba, Jordan). This consideration would suggest that the area in

---

[324] Noth M (1960).

question was one that was fairly unfamiliar to the compilers of the Torah and would thus tend to exclude the Sinai Peninsula as the site of Mt. Sinai. Again, this consideration would be consistent with a site in the northern Hijaz. Secondly, the Israelites were reportedly attacked during the Exodus from Egypt at Rephidim, i.e., the final stopping point before Mt. Sinai, by the Amalekites. [325] The Amalekites were reportedly an offshoot of the Edomites [326] and were apparently located in a southerly direction from the Edomites of southern Jordan. Third, Kibrothhattaavah, which was apparently the first stopping point after Mt. Sinai, was apparently located close to Massah.[328] While Exodus provides an interesting origin myth regarding the place name of Massah, one cannot help but be struck by the similarity of this place name to the personal name of Massa. Of note, Massa is the name of one of the sons of Ishmael, the son of Abraham, [329] and the name occurs nowhere else in the entire Old Testament except in reference to the son of Ishmael.[330] If the place name of Massah was actually derived from the personal name of Massa, this would suggest an area inhabited by the Ishmaelites, which would again point to Mt. Sinai being located in the northern Hijaz.

As can be seen by the sum total of the above considerations, while no one consideration definitively proves that Mt. Sinai was located in the northern Hijaz, four of the five considerations point to the Hijaz as the probable location of Mt. Sinai, while the fifth consideration is uninformative. Certainly, the probabilistic weight of the evidence suggests a high likelihood that Mt. Sinai was actually located in the northern Hijaz, probably southeast of Tabuk.

---

[325] Exodus 17:1b-2, 4-6, & 8-16.
[326] Genesis 36:9-12.
[327] Deuteronomy 9:22.
[328] (A) Exodus 17:2c-3 & 7; (B) Exodus 17:1b-2b & 4-7.
[329] (A) Genesis 25:12-14; (B) I Chronicles 1:28-30.
[330] Kohlenberger III JR (1991).

MOSES' FIRST WIFE

From the Jewish and ancient Israelite perspectives, Moses was the great "national liberator"[331] of the Israelite people from the slavery of 15th-century BCE Egypt. He was the one who lead them out of bondage in Egypt and through their 40 years of wandering in the wilderness. From the Jewish perspective, he was the "greatest name in the history and religious development of Israel," and was the recipient of the Torah and of the Mosaic covenant.[332] The story of Moses' birth and infancy is told in Exodus. Briefly summarized, the reported events were as follows: (1) Moses was born into the Israelite tribe of Levi during a time in which all male children of the Israelites in Egypt were being killed at birth by the Egyptians; (2) in order to save her son, Moses' mother placed him in a basket and set him adrift on the, presumably Nile, river; and (3) he was then discovered by a daughter of the pharaoh of Egypt, who adopted him.[333] This princess of Egypt, who adopted Moses and raised him as a prince of Egypt, is variously identified within the Jewish tradition as having been Hatshepsut[334] and Thermuthis.[335]

The *Bible* repeatedly refers to Moses' wife as a Midianite, i.e., a descendant of Abraham's son Midian out of Keturah, who was a Canaanite woman, although different passages in the Bible give slightly discrepant information about Moses' wife. (1) In Exodus 2:15b-22, she is identified as Zipporah, the daughter of Reuel, a priest of Midian. (2) In Exodus 3:1, 4:18, and 18:1-12, Zipporah is identified as being the daughter of Jethro, a priest of Midian. (3) Further, in Numbers 10:29, she is identified as

---

[331] Epstein I (1966).
[332] Schonfield HJ (1967).
[333] Exodus 2:1-10.
[334] Epstein I (1966).
[335] Josephus F (1988).

being the daughter of Hobab, the son of Reuel, a Midianite. (4) Finally, Judges 1:16 refers to her as being the daughter of Hobab, a Kenite. Presumably, the Kenites were a clan of the Midianites.[336]

Exodus 2:21-22 identifies Zipporah as having had at least one son, i.e., Gershom, by Moses. In contrast, Exodus 18:2-4 identifies Zipporah as having two sons, i.e., Gershom and Eliezer, by Moses. Finally, I Chronicles 23:15 identifies Moses as having had two sons, i.e., Gershom and Eliezer, but does not identify their mother.

So when did Moses live? While some Biblical scholars tend to place Moses as living in the 13th century BCE and date the Israelite Exodus from Egypt as occurring circa 1250 BCE,[337] actual Biblical dating places the life of Moses a couple of centuries earlier than that. To illustrate that fact, a brief digression is needed.

Almost all scholars place the 40-year reign of King Solomon in the 10th century BCE, with various estimates ranging from 973-933 BCE,[338] 971-931 BCE,[339] 970-931 BCE,[340] 965-926 BCE,[341] and 962-922 BCE.[342] For purposes of this discussion, it is assumed that Solomon began his reign in 970 BCE. Given this date, the following Biblical verse becomes crucial.

> And it came to pass in the four hundred and eightieth year after
> the children of Israel were come out of the land of Egypt, in the

---

[336] (A) Schonfield HJ (1967); (B) --- (2003cd); (C) McNutt PM (1993).
[337] (A) Duncan GB (1971a); (B) Leslie EA (1929).
[338] (A) Leslie EA (1929); (B) Asimov I (1968).
[339] (A) Epstein I (1966); (B) Packer JI, Tenney MC, White W (1980).
[340] Duncan GB (1971a).
[341] (A) Hebert G (1965); (B) Noth M (1960).
[342] (A) Murphy RE (1993); (B) Fredericksen L (2003).

fourth year of Solomon's reign over Israel, in the month Zif, which is the second month, that he began to build the house of the Lord. (I Kings 6:1, King James Version)

If Solomon began his reign circa 970 BCE, then construction of the temple would have begun in about 966 BCE. Given a 480 year gap between the Israelite Exodus from Egypt and the beginning of the temple, then the Exodus would have been approximately 1,446 BCE. As Exodus 7:7 states that Moses was 80 years old at the time of the Exodus, Moses would have been born circa 1,526 BCE. According to Deuteronomy 34:7, Moses was 120 years old when he died, suggesting a death date of 1,406 BCE. These dates will become important later when assessing a story about Moses from Flavius Josephus, the first-century Jewish historian.

Having set the stage, it's time to turn to the story of Moses and Zipporah, a story often repeated in Sunday school classes.

Now when Pharaoh heard this thing, he sought to slay Moses. But Moses fled from the face of Pharaoh, and dwelt in the land of Midian: and he sat down by a well. Now the priest of Midian had seven daughters: and they came and drew water, and filled the troughs to water their father's flock. And the shepherds came and drove them away: but Moses stood up and helped them, and watered their flock. And when they came to Reuel their father, he said, How is it that ye are come so soon to day? And they said, An Egyptian delivered us out of the hand of the shepherds, and also drew water enough for us, and watered the flock. And he said unto his daughters, And where is he? why is it that ye have left the man? call him, that he may eat bread. And Moses was content to dwell with the man: and he gave Moses Zipporah his daughter. And she bare him a son, and he called his name Gershom: for he said, I have been a stranger in a strange land. (Exodus 2:15-22, King James Version)

As noted in the above passage and in the previously cited verses of the *Bible*, Zipporah was a Midianite, a descendant of Abraham's son Midian out of Keturah.[343] However, there is a verse in Numbers that clearly states that Moses also had a different wife, a Cushite or Ethiopian woman.

And Miriam and Aaron spake against Moses because of the Ethiopian woman whom he had married: for he had married an Ethiopian woman. (Numbers 12:1; King James Version)

The Hebrew word that is translated as "Ethiopian" in the above verse is "*Kushiyt*," and most modern translations of the *Bible*, including the American Standard Version, the Living *Bible*, the Revised Standard Version, the New Revised Standard Version, the New Jerusalem Version, Young's *Bible*, Webster's *Bible*, and the New Living Translation, simply transliterate the Hebrew word "*Kushiyt*" as "Cushite." Both approaches are technically correct, as it also would be to translate the word "*Kushiyt*" as "Nubian."[344]

The alleged historical setting of the above verse is the Israelite wanderings in the wilderness following the Israelite Exodus from Egypt. According to Exodus 7:7, Moses was approximately 80 years old at the start of the Israelite Exodus from Egypt. How many years had past between the Exodus from Egypt and the alleged historical setting of this verse is unknown. However, the average reader of the above passage will probably conclude that the Cushite woman was the wife of Moses' old age.

---

[343] Genesis 25:1-2.
[344] Bennett RA (1993).

There are, however, several problems with this assumption. (1) There is nothing in the above quoted verse that states that Moses had only recently taken a Cushite wife. Given the stated information in the verse, he might have taken the Cushite wife a year before, five years before, or even 60 years before. The above quoted verse only purports to give the time at which Moses' siblings allegedly complained about Moses having taken a Cushite wife. (2) According to Genesis 10:6, Cush was the son of Ham, who was the son of Noah. Further, Cush was the father of the Nubian people of Ethiopia and Sudan.[345] This raises a significant problem in maintaining that Moses married his Cushite wife during the Israelite wanderings in the wilderness. How would Moses have ever found a black Nubian wife from Sudan or Ethiopia during the midst of the Israelite wanderings in the wilderness of the Sinai and its environs? (3) Finally, Josephus, the first-century Jewish historian, specifically reports that Moses married an "Ethiopian" wife while still a young man living in Egypt, and before he ever left Egypt to journey to Midian. Josephus' account appears to have been drawn from the no longer extant *Peri Ioudaion*, which was written by Artapanus, a Jewish historian of the third century BCE.[346] Further, it is quite probable that Artapanus, who was writing over 2,200 years ago, had access to various Egyptian and Jewish records that no longer exist.

According to Josephus, a major war broke out between Egypt and Nubia, i.e., the Sudan, while Moses was yet a young man living in Egypt. After a series of initial Egyptian losses, in which the Nubians managed to invade well into northern Egypt, the reigning pharaoh of Egypt finally placed Moses in charge of the Egyptian army. Responding to the

---

[345] (A) Marks JH (1971); (B) --- (2003c); (C) May HG (1971a); (D) Asimov I (1968); (E) Bennett RA (1993); (F) McKenzie SL (1993).
[346] Rohl DM (1995).

challenge, and utilizing the combination of a surprise counterattack and a great flanking maneuver through a snake-infested area, Moses then achieved a great military victory against the invading Nubians. As a result, the Nubians fled back into the Sudan in panicky flight, with the Egyptian army of Moses in hot pursuit. Arriving back in the Sudan, the Nubians barricaded themselves in their capital city, which was well fortified and practically impervious to frontal assault. As such, the Egyptians laid siege and prepared to wait out the Nubians. However, a long, drawn out siege was reportedly avoided when Tharbis, the daughter of the king of the Nubians, saw Moses down below her from her position high on the city's walls and ramparts and fell in love with him. Apparently wasting no time, Tharbis quickly sent a courier to Moses with a letter proposing marriage. Moses reportedly accepted this marriage proposal, with the stipulation that the city be surrendered to him and his military forces. After consultation between Tharbis and her father, this stipulation was accepted, and Moses and Tharbis were reportedly married.[347]

After the above narrative from Josephus, Tharbis was apparently lost to the pages of history. Nothing of substance is known about her marriage to Moses. Further, nothing is known of any possible children from this marital union. All that is known is that the marriage had taken place, that Josephus recorded it, and that Numbers alluded quite briefly and quite obliquely to it.

If the sum total of Josephus' account seems a little hard to swallow, it should be noted that there is some indirect and circumstantial support from the pages of the secular history of Nubia and Egypt. In that regard,

---

[347] Josephus F (1988).

the following historical facts are noted. (1) Nubia was that region of ancient northeastern Africa that extended on a north-south axis from near the first cataract of the Nile River in Upper Egypt to about the location of modern Khartoum, Sudan. It extended on an east-west axis from the Red Sea to the Libyan Desert. (2) The southern portion of Nubia was known as Cush by at least as early as the 12th dynasty of Egypt. (3) By 1,650 BCE, the Cushites had grown strong enough militarily, that they had advanced north into Egypt as far as the current Aswan Dam. Subsequently, the Cushites were to extend their military conquests in Egypt and were to advance as far north as northern Egypt. (4) However, the armies of Pharaoh Amenhotep I (reigned circa 1,514-1,493 BCE) mounted a major counterattack against Cush, were able to drive the Cushites out of Egypt, invaded Cush, destroyed the capital city, and made Cush a colony of Egypt.[348]

In reviewing the above secular history of the relations between Cush and Egypt, the reader should note several important considerations. (1) Consistent with the story in Josephus, the Cushites had managed to invade all the way into northern Egypt. (2) Consistent with the story in Josephus, the Egyptians were successful in a major counterattack, which resulted in the surrender of the capital city of Cush and in Cush being controlled by Egypt. (3) The estimated dates for the reign of Pharaoh Amenhotep I, i.e., 1,514-1,493 BCE, are totally within Biblically-based estimates for the life of Moses, i.e., 1,526-1,406 BCE. In fact, Moses would have been about 12 years old when Amenhotep I began to rule and would have been about 33 years old at the death of Amenhotep I. This is certainly consistent with Josephus' account that Moses led this military campaign while still a young man.

---

[348] --- (2003c).

AARON'S GRANDSON

Did Aaron and Miriam really speak out against Moses because he had taken a Nubian wife while still a young man? Were these two siblings of Moses really so racist? Were the early Israelites of the Exodus so racist? On the surface, it would appear that the *Bible* would have us belief so, as the following passage so clearly indicates.

> And, behold, one of the children of Israel came and brought unto his brethren a Midianitish woman in the sight of Moses, and in the sight of all the congregation of the children of Israel, who were weeping before the door of the tabernacle of the congregation. And when Phinehas, the son of Eleazar, the son of Aaron the priest, saw it, he rose up from among the congregation, and took a javelin in his hand: and he went after the man of Israel into the tent, and thrust both of them through, the man of Israel, and the woman through her belly. So the plague was stayed from the children of Israel. And those that died in the plague were twenty and four thousand. And the Lord spake unto Moses, saying, Phinehas, the son of Eleazar, the son of Aaron the priest, hath turned my wrath away from the children of Israel, while he was zealous for my sake among them, that I consumed not the children of Israel in my jealousy. Wherefore say, Behold, I give unto him my covenant of peace: and he shall have it, and his seed after him, even the covenant of an everlasting priesthood; because he was zealous for his God, and made an atonement for the children of Israel. (Numbers 25:6-13, King James Version)

A man of Israel, identified in Numbers 25:14 as being Zimri, the son of Salu of the tribe of Simeon, takes a Midianite woman, identified in Numbers 25:15 as being Cozbi, the daughter of Zur, to be his wife. Because Zimri and Cozbi have entered into an interethnic marriage,

Phinehas, the grandnephew of Moses, kills both of them.[349] So how does this square with Moses himself having married a Midianite, much less with his having married a Nubian? There are no easy answers to these questions. However, there is one additional wrinkle to the story, which concerns Aaron's grandson.

In the above quoted passage, Aaron's grandson is Phinehas, who is the son of Aaron's son Eleazar. This genealogy is also confirmed in several other passages of the *Bible*.

> And Eleazar Aaron's son took him one of the daughters of Putiel to wife; and she bare him Phinehas: these are the heads of the fathers of the Levites according to their families. (Exodus 6:25, King James Version)

> And Moses sent them to the war, a thousand of every tribe, them and Phinehas the son of Eleazar the priest, to the war, with the holy instruments, and the trumpets to blow in his hand. (Numbers 31:6, King James Version)

> And the children of Israel sent unto the children of Reuben, and to the children of Gad, and to the half tribe of Manasseh, into the land of Gilead, Phinehas the son of Eleazar the priest...And Phinehas the son of Eleazar the priest said unto the children of Reuben, and to the children of Gad, and to the children of Manasseh, This day we perceive that the Lord is among us, because ye have not committed this trespass against the Lord: now ye have delivered the children of Israel out of the hand of the Lord. And Phinehas the son of Eleazar the priest, and the princess, returned from the children of Reuben, and from the

---

[349] (A) Guthrie HH (1971a); (B) Eisenman R (1997).

children of Gad, out of the land of Gilead, unto the land of Canaan, to the children of Israel, and brought them word again. (Joshua 22:13, 31-32, King James Version)

And Eleazar the son of Aaron died; and they buried him in a hill that pertained to Phinehas his son, which was given him in mount Ephraim. (Joshua 24:33, King James Version)

And Phinehas, the son of Eleazar, the son of Aaron, stood before it in those days... (Judges 20:28, King James Version)

And the children of Amram; Aaron, and Moses, and Miriam. The sons also of Aaron; Nadab, and Abihu, Eleazar, and Ithamar. Eleazar begat Phinehas... And these are the sons of Aaron; Eleazar his son, Phinehas his son... (I Chronicles 6:3-4, 50, King James Version)

And Phinehas the son of Eleazar was the ruler over them in time past, and the Lord was with him. (I Chronicles 9:20, King James Version)

The son of Abishua, the son of Phinehas, the son of Eleazar, the son of Aaron the chief priest. (Ezra 7:5, King James Version)

So what is so important about establishing the lineage of Phinehas as Aaron's grandson? Quite simply, the importance is in Phinehas' name. While some may try to render this name as meaning either "mouth of a serpent" from the Hebrew "*peh nachash*"[350] or "mouth of brass" from the Hebrew "*peh nchosheth*" or "*peh nchuwshah*,"[351] the name actually comes from the Egyptian language, i.e., "*pa nehas*," not from the Hebrew.[352]

---

[350] *Strong's Old Testament Dictionary.* In --- (2001).
[351] *Vine's Old Testament Dictionary.* In --- (2001).
[352] (A) Bennett RA (1993); (B) Smith DA (1997).

In Egyptian, "*pa*" is simply the article "the," while "*nehas*" means "southerner or southern neighbor."[353] As the Nubians of the Sudan were the Egyptians' southern neighbors, "*pa nehas*" eventually came to mean "the dark-skinned one," "the black," or "the Nubian."[354]

If Aaron's grandson was named "the black" or "the Nubian," then it certainly appears that Moses was not the only member of the family to have a Nubian wife. So just how could Aaron have justified his verbal attack against Moses for taking a Nubian wife? Even more perplexing, how could Phinehas himself have ever justified killing an Israelite man and a Midianite woman merely because they were involved in an interethnic marriage? How could the ancient Israelites have maintained a stance of rigid ethnic purity in the face of both Moses and Aaron, or perhaps Aaron's son Eleazar, having taken Nubian wives? Sensible answers are not readily forthcoming.

GOLIATH

And there went out a champion out of the camp of the Philistines, named Goliath of Gath, whose height was six cubits and a span. And he had an helmet of brass upon his head, and he was armed with a coat of mail; and the weight of the coat was five thousand shekels of brass. And he had greaves of brass upon his legs, and a target of brass between his shoulders. And the staff of his spear was like a weaver's beam; and his spear's head weighed six hundred shekels of iron: and one bearing a shield went before him. And he stood and cried unto the armies of Israel, and said unto them, Why are ye come out to set your battle in array? am

---

[353] Bennett RA (1993).
[354] (A) Bennett RA (1993); (B) Smith DA (1997).

not I a Philistine, and ye servants to Saul? choose you a man for you, and let him come down to me. If he be able to fight with me, and to kill me, then will we be your servants: but if I prevail against him, and kill him, then shall ye be our servants, and serve us. And the Philistine said, I defy the armies of Israel this day; give me a man, that we may fight together. When Saul and all Israel heard those words of the Philistine, they were dismayed, and greatly afraid. (I Samuel 17:4-11, King James Version)

The above portrait of Goliath paints the picture of an imposing giant of a warrior. His height of six cubits and a span translates to nine feet, nine inches,[355] although in the Greek Septuagint and Dead Sea Scrolls the above passage reads a more modest four cubits and a span,[356] i.e., about six feet, nine inches,[357] still a most imposing height in that ancient day. His coat of mail reportedly weighed 5,000 shekels of brass, which was equivalent to 103-125 pounds, depending upon whether the sanctuary or commercial weight standard was being used, and at 600 shekels, his spear's head weighed between 12 and 15 lbs.[358]

While the above text clearly identifies Goliath as being a Philistine from the city of Gath, some have speculated that Goliath was actually a member of the Anakim, a tribe of giants whose descendants lived in Gath.[359] In contrast, Jewish Rabbinic tradition[360] states that Goliath's mother was Orpah, a Moabite and the sister-in-law of Ruth mentioned

---

[355] Duncan GB (1971b).

[356] Avalos HI (1993).

[357] Duncan GB (1971b).

[358] Duncan GB (1971b).

[359] (A) Polhill JB (1997); (B) For Biblical passages pertaining to the Anakim, see Deuteronomy 1:28; 2:10-11 & 21; 9:2; and Joshua 11:21-22; 14:12 & 15.

[360] Midrash Ruth 1:14 and Tan, Wayiggash 8 as cited in ---; Hirsch EG (2002).

in Ruth 1:4 & 14. According to this tradition, Orpah led a promiscuous lifestyle after separating from Naomi and Ruth, resulting in her having four illegitimate sons, all giants, by various unknown men.

Regardless of Goliath's exact height (nine foot, nine inches vs. six foot, nine inches) and origin (Philistine, Anakim, or Moabite), he was a most formidable figure to the Israelite army of King Saul, and no Israelite soldier was willing to face Goliath in single, man-to-man combat. At this point, David, a young shepherd boy from Bethlehem, enters the story, having brought provisions for his three oldest brothers, all of whom were serving in the Israelite army.[361] Hearing the challenge of Goliath, David volunteers to fight Goliath for King Saul and his army, and after some hesitancy on Saul's part, David's offer is accepted.[362]

> And he took his staff in his hand, and chose him five smooth stones out of the brook, and put them in a shepherd's bag which he had, even in a scrip; and his sling was in his hand: and he drew near to the Philistine...And it came to pass, when the Philistine arose, and came and drew nigh to meet David, that David hasted, and ran toward the army to meet the Philistine. And David put his hand in his bag, and took thence a stone, and slang it, and smote the Philistine in his forehead, that the stone sunk into his forehead; and he fell upon his face to the earth. So David prevailed over the Philistine with a sling and with a stone, and smote the Philistine, and slew him: but there was no sword in the hand of David. Therefore David ran, and stood upon the Philistine, and took his sword, and drew it out of the sheath thereof, and slew him, and cut off his head therewith. And when

---

[361] I Samuel 17:12-31.
[362] I Samuel 17: 32-39.

the Philistines saw their champion was dead, they fled. (I Samuel
17:40-41, 48-51, King James Version)

Generation after generation of Sunday school attendees have been taught
the above quoted story of how David, a young shepherd boy, slew the
mighty Goliath with nothing but a stone and a sling. At least one other
Biblical passage, i.e., I Samuel 21:8-9, directly states that David killed
Goliath. Yet, there is a Biblical passage that totally contradicts the
oft-taught Sunday school lesson concerning David's triumph over
Goliath.

And there was again a battle in Gob with the Philistines, where
Elhanan the son of Jaareoregim, a Bethlehemite, slew the brother of
Goliath the Gittite, the staff of whose spear was like a weaver's beam.
(II Samuel 21:19, King James Version)

The casual reader of the above verse will probably see no contradiction
between it and the traditional story of David and Goliath. However, in the
above verse, the translators of the King James Version have added the words
"the brother of," which appear nowhere in the original Hebrew text. In short,
the verse actually says that Elhanan of Bethlehem slew Goliath, which, as is
seen in the following, is what most modern translations say.

And there was again war with the Philistines at Gob; and
Elhanan the son of Jaareoregim, the Bethlehemite, slew Goliath
the Gittite, the shaft of whose spear was like a weaver's beam. (II
Samuel 21:19, Revised Standard Version)

Then there was another battle with the Philistines at Gob; and
Elhanan son of Jaareoregim, the Bethlehemite, killed Goliath the
Gittite, the shaft of whose spear was like a weaver's beam. (II
Samuel 21:19, New Revised Standard Version)

Again war with the Philistines broke out at Gob, and Elhanan son of Jair from Bethlehem killed Goliath of Gath, the shaft of whose spear was like a weaver's beam. (II Samuel 21:19, Jerusalem Version)

Again, war with the Philistines broke out at Gob, and Elhanan son of Jair, of Bethlehem, killed Goliath of Gath, the shaft of whose spear was like a weaver's beam. (II Samuel 21:19, New Jerusalem Version

And there was again a battle at Gob with the Philistines; and Elhanan the son of Jaareoregim, a Bethlehemite, smote Goliath the Gittite; now the shaft of his spear was like a weaver's beam. (II Samuel 21:19, Darby Version)

There was another battle with the Philistines in Gob, in which Elhanan, son of Jair from Bethlehem, killed Goliath of Gath, who had a spear like a weaver's heddle-bar. (II Samuel 21:19, New American Version)

And there was again war with the Philistines at Gob; and Elhanan the son of Jaareoregim the Bethlehemite slew Goliath the Gittite, the staff of whose spear was like a weaver's beam. (II Samuel 21:19, American Standard Version)

There was war with the Philistines at Gob, and Elhanan the son of Jaareoregim the Bethlehemite killed Goliath the Gittite, the shaft of whose spear was like a weaver's beam. (II Samuel 21:19, New American Standard Version)

Why did the translators of the King James Version alter the actual text of II Samuel 21:19? Undoubtedly, it was to harmonize the two accounts of Goliath's death, leaving David as the one who slew him. Why did those translators alter the text the way they did? The answer is to be found in another passage of the *Bible*, which is quoted immediately below.

And there was war again with the Philistines; and Elhanan the son of Jair slew Lahmi the brother of Goliath the Gittite, whose spear staff was like a weaver's beam. (I Chronicles 20:5, King James Version)

While the above verse is quoted from the King James Version, the statement that Elhanan slew Lahmi, the brother of Goliath the Gittite, i.e., a person from Gath, is actually present in the Hebrew text. As such, all translations basically state the same thing as the King James Version. However, before using I Chronicles 20:5 to justify the action of the King James Version translators in adding words to the text of II Samuel 21:19, one must consider the actual dating to be assigned to I Samuel, II Samuel, and I Chronicles.

Jewish tradition and the *Babylonian Talmud* attribute the authorship of I and II Samuel to Samuel,[363] the 11th-century BCE judge of the Israelite tribe of Ephraim. However, in reality, these books were compiled from various prior sources, by an unknown member of the Deuteronomic School, perhaps the same one who compiled Joshua and/or Judges. Some of the prior sources utilized by the unknown Deuteronomist can be identified. In that regard, one can identify: (1) the Court History of David, as found in chapters nine through 20 of II Samuel, and which dates to the early 10th century BCE; (2) the Shiloh stories of I Samuel 1:1-2:26 and 3:1-21, which appear to reflect an early, northern Israelite tradition; (3) the Military Source Document, as found in II Samuel 10: 1-19 and 12:26-31, and which appears to date from early in the 10th century BCE; and (4) various poems, local traditions, Saul stories, David stories, Ark of the Covenant stories, etc. While the content of I and II

---

[363] (A) Silberman LH (1971); (B) Cate RL (1997).

Samuel is Deuteronomic history for the era spanning the time from the birth of Samuel until the death of King David, and while the Court History of David and the Military Source Document represent sources from early in the 10th century BCE, I and II Samuel were not compiled until the middle of the sixth century BCE.[364]

The *Babylonian Talmud* attributes at least part of I Chronicles to Ezra, while the Christian tradition usually attributes I Chronicles to the anonymous Chronicler. Most likely, the author of I Chronicles is the same as the author of Ezra and Nehemiah. I and II Chronicles are basically a purported history of the Israelite people until early in the fourth century BCE. In that regard, they overlap greatly with portions of I and II Samuel and of I and II Kings. However, while the latter four books represent the historical perspective of the earlier Deuteronomic School, I Chronicles represents the historical perspective of the later Priestly School. As such, the compilation date may comfortably be assigned to early in the fourth century BCE.[365]

Given that I Chronicles was written almost two centuries after I and II Samuel, it is hardly justifiable to use I Chronicles 20:5 to alter II Samuel 21:19. So how does one explain the clear contradiction between I Samuel and II Samuel when it comes to the identity of the person who slew Goliath? Several different hypotheses have been offered in the past, but none of them is really satisfying.

One explanation is to hypothesize that it actually was Elhanan who slew Goliath. However, as time went on and David assumed the kingship of

---

[364] (A) Hyatt JP (1971); (B) Wevers JW (1971); (C) Cate RL (1997).
[365] (A) Fritsch CT (1971); (B) Silberman LH (1971).

Israel, the legendary killing of Goliath was later attributed to him. This is a theory that has been advanced by several Biblical scholars,[366] but it is one that is going to be rejected by most observant Jews and Christians. Likewise, Muslims would reject this possible explanation because the *Qur'an* clearly states that it was David who killed Goliath.

> When Saul set out with his army (to face the Philistines), he addressed (his men), saying, "God will test you by that stream. Whoever drinks from it won't be allowed to march any farther with me. Only those who abstain from it will go with me, or who at the very least drink only a sip from their hand." All of them, save for a few, drank from the stream. Then after they crossed over (the stream), the (few remaining) faithful (soldiers) lamented, "We're no match for Goliath and his army today." However, those who were certain they would meet God one day said, "How many were the times when a small force defeated a larger one by God's will? God is with those who persevere!" As they advanced upon Goliath and his forces, they prayed, "Our Lord, pour determination down upon us, make our stance firm and help us against this nation that rejects (faith)." And so by God's will they routed them, and David killed Goliath. (*Qur'an* 2:249-251, Emerick translation)

A second explanation is to maintain that David killed Goliath and that Elhanan actually did kill a brother or son of the Goliath that David killed. Again, this position has its supporters.[367] However, this hypothesis does absolutely nothing to explain away the contradiction to be found between I Samuel 17 and II Samuel 21:19, unless one goes on to posit that there is a serious omission in the latter verse that completely changes

---

[366] For example: (A) Hirsch EG, Levi GB (2002); (B) Avalos HI (1993); (C) Asimov I (1968); (D) Micklem N (1929).
[367] For example, Reeve JJ (2001).

its meaning.

A third possibility is that David and Elhanan are actually the same person, with David perhaps being the regnal name taken by Elhanan upon becoming king. That David and Elhanan are the same person was a theory advanced by Saint Jerome (circa 347-420 CE) that continues to attract some adherents to this day.[368] In favor of such a theory is the fact that both David and Elhanan are said to be from Bethlehem. However, there are at least two important considerations weighing heavily against this theory. The first is that David's father is consistently said to be Jesse,[369] while Elhanan's father is said to be Jair, Jaareoregim, or Dodo.[370] The second is that II Samuel 21:17-19 clearly states that David was not on the battlefield when Elhanan slew Goliath.

In short, the *Bible* leaves the reader with a rather blatant contradiction when it comes to the person who killed Goliath, the Philistine giant from Gath. The popular version is that it was David who killed Goliath. The other version has Elhanan killing Goliath. How does one resolve this discrepancy? Surely, one cannot do it by resorting to the passage in I Chronicles, a passage that was written almost two centuries after the contradictory accounts found in I and II Samuel and that quite clearly was groping for a way to resolve the previously recorded contradiction.

"DOUBTING" THOMAS

But Thomas, one of the twelve, called Didymus, was not with them

---

[368] Sampey JR (2001).

[369] (A) Ruth 4:17 & 18-22; (B) I Samuel 16:10-13 & 19-20; 17:12, 17, &58; 20:25-27; 25:10; (C) II Samuel 20:1; 23:1; (D) I Kings 12:16; (E) I Chronicles 2:13-15; 10:14; 12:18; 29:26; (F) II Chronicles 10:16; (G) Psalms 72:20; (H) Matthew 1:6; (I) Luke 3:31-32; (J) Acts 13:22.

[370] (A) II Samuel 21:19 & 23:24; (B) I Chronicles 11:26 & 20:5.

when Jesus came. The other disciples therefore said unto him, We have seen the Lord. But he said unto them, Except I shall see in his hands the print of the nails, and put my finger into the print of the nails, and thrust my hand into his side, I will not believe. And after eight days again his disciples were within, and Thomas with them: then came Jesus, the doors being shut, and stood in the midst, and said, Peace be unto you. Then saith he to Thomas, Reach hither thy finger, and behold my hands; and reach hither thy hand, and thrust it into my side: and be not faithless, but believing. And Thomas answered and said unto him, My Lord and my God. Jesus saith unto him, Thomas, because thou hast seen me, thou hast believed: blessed are they that have not seen, and yet have believed. (John 20:24-29, King James Version)

Generations of Sunday school attendees have been regaled with the above story of "Doubting" Thomas. Yet, aside from this story, precious little is taught in Sunday school about this disciple. Occasionally, Sunday school students might learn that Christian tradition holds that Thomas was assigned Parthia as his missionary field,[371] that he founded the church in Edessa, Syria,[372] and that later in his missionary efforts he migrated to India.[373] However, precious little exists in the New Testament about this member of the 12 disciples. The Gospels of Matthew, Mark, and Luke each name him only once, and in each case that is in a simple listing of the 12 disciples.[374] Likewise, he is named only once in Acts, and that is in a listing of the 11 disciples (Judas Iscariot having reportedly died by this time) gathered in an upper room.[375] Aside from the above quoted passage, the Gospel of John names Thomas a grand total of only three times.

[371] Eusebius (1999).
[372] Koester H (1990).
[373] (A) Coogan MD (1993); (B) Koester H (1990); (C) Turner JD (1990); (D) May DM (1997).
[374] (A) Matthew 10:3; (B) Mark 3:18; (C) Luke 6:15.
[375] Acts 1:13.

Then said Jesus unto them plainly, Lazarus is dead. And I am glad for your sakes that I was not there, to the intent ye may believe; nevertheless let us go unto him. Then said Thomas, which is called Didymus, unto his fellow disciples, Let us also go, that we may die with him. (John 11:14-16, King James Version)

Thomas saith unto him, Lord, we know not whither thou goest; and how can we know the way? (John 14:5, King James Version)

There were together Simon Peter, and Thomas called Didymus, and Nathanael of Cana in Galilee, and the sons of Zebedee, and two other of his disciples. (John 21:2, King James Version)

So just who was Thomas? The King James Version of the New Testament gives little information as to his identity. However, there is more to be found in the Greek New Testament than the translators of the King James Version were willing to say. The keys to unlocking this information lie in the two names given to this disciple, i.e., "Thomas" and "Didymus." With regard to these two names, "Thomas" is merely the Greek transcription of the Aramaic "*toma*," which means "twin;" likewise, "*didymus*" is merely the Greek word for "twin."[376] So when Thomas is referred to as "Thomas called Didymus," what is really being said is "the twin called the twin." Why this double emphasis on Thomas being a twin, and what was Thomas' real name? Let's begin with the second question and work our way backward to the first question.

Bishop Eusebius of Caesarea (circa 260-339 CE) wrote in his fourth-century *Ecclesiastical History* that King Abgar V and Jesus had an exchange

---

[376] (A) Koester H (1982); (B) Koester H (1990); (C) Humphreys F (1997); (D) Coogan MD (1993); (E) Eisenman R (1997).

of letters and that these letters were preserved in the archives at Edessa. Eusebius then went on to state that appended to those letters in Syriac is the following statement: "After the ascension of Jesus, Judas, who is also called Thomas, sent Thaddeus, one of the Seventy, to (Abgar), and he stayed with Tobias, son of Tobias."[377]Of note, Eusebius is not the only source for concluding that Thomas' real name was Judas, alternative spellings of which include Juda, Judah, and Jude. The same identification can be found in one of the apocryphal gospels.

The Gospel of Thomas was discovered at Nag Hammadi, Egypt, in 1945.[378] Written in the Sahidic dialect of Coptic, the Nag Hammadi copy of this gospel probably dates to the middle of the fourth century CE.[379] However, this gospel was known and quoted by Origen (circa 185-254 CE) and Hippolytus (circa 170-235 CE) early in the third century CE.[380] Further, the dating of this gospel does not stop there. The Coptic version discovered at Nag Hammadi is a translation from a Greek original,[381] fragments of which have been preserved in Oxyrhynchus Papyri 1, 654, and 655, one of which was written before 200 CE.[382] Given the above, it appears that the Greek version of this gospel was used in Egypt as early as the second century,[383] and most Biblical scholars date this gospel in its original form to first-century Palestine or Syria.[384] The importance of this apocryphal gospel in corroborating Eusebius' report that Thomas' real name was Judas is found in its incipit or title, which reads as follows: "These are the secret words which the Living

---

[377] Eusebius (1999), p. 49.

[378] (A) Peel ML (1997a); (B) Guillaumont A, Puech H, Quispel G, Till W, 'Abd Al-Masih Y (1959).

[379] (A) Hedrick CW (1997); (B) Guillaumont A, Puech H, Quispel G, Till W, 'Abd Al-Masih Y (1959).

[380] Hedrick CW (1997).

[381] (A) Hedrick CW (1997); (B) Mack BL (1995); (C) Koester (1990); (D) Guillaumont A, Puech H, Quispel G, Till W, 'Abd Al-Masih Y (1959).

[382] (A) Koester (1990); (B) Hedrick CW (1997).

[383] Koester (1990).

[384] (A) Koester (1990); (B) Koester H (1982); (C) Hedrick CW (1997); (D) Mack BL (1995).

Jesus spoke and Didymos Judas Thomas wrote."[385]

Thomas' real name was Judas/Jude/Juda/Judah. However, the question still remains as to who this disciple really was. The beginnings of this answer may be found in three Biblical passages.

> Is not this the carpenter, the son of Mary, the brother of James and Joses, and of Juda, and Simon? and are not his sisters here with us? (Mark 6:3, King James Version)

> Is not this the carpenter's son? is not his mother called Mary? and his brethren, James, and Joses, and Simon, and Judas? (Matthew 13:55, King James Version)

> Jude, the servant of Jesus Christ, and brother of James... (Jude 1:1, King James Version)

In the first two passages quoted above, Judas is identified as being the brother of Jesus, James the Just, Joses, and Simon. In the third passage, he is identified as being the brother of James the Just, which would make him the brother of Jesus.[386] In point of fact, the Syrian church has a long tradition that Judas (Thomas) was none other than one of the brothers of Jesus. Was "Doubting" Thomas really Jesus' own brother? That identification is made even more explicit in yet another book from the New Testament Apocrypha.

The Book of Thomas the Contender is an eight-page Coptic text, translated from a Greek original, with authorship attributed to one Mathaias, who most likely is to be identified with Matthew, one of the 12 disciples.[387] The book was most likely composed in the first half of the

---

[385] Guillaumont A, Puech H, Quispel G, Till W, 'Abd Al-Masih Y (1959), p. 3.
[386] Koester H (1990).

third century in Syrian Edessa and was most likely originally written in Greek.[388] This book not only states quite explicitly that Judas Thomas was the brother of Jesus; it also gives an identification as to Thomas' twin.

> The secret words that the savior spoke to Judas Thomas which I, even I Mathaias, wrote down, while I was walking, listening to them speak with one another. The savior said, "Brother Thomas, while you (sg.) have time in the world, listen to me, and I will reveal to you the things you have pondered in your mind. Now since it has been said that you are my twin and true companion, examine yourself and learn who you are, in what way you exist, and how you will come to be.[389]

In the above passage, "Doubting" Thomas (Judas, the twin) is not just identified as Jesus' brother. He is also identified as Jesus' twin brother! Clearly, those Christians who believe in the virgin birth of Jesus will be quick to reject this identification of Thomas as Jesus' twin. Likewise, as the *Qur'an* upholds the virgin birth of Jesus,[390] Muslims will also find this identification unsatisfactory. However, if "Doubting" Thomas was Jesus' brother, and there is a strong tradition that he was, and if he was a twin, as attested to by his being called both Thomas and Didymus, then whose twin was he? The most likely identification would seem to be with James the Just, the brother of Jesus who headed the early Jerusalem church.[391] After all, Judas Thomas only identifies himself as being James' brother in Jude 1:1. Further, the fact that none of the gospel writers felt it necessary to identify whose twin Judas was suggests that Judas' twin was so promi-

---

[387] Peel ML (1997b).
[388] Turner JD (1990).
[389] Turner JD (1990), p. 201.
[390] See chapter six of this book.
[391] (A) Wilson RF (1997); (B) Galatians 1:19; 2:12; (C) I Corinthians 15:7; (D) Acts 12:17; 15; 21:17-18.

nent that no identification was needed. Certainly, that consideration would apply only to Jesus and to James the Just.

THE DEATH OF JUDAS ISCARIOT

The New Testament is quite consistent in maintaining that Judas Iscariot was the disciple who betrayed Jesus. However, as is illustrated below, the New Testament offers two radically different stories regarding the death of Judas.

> Then Judas, which had betrayed him, when he saw that he was condemned, repented himself, and brought again the thirty pieces of silver to the chief priests and elders, Saying, I have sinned in that I have betrayed the innocent blood. And they said, What is that to us? see thou to that. And he cast down the pieces of silver in the temple, and departed, and went and hanged himself. And the chief priests took the silver pieces, and said, It is not lawful for to put them into the treasury, because it is the price of blood. And they took counsel, and bought with them the potter's field, to bury strangers in. (Matthew 27:3-7, King James Version)

> Men and brethren, this scripture must needs have been fulfilled, which the Holy Ghost by the mouth of David spake before concerning Judas, which was guide to them that took Jesus. For he was numbered with us, and had obtained part of this ministry. Now this man purchased a field with the reward of iniquity; and falling headlong, he burst asunder in the midst, and all his bowels gushed out. (Acts 1:16-18, King James Version)

According to the Gospel of Matthew, Judas committed suicide by hanging, and the Jewish priests took the 30 pieces of silver that Judas had been paid, and with the silver they purchased a field to serve as a cemetery. In marked contrast, Acts maintains that Judas purchased the field with his ill-gotten gains and that Judas suffered an accidental death when he fell down and was thus disemboweled. How could these two New Testament books have such discrepant accounts regarding the death of Judas Iscariot? Unfortunately, there is no satisfactory answer to that question.

THE AUTHORS OF THE CANONICAL GOSPELS

INTRODUCTION

The canonical Gospels of Matthew, Mark, Luke, and John are the only four gospels to be found in each of the different *Bibles* recognized by one or another branch of contemporary Christianity. Untold millions of Christians read these gospels content with the knowledge that each gospel was authored by the person whose name it bears. After all, each gospel is entitled "The Gospel According to _____," with the blank being filled in by the corresponding name of the person who supposedly wrote the gospel in question. Unfortunately, few readers of those gospels understand that those titles are not actually part of the text of those gospels; rather, they are later attributions of authorship that are based on tradition, traditions that are less than optimally sound and that trace back only to the second century CE.[392] In what follows, those traditions are examined for each of the four canonical gospels.

THE GOSPEL OF MATTHEW

The authorship of the Gospel of Matthew has traditionally been assigned

---

[392] (A) Fitzmyer JA (1993); (B) Eisenman R (1997).

to Matthew, one of the 12 disciples of Jesus who is mentioned in two different passages in this gospel. Of note, these are the only two places in this gospel where Matthew is even named.

> And as Jesus passed forth from thence, he saw a man, named Matthew, sitting at the receipt of custom: and he saith unto him, Follow me. And he arose, and followed him. (Matthew 9:9, King James Version)

> Now the names of the twelve apostles are these; The first, Simon, who is called Peter, and Andrew his brother, James the son of Zebedee, and John his brother; Philip, and Bartholomew; Thomas, and Matthew the publican; James the son of Alphaeus, and Lebbaeus, whose surname was Thaddaeus; Simon the Canaanite, and Judas Iscariot, who also betrayed him. (Matthew 10:2-4, King James Version)

How does one get from the above two passages to attributing this entire gospel to a person who is named in it only two times? To answer that question, one needs to examine when this gospel was written, how it was written, and the later traditions associating this gospel with Matthew, the disciple of Jesus.

The Gospel of Matthew is typically acknowledged by Biblical scholars to have been the second of the canonical gospels to be compiled, with the Gospel of Mark being considered the oldest of the canonical gospels. The Gospel of Matthew's date of composition is usually placed between the years 80 and 90 CE.[393] It appears to have been compiled in Syria,[394] probably in the vicinity of Antioch, and was written in Greek (Koine)[395] by a person whose Old Testament was the Greek

---

[393] (A) Duncan GB (1971a); (B) Sundberg AC (1971); (C) Kee HC (1971); (D) Leon-Dufour X (1983); (E) Mack BL (1995); (F) Fenton JC (1973); (G) Filson FV (1971); (H) Peritz IJ (1929); (I) Kingsbury JD (1993).

Septuagint, as opposed to a Hebrew text of the Old Testament.[396] This latter consideration, which is squarely based on an analysis of the Old Testament passages quoted in the Gospel of Matthew, as well as on the obvious reliance of the Gospel of Matthew on the Greek Gospel of Mark,[397] contraindicates that the gospel was written by a disciple of Jesus living in Palestine, whether or not that disciple was named Matthew,[398] because such a disciple would not have been using the Greek Septuagint. Rather, such a person would have been using the Hebrew manuscripts and texts of Jewish scripture.

As noted previously, the Gospel of Matthew was compiled. It was not written as a new literary work as much as it was edited in a cut-and-paste manner. In that regard, the sources used by the compiler of the Gospel of Matthew included at least two earlier, written sources: (1) the Gospel of Mark or an earlier proto-Mark; and (2) a collection of reported sayings of Jesus, which can be termed Q, which stands for the German word "*Quelle*" meaning "source." In addition to these two written sources, the compiler of the Gospel of Matthew utilized material that was not included in the other canonical gospels. This material may have been written or oral, may or may not have been confined to a single source, and may or may not have originated with the compiler of Gospel of Matthew. For the sake of convenience, this material can be referred to as M.[399]

---

[394] (A) Leon-Dufour X (1983); (B) Kee HC (1971); (C) Davies JN (1929b); (D) Hamilton W (1959); (E) Koester H (1982).

[395] (A) Leon-Dufour X (1983); (B) Kee HC (1971); (C) Filson FV (1971); (D) Burch EW (1929); (E) Cadbury HJ (1929); (F) Moffatt J (1929); (G) Grobel K (1971); (H) Robertson AT (1929); (I) Koester H (1982).

[396] (A) Davies JN (1929b); (B) Kee HC (1971); (C) Moffatt J (1929); (D) Koester H (1982).

[397] (A) Kee HC (1971); (B) Filson FV (1971); (C) Davies JN (1929b); (D) Hamilton W (1959).

[398] (A) Filson FV (1971); (B) Davies JN (1929b); (C) Fenton JC (1973); (D) Hamilton W (1959); (E) Mack BL (1995); (F) Koester H (1982).

[399] (A) Filson FV (1971); (B) Kee HC (1971); (C) Leon-Dufour X (1983); (D) Davies JN (1929b); (E) Burch EW (1929); (F) Wilson RM (1971); (G) Fenton JC (1973); (H) Hamilton W (1959); (I) Koester H (1982).

Given the above background, one is now ready to consider the tradition that claims that this gospel was written by Matthew. This tradition goes back to around the year 130 CE, i.e., 40 to 50 years after the gospel was actually compiled. At about that time, Papias, the Bishop of Hierapolis, wrote *Exposition of the Oracles of the Lord*, a book that has been preserved only in fragments quoted by later authors. In this book, according to a quotation made from it by Bishop Eusebius of Caesarea (circa 260-339 CE) in his fourth-century *Ecclesiastical History*, Papias wrote: "Matthew compiled the sayings (logia of Christ) in the Hebrew language, and each interpreted them as best he could." [400] Later writers, without any apparent basis, applied this statement by Papias to the gospel currently under consideration, claiming that Papias' statement demonstrated that Matthew wrote the gospel. [401]

As can be seen, the above tradition is a rather weak reed upon which to hang the authorship of this gospel. However, it is not just that the reed is feeble; it is positively broken, as the following considerations illustrate. (1) Papias referred only to a collection of sayings, not to a complete gospel with biographical material, miracle stories, etc.[402] (2) The Gospel of Matthew was written in Greek, relied upon the Greek Septuagint for many of its Old Testament quotations and upon the Greek Gospel of Mark for much of its material about Jesus, and gives no sign of having been translated from Hebrew into Greek. In contrast, the manuscript to which Papias was referring was written in Hebrew.[403] (3) There is absolutely nothing to link Papias' statement with the current gospel other

---

[400] Eusebius (1999), p. 130.
[401] (A) Kee HC (1971); (B) Michaels JR (1997); (C)Davies JN (1929b); (D) --- (2003d).
[402] Kee HC (1971).
[403] (A) Kee HC (1971); (B) Michaels JR (1997).

than much later speculation. Given the sum total of the above, most Biblical scholars readily admit that they have absolutely no idea who actually wrote the Gospel of Matthew.[404]

THE GOSPEL OF MARK

The earliest of the canonical gospels is the Gospel of Mark. An analysis of this gospel suggests that its author made extensive cut-and-paste use of a prior miracles or signs source, various pronouncement stories in circulation, and some probable use of Q.[405] The initial author arranged individual pericopes from these sources into some, perhaps arbitrary, chronological order and then joined them with his own editorial glosses. This resulting document may be termed proto-Mark (*Urmarkus*). Later revision by unknown redactors, probably coupled with the addition of material not originally included in proto-Mark, resulted in the Gospel of Mark, which can be dated to some point circa 70-75 CE.[406]

So how did this gospel come to be associated with authorship by Mark? Once again, the tradition goes back to Bishop Papias' *Exposition of the Oracles of the Lord,* which was written circa 130 CE, but which is preserved only in Bishop Eusebius' (circa 260-339 CE) fourth-century CE *Ecclesiastical History*, and which was written by Papias a good 55 years after the Gospel of Mark was compiled.[407] As Bishop Eusebius quotes him, Papias reportedly wrote:

---

[404] For example: (A) Kee HC (1971); (B) Michaels JR (1997); (C) Kingsbury JD (1993); (D) Davies JN (1929b).

[405] (A) Mack BL (1995); (B) Hooker MD (1993).

[406] (A) Duncan GB (1971a). (B) Davies JN (1929a); (C) Moffatt J (1929); (D) Sundberg AC (1971); (E) Pherigo LP (1971); (F) Mack BL (1995); (G) Nineham DE (1973); (H) Leon-Dufour X (1983).

[407] (A) Garland DE (1997); (B) Hooker MD (1993); (C) Nineham DE (1973).

The Presbyter used to say this also: "Mark became Peter's interpreter and wrote down accurately, but not in order, all that he remembered of the things said and done by the Lord. For he had not heard the Lord or been one of his followers, but later, as I said, a follower of Peter. Peter used to teach as the occasion demanded, without giving systematic arrangement to the Lord's sayings, so that Mark did not err in writing down some things just as he recalled them. For he had one overriding purpose: to omit nothing that he had heard and to make no false statements in his account."[408]

So who was this Mark to whom Papias credits the authorship of this gospel, and who was the unnamed presbyter who gave Papias his information? As to the latter question, it appears to have been a person variously known as John the Elder and John the Presbyter. Unfortunately, we have absolutely no way to judge either his credibility or the accuracy of his information. As to the former question, three answers have traditionally been given. (1) Mark was the unidentified young man wearing only a linen cloth reported in Mark 14:51-52 to have been the only person who attempted to follow Jesus after his arrest, but whose linen cloth was grabbed, leaving him to run off naked into the night.[409] However, there is absolutely no basis for claiming this unknown person was named Mark and that he was the author of this gospel except for the fact that this particular story occurs only in the Gospel of Mark, and not in the other gospels. Furthermore, Eusebius reports Papias as saying that the author of the Gospel of Mark "had not heard the Lord or

---

[408] Eusebius (1999), p. 129-130. Eusebius also maintained that Clement said that Mark was a follower of Peter and wrote the gospel that bears his name (p. 73).

[409] "And there followed him a certain young man, having a linen cloth cast about his naked body; and the young men laid hold on him: and he left the linen cloth, and fled from them naked." (Mark 14:51-52, King James Version)

been one of his followers," which flatly contradicts the theory that this Mark was the young man referred to in Mark 14:51-52. Clearly, this is a slender and shaky reed to grasp for support. (2) He was, as Papias reportedly said, the interpreter of Peter, the disciple. However, the only known New Testament sources for a person named Mark being with Peter is the statement in I Peter 5:13 in which the author of this epistle refers to a Mark as being his son[410] and the statement in Acts that is quoted below and that says that Peter once entered the house of John Mark's mother. However, there is absolutely nothing in the New Testament that lists a person named Mark being the interpreter of Peter. (3) He was the John Mark who lived in Jerusalem, who was a close relative of Barnabas, who was briefly associated with Paul, and who was mentioned some four times in Acts by the name Mark, once in Colossians, once in II Timothy, and most likely once in Philemon.

> And when he (Peter) had considered the thing, he came to the house of Mary the mother of John, whose surname was Mark; where many were gathered together praying. (Acts 12:12, King James Version)

> And Barnabas and Saul (Paul) returned from Jerusalem, when they had fulfilled their ministry, and took with them John, whose surname was Mark...and John departing from them returned to Jerusalem. (Acts 12:25 & 13:13, King James Version)

> And some days after Paul said unto Barnabas, Let us go again and visit our brethren in every city where we have preached the word of the Lord, and see how they do. And Barnabas determined to take with them John, whose surname was Mark. But Paul

---

[410] "The church that is at Babylon, elected together with you, saluteth you; and so doth Marcus my son." (I Peter 5:13, King James Version) The "Babylon" in the above passage is a coded reference to Rome.

thought not good to take him with them, who departed from them from Pamphylia, and went not with them to the work. And the contention was so sharp between them, that they departed asunder one from the other: and so Barnabas took Mark, and sailed unto Cyprus; and Paul chose Silas, and departed… (Acts 15:36-40, King James Version)

Aristarchus my fellowprisoner saluteth you, and Marcus, sister's son to Barnabas… (Colossians 4:10, King James Version)

Only Luke is with me. Take Mark and bring him with thee: for he is profitable to me for the ministry. (II Timothy 4:11, King James Version)

There salute thee Epaphras, my fellowprisoner in Christ Jesus; Marcus, Aristarchus, Demas, Lucas, my fellowlabourers. (Philemon 1:23-24, King James Version)

There are several reasons to reject the identification of the author of the Gospel of Mark with the John Mark of the above verses. (1) Mark was a very common name in the first century, being the most frequent Latin name used in the Roman Empire.[411] As such, there is absolutely no reason to link the Mark of Papias' statement with the John Mark of the New Testament.[412] (2) The author of this gospel demonstrates a poor knowledge of the geography of first-century Palestine, something that would not have been the case with the John Mark who lived in Jerusalem.[413] (3) As seen in the above quoted verses, John Mark was primarily associated with Paul and Barnabas, not with Peter.[414] (4) The

---

[411] (A) Hooker MD (1993); (B) Nineham DE (1973); (C) Garland DE (1997).
[412] Nineham DE (1973).
[413] (A) Hooker MD (1993); (B) Pherigo LP (1971).
[414] Hooker MD (1993).

author of the gospel treats Palestinian Judaism as an outsider, which would not have been the case with John Mark of Jerusalem.[415]

In summary, most Biblical scholars reject the claim that this gospel was written by the John Mark of Jerusalem, by the unnamed youth in Mark 14:51-52, and by a Mark who was an interpreter for Simon Peter. Perhaps it was written by someone named Mark, but who that Mark was really remains unknown. As such, it is probably best to maintain that the author of this gospel remains anonymous.

THE GOSPEL OF LUKE

A structural analysis of the Gospel of Luke demonstrates that it was composed in a cut-and-paste procedure from the Gospel of Mark (or possibly proto-Mark), Q, and oral or written sources unique to the Gospel of Luke, which may be termed L.[416] The compilation of the Gospel of Luke is frequently dated to circa 95 CE.[417] Although a few Biblical scholars place it closer to the years 80-85 CE,[418] one suggests it could have been written as late as the year 100 CE,[419] and one goes so far as to suggest a date as late as 120 CE.[420] However, a date around the year 95 CE is the most probable. As to authorship of this gospel, most Christians assume that it was written by Luke, the physician and

---

[415] Pherigo LP (1971).

[416] (A) Mack BL (1995); (B) Baird W (1971a); (C) Filson FV (1971); (D) Burch EW (1929); (E) Fitzmyer JA (1993).

[417] (A) Asimov I (1969); (B) Duncan GB (1971a); (C) Baird W (1971a); (D) Sundberg AC (1971); (E) Some scholars argue that there was an earlier version of the Gospel of Luke, which can be called proto-Luke, which was composed around 60 CE, and which began with the baptism of Jesus, just as the Gospel of Mark had. Caird GB (1972).

[418] For example, Fitzmyer JA (1993).

[419] Talbert CH (1997).

[420] Mack BL (1995).

companion of Paul, who is mentioned only three times by name in the
New Testament (Philemon 1:24, Colossians 4:14, and II Timothy 4:11),
and to whom the authorship of Acts is often credited.

> There salute thee Epaphras, my fellowprisoner in Christ
> Jesus; Marcus, Aristarchus, Demas, Lucas, my fellowlabourers.
> (Philemon 1:23-24, King James Version)

> Luke, the beloved physician, and Demas, greet you. (Colossians
> 4:14, King James Version)

> Only Luke is with me. Take Mark, and bring him with thee: for
> he is profitable to me for the ministry. (II Timothy 4:11, King
> James Version)

How solid is that attribution of authorship? The fact is that the earliest
known attribution that Luke was the author of this gospel is to be
found in Bishop Irenaeus' (130-200 or 140-210 CE) *Adversus Omnes
Haereses*, a book that was written circa 180 CE.[421] Other sources for Luke
being the author of this gospel include Papyrus #75 (175-225 CE), in
which the words "Gospel according to Luke" are appended to the end of
the gospel, the Muratorian Canon (circa 200 CE), *Adversus Marcionem*
by Tertullian (circa 155-post 220 CE), Origen (circa 185-254 CE)
as later quoted by Bishop Eusebius (circa 260-339 CE) in his fourth-
century *Ecclesiastical History*, and *De Viris Illustribus* by Saint Jerome
(circa 347-420 CE).[422]

> Luke, the follower of Paul, wrote down in a book the Gospel
> preached by him.[423]

---

[421] (A) Talbert CH (1997); (B) Caird GB (1972); (C) Baird W (1971a).
[422] (A) Talbert CH (1997); (B) Caird GB (1972).
[423] Irenaeus in *Adversus Omnes Haereses*, as quoted by Eusebius (1999), p. 183.

The third is by Luke, who wrote the Gospel praised by Paul for Gentile believers.[424]

Luke, an Antiochene by birth and a physician by profession, was long a companion of Paul and was closely associated also with the other apostles. In two divinely inspired books, the Gospel and the Acts of the Apostles, he has left us examples of the soul healing that he learned from them.[425]

All of these sources were written a good 80 years or more after the most likely date for the gospel in question, and many of them more than 100 years later. Additionally, it is quite possible that the additional sources noted above were merely relying on Irenaeus in making their attribution of authorship, in which case they are not independent sources.[426] Given these considerations, many Biblical scholars maintain that the author of this gospel remains anonymous.

THE GOSPEL OF JOHN

The fourth gospel does not share the same commonalities of construction that are found in the first three. To a great extent, the prior sources utilized by this gospel are veiled in mystery,[427] and there is some disagreement among scholars as to how familiar the author of this gospel was with the other three canonical gospels.[428] There is also a fair amount of disagreement among Biblical scholars as to when this gospel was

---

[424] Origen in *Commentary on Matthew*, as quoted by Eusebius (1999), p. 226.

[425] Eusebius (1999), p. 94.

[426] For example: (A) Baird W (1971a); (B) Talbert CH (1997); (C) Mack BL (1995); (D) Koester H (1982).

[427] Shepherd MH (1971b).

[428] Clement of Alexandria, writing circa 190 CE, specifically stated that the author of the fourth gospel was familiar with the other three canonical gospels (Shepherd MH, 1971b), which would imply that the Gospel of John may be based, in part, on the Gospel of Mark, as some Biblical scholars maintain (Mack BL, 1995; Garvie AE, 1929).

written. Estimates range from as early as 85 CE for the first draft of the gospel, which was then followed by a final draft some years later,[429] to the 90s CE,[430] to the first two decades of the second century CE.[431] However, one thing that most scholars[432] are agreed upon is that this gospel was composed in stages by different people. In support of this position, the internal evidence of John 21:24-25 clearly identifies an original author and a later editor, with the editor appending the last chapter[433] and the Prologue (1:1-18)[434] to the original gospel.

> This is the disciple which testifieth of these things, and wrote these things: and we know that his testimony is true. And there are also many other things which Jesus did, the which, if they should be written every one, I suppose that even the world itself could not contain the books that should be written. Amen. (John 21:24-25, King James Version)

Tradition holds that this gospel was written by John, a Galilean fisherman, the son of Zebedee, the brother of James, and one of the twelve disciples of Jesus, the one that is often believed to be "the beloved disciple" or "the disciple whom Jesus loved." This is what most Christians are taught as children in their Sunday school lessons. However, two questions need to be answered before accepting that Sunday school lesson. Firstly, from where does that tradition originate? Secondly, just how strong is the evidence behind that tradition?

---

[429] Smalley SS (1993).
[430] (A) Mack BL (1995); (B) Culpepper RA (1997).
[431] (A) Marsh J (1972); (B) Peritz IJ (1929); (C) Bullard RA (1997).
[432] For example: (A) Garvey AE (1929); (B) Shepherd MH (1971b).
[433] (A) Shepherd MH (1971b); (B) Moffat J (1929).
[434] (A) Garvie AE (1929); (B) Smalley SS (1993).

To some extent, the tradition goes back to the gospel itself. In the last chapter of the gospel, in the section added by the unknown editor, it is said that this gospel was written by the disciple who leaned on Jesus' breast during the Last Supper and who asked the question about which of the disciples would betray Jesus.[435] The relevant verses are quoted immediately below.

> Then Peter, turning about, seeth the disciple whom Jesus loved following; which also leaned on his breast at supper, and said, Lord, which is he that betrayeth thee? Peter seeing him saith to Jesus, Lord, and what shall this man do? Jesus saith unto him, If I will that he tarry till I come, what is that to thee? follow thou me. Then went this saying abroad among the brethren, that that disciple should not die: yet Jesus said not unto him, He shall not die: but, If I will that he tarry till I come, what is that to thee? This is the disciple which testifieth of these things, and wrote these things: and we know that his testimony is true. (John 21:20-24, King James Version)

We have the above statement solely on the word of the unknown editor of this gospel. We don't know who the editor was, and we don't know from where he obtained his information. Further, the statement does not identify the "disciple whom Jesus loved" with John, the son of Zebedee. Additionally, as we shall subsequently see, there are a number of reasons for doubting the accuracy of the statement. Therefore, we need to examine what other sources there are to support the Sunday school tradition.

---

[435] "When Jesus had thus said, he was troubled in spirit, and testified, and said, Verily, verily, I say unto you, that one of you shall betray me. Then the disciples looked one on another, doubting of whom he spake. Now there was leaning on Jesus' bosom one of his disciples, whom Jesus loved. Simon Peter therefore beckoned to him, that he should ask who it should be of whom he spake. He then lying on Jesus' breast saith unto him, Lord, who is it?" (John 13:21-25, King James Version)

Aside from the statement in the gospel, the tradition of John's authorship of the fourth gospel goes back to Bishop Irenaeus (130-200 or 140-210 CE). Writing circa 180 CE in his *Adversus Omnes Haereses*, Ireneaus noted the following.

> All the elders in Asia associated with John, the Lord's disciple, testify that John taught them the truth, for he remained with them until the time of Trajan…Now the church at Ephesus was founded by Paul, but John remained there until Trajan's time (98-117 CE), and it is a true witness of the apostolic tradition…Then John, the disciple of the Lord who had rested on his breast, produced a Gospel while living at Ephesus in Asia.[436]

In addition to the above, Bishop Eusebius (260-339 CE) states that Clement of Alexandria (died 215 CE) reported that John wrote the last of the four canonical gospels, which was a "spiritual Gospel."[437] In his *Commentary on John*, Origen (circa 185-254 CE) wrote the following in the third century.

> Need I say anything about John, who leaned on Jesus' breast? He left one Gospel, while claiming he could write so many that the world itself could not contain them [John 21:25].[438]

Finally, writing in his fourth-century *Ecclesiastical History*, Bishop Eusebius stated his summary conclusions regarding the authorship of the fourth gospel.

---

[436] Irenaeus in *Adversus Omnes Haereses*, as quoted in Eusebius (1999), p. 110 & 183.
[437] Eusebius (1999), p. 218.
[438] Eusebius (1999), p. 232. The reference to so many books the world could not contain them all refers to John 21:25, which reads as follows. "And there are also many other things which Jesus did, the which, if they should be written every one, I suppose that even the world itself could not contain the books that should be written. Amen." (King James Version)

Now let me indicate the undisputed writings of this apostle. His Gospel read by all the churches under heaven, must be recognized as first of all. That the early Fathers assigned it to the fourth place after the other three is understandable...Yet of all those who had been with the Lord, only Matthew and John have left us their memoirs...The three written Gospels in general circulation also came into John's hands. He welcomed them, it is said, and affirmed their accuracy, but noted that the narrative lacked only the account of what Christ had done at the beginning of his mission...They say, then, that for this reason John was urged to record in his own gospel the Savior's deeds during the period passed over in silence by the earlier Evangelists—that is, the events before the Baptist's imprisonment.[439]

It should be noted that the sum total of the above tradition makes two separate claims: (1) that the gospel was written by John, the son of Zebedee; and (2) that John, the son of Zebedee, was "the disciple whom Jesus loved" and who leaned on Jesus' breast.[440] The second claim is based on one fact and a huge assumption. The fact is that the fourth gospel is the only one to use the phrase "the disciple whom Jesus loved" and to report this disciple leaning on Jesus' breast. The assumption is that John, the son of Zebedee, wrote the fourth gospel. As such, if the first claim can be cast into doubt, the second claim has nothing more to stand on than the fact that the fourth gospel is unique in using the phrase "the disciple whom Jesus loved." As such, it is time to examine the many reasons for doubting that the fourth gospel was written by John, the son of Zebedee.

---

[439] Eusebius (1999), p. 113-114.
[440] John 13:23; 19:26; 20:2; 21:7 &20.

(1) The first argument against this gospel being written by John follows from the issue of age. However, before addressing this, one needs to note that the Gospel of John was written early in the second century. This date can be verified by noting that in only three passages in the entire New Testament is the Sea of Galilee referred to as the Sea of Tiberias, and all three passages are in the Gospel of John.[441] What makes this fact so important is that the Sea of Galilee was never called Tiberias until the second century.[442] As such, the fourth gospel cannot have been written before 100 CE. However, John, the son of Zebedee, was already an adult fisherman in Galilee at the time Jesus called him to be a disciple,[443] in 28 or 29 CE.[444] Assuming that John was 25 years old at the time, he would have been born around four CE, making him at least 96 years old, and perhaps over 100, when the fourth gospel was written. While this is not impossible, it certainly is improbable. Furthermore, in contrast to the above quoted traditions, there is also an early Christian tradition that John was martyred at the same time as his brother James.[445] As James was martyred circa 41 CE,[446] that tradition, if accepted, would clearly rule out John as being the author of the fourth gospel. Given the above considerations having to do with age, John's authorship of the fourth gospel must be seriously questioned.

(2) The fourth gospel implies in three different verses that the high priest of Judaism served for only one year at a time.[447] This is totally false, as can be easily seen by referring to Josephus' listing of the high priests.[448] One

---

[441] John 6:1 & 23; 21:1.
[442] Marsh J (1972).
[443] (A) Matthew 4:18-22; (B) Mark 1:16-20; (C) Luke 5:1-11.
[444] Duncan GB (1971a).
[445] Marsh J (1972).
[446] Eusebius (1999).
[447] John 11:49 & 51; 18:13.
[448] Josephus F (1988).

would certainly expect that a Jew living in first-century Palestine would have known this and would not have made the mistake implied three different times in the fourth gospel.[449]

(3) The fourth gospel totally fails to report anything at all about certain events where John, the son of Zebedee, was a key player or observer. This includes John's call to be a disciple,[450] his witnessing of the transfiguration of Jesus,[451] his witnessing the raising of Jairus' daughter,[452] and Jesus' agony in Gethsemane, the latter three events being ones where only Peter, James, and John were reportedly present. Certainly, it seems more than a little strange that all three of the other canonical gospels reported these events, but that John would have failed to record these events that must have been so important to him in any gospel he may have written.[453]

(4) "The disciple whom Jesus loved" is sometimes identified with the unnamed disciple who, with Simon Peter, followed Jesus after his arrest to Jesus' appearance before Caiaphas, the high priest of Judaism.[454] This event, which is recorded in John 18:15-18, clearly states that the unnamed disciple knew Caiaphas, the high priest. However, John, the son of Zebedee, was a simple, Galilean fisherman, and it is highly unlikely that he would have been on personal terms with the high priest.[455] Thus, either John was not "the disciple whom Jesus loved," or that disciple was not the unnamed disciple that knew the high priest.

---

[449] Marsh J (1972)

[450] (A) Matthew 4:18-22; (B) Mark 1:16-20; (C) Luke 5:1-11.

[451] (A) Matthew 17:1-13; (B) Mark 9:2-13; (C) Luke 9:28-36.

[452] (A) Matthew 9:18-26; (B) Mark 5:22-43; (C) Luke 8:40-56.

[453] Culpepper RA (1997).

[454] Culpepper RA (1997).

[455] Culpepper RA (1997).

(5) Finally, it is noted that the fourth gospel focuses on Jesus' Judaean ministry, not on his Galilean ministry.[456] This is not something that one would expect from a Galilean fisherman.

For all of the above reasons, the tradition that the fourth gospel was written by John, the son of Zebedee, must be rejected. However, if John didn't write this gospel, who did? Biblical scholars have come up with several different hypotheses regarding the authorship of the fourth gospel, and these are briefly reviewed below.

One hypothesis is that the fourth gospel was written by another person named John who is typically referred to as John the Presbyter or John the Elder.[457] Factors to consider in support of this hypothesis include the fact that in his *Exposition of the Oracles of the Lord,* which was written circa 130 CE, but which is preserved only in Bishop Eusebius' (260-339 CE) fourth-century *Ecclesiastical History,* Bishop Papias wrote that there were two Johns in Ephesus, one an actual member of the 12 disciples and the other an otherwise unknown presbyter, each having been buried in a tomb in Ephesus.[458] Further, Dionysius of Alexandria (circa 200-265 CE) identified John the Presbyter as being the author of Revelation[459] and hence the John who was imprisoned on Patmos.[460] These considerations suggest the possibility that the two Johns were confused during the second century and that the fourth gospel was mistakenly attributed to the wrong John.

---

[456] (A) Culpepper RA (1997); (B) Garvie AE (1929).
[457] (A) Marsh J (1972); (B) Garvie AE (1929).
[458] Eusebius (1999).
[459] Eusebius (1999).
[460] Revelation 1:9.

Another theory is that the author of the fourth gospel was Nicodemus.[461] Still other Biblical scholars[462] have suggested that "the disciple whom Jesus loved" was Lazarus, the young man Jesus raised from the dead. Two different Biblical verses support this hypothesis and give some measure of credence, however slight, to the hypothesis that Lazarus was the author of the fourth gospel.

> Now Jesus loved Martha, and her sister, and Lazarus. (John 11:5, King James Version)

> Jesus wept. Then said the Jews, Behold how he (Jesus) loved him (Lazarus)! (John 11:35-36, King James Version)

In summary, it is extremely unlikely that the fourth gospel was written by the John who was one of the 12 actual disciples of Jesus. The same age issue that tends to rule out this John as being the author also tends to rule out Nicodemus and Lazarus as candidates for authorship. While John the Elder cannot be ruled out as the author, the most realistic conclusion is that the authorship of the fourth gospel remains unknown.

CONCLUSIONS

The authorship of none of the four canonical gospels can be reliably attributed to the names traditionally associated with those gospels. In the final analysis, tradition breaks down, and one is left with gospels written many years after the fact by unknown authors, probably none of whom were actual eyewitnesses to the events they chronicled.

THE TWELVE DISCIPLES

That Jesus had two groups of disciples, an inner core of 12 and a larger group of 70, is a frequently taught lesson in Sunday school. However, it

---

[461] Garvie AE (1929).

[462] For example, (A) Culpepper RA (1997); (B) Garvie AE (1929).

is seldom mentioned in those Sunday school classes that the New Testament lists of the people comprising the select group of 12 disciples are discrepant with each other. Four different lists of the 12 disciples can be found in the New Testament, one each in Matthew 10:1-4, Mark 3:13-19, Luke 6:12-16, and Acts 1:12-17. While these lists agree with regard to 11 of the 12 disciples, there is disagreement regarding the 12th disciple. Matthew and Mark list him as being Thaddaeus (Lebbaeus whose surname was Thaddaeus in some manuscripts), while Luke and Acts list him as being Judas the son of James (perhaps Judas the brother of James). The four lists are presented below in Figure #7.

Figure #7

THE TWELVE DISCIPLES

MATTHEW	MARK	LUKE	ACTS
Simon Peter	Simon Peter	Simon Peter	Peter
Andrew	Andrew	Andrew	Andrew
James b. Zebedee	James b. Zebedee	James	James
John b. James	John b. of James	John	John
Philip	Philip	Philip	Philip
Bartholomew	Bartholomew	Bartholomew	Bartholomew
Thomas	Thomas	Thomas	Thomas
Matthew	Matthew	Matthew	Matthew
James b. Alphaeus	James b. Alphaeus	James b. Alphaeus	James b. Alphaeus
Thaddaeus*	Thaddaeus		
Simon**	Simon**	Simon the Zealot**	Simon the Zealot**
Judas Iscariot	Judas Iscariot	Judas Iscariot	Judas***
		Judas b. James****	Judas b. James****

*Listed as Lebbaeus whose surname is Thaddaeus in some manuscripts.

**Called the Cananaean in Matthew and Mark and the Zealot in Luke and Acts. Cananaean and Zealot were both terms referring to an extremist nationalist movement in first-century Palestine, so there is no discrepancy here.[463]

***It is clear by context that this is Judas Iscariot.

****It could be read as Judas the brother of James.

What is one to make of this inconsistency? Quite clearly, the New Testament is giving discrepant lists. Was the 12th disciple a Judas who was the son or brother of James, or was he Thaddaeus or Lebbaeus who was surnamed Thaddaeus? There simply is no satisfactory answer to be found within the pages of the New Testament text.

Complicating the picture a little further, Mark 2:13-17 and Luke 5: 27-32 recount the story of Jesus calling a tax collector named Levi to follow him, presumably indicating that Levi was to be a disciple. In Mark's story, this Levi is identified as being the son of Alphaeus, the same name given to the father of one of the two disciples named James in all four lists of the 12 disciples. However, the same story told in Matthew 9:9-13 calls this tax collector Matthew! What is going on here? Is Levi the same person as James the son of Alphaeus? Is Levi the brother of James the son of Alphaeus? Is Levi the same person as Matthew? Are Matthew, Levi, and James the son of Alphaeus all the same person? Unfortunately, there is nothing but speculation to go on, as the New Testament fails to clear up this confusion.

---

[463] Pherigo LP (1971).

CHAPTER 5

ADDITIONS, DELETIONS, AND MISLEADING TRANSLATIONS

INTRODUCTION

OVER THE CENTURIES, THE TEXT of the *Bible* has suffered from a variety of later additions, deletions, and misleading translations. Some of these corruptions of the Biblical text were probably no more insidious than a copyist's inadvertent deletion of a word or a phrase. Unfortunately, when later scribes copied the now defective text of the copyist who made the original deletion, the deletion spread to other manuscripts and eventually became the common standard. Fortunately, in some cases, manuscripts that predate the original deletion continue to exist and allow us to reconstruct the text in its more original format.

Other cases of corruption of the Biblical text appear to have a more malevolent origin. This is especially true when it comes to later additions to the Biblical text. Sometimes such additions were in the service of promoting a particular theological doctrine or point of view, such as in the case of the Johannine Comma, which is discussed below. In other cases, the motive for the addition to the Biblical text is less clear.

It is quite outside the scope of the present chapter to present an encyclopedic listing of every addition to, deletion from, and misleading translation of the *Bible*. However, the following listing serves as a representative sample of examples from the Protestant canon of the *Bible*. In some cases, the when, where, and why of the corruption of the Biblical text are known. In other cases, they are not.

ADDITIONS TO THE ORIGINAL TEXT OF THE *BIBLE*
THE JOHANNINE COMMA

> For there are three that bear record in heaven, the Father, the
> Word, and the Holy Ghost: and these three are one. And there
> are three that bear witness in earth, the Spirit, and the water,
> and the blood: and these three agree in one. (I John 5:7-8, King
> James Version)

The above verses from the King James Version of I John 5:7-8 appear to
supply a clear Biblical basis for the Doctrine of the Trinity. After all, what
clearer and more definitive Trinitarian statement could there be? These
verses specifically tell us that there are three in heaven, that these three are
one, and that these three are the Father, the Word (Jesus Christ), and the
Holy Spirit. When confronted with the fact that the word "Trinity" never
appears in the *Bible*, many Christians find comfort and support for their
Trinitarian views in this passage from the King James Version of the *Bible*.
However, when one examines other translations of the *Bible* than the
King James Version, one is immediately confronted with a very different
message, as the following quotations illustrate.

> And the Spirit is the witness because the Spirit is the truth. There
> are three witnesses, the Spirit, the water, and the blood; and these
> three agree. (I John 5:7-8, Revised Standard Version)

> There are three that testify: the Spirit and the water and the
> blood, and these three agree. (I John 5:/-8, New Revised
> Standard Version)

> so that there are three witnesses, the Spirit, the water and the
> blood, and all three of them agree. (I John 5:7-8, Jerusalem
> Version)

In none of the immediately above quoted translations do we find any reference to three beings in heaven, nor do we find a statement that these three beings are somehow one. Finally, there is absolutely no statement that these three beings are comprised of the Father, the Word, and the Holy Spirit. Quite simply, the Trinitarian trappings to be found in the King James Version completely disappear. What is going on here?

The simple answer is that the King James Version includes a relatively late addition to the Biblical text, known as the Johannine Comma, which is not found in any of the earliest manuscripts of the *Bible*, [464] including Greek (Koine Greek being the language in which the New Testament was originally written), Syriac, Coptic, Armenian, Ethiopic, Arabic, Slavonic, and Old Latin manuscripts. [465] Furthermore, none of the early Greek Fathers quoted the Johannine Comma, suggesting that it was unknown to them, because had they known of it, they surely would have quoted it against Sabellius' and Arius' arguments against the Trinity. [466]

The Johannine Comma (here "comma" refers not to a punctuation mark but to a clause or sentence) is an insertion of extra words into I John 5: 7-8. This insertion was initiated circa 380 CE in a Latin text in Spain, [467] and our first written record in which this insertion is found is *Liber Apologeticus*, a fourth century CE Latin treatise that is variously attributed to Priscillian, the Spanish heretic who died circa 385 CE, and to Bishop Instantius, a follower of Priscillian. [468] By the fifth century CE, the insertion was being quoted by Latin-speaking Church Fathers in

---

[464] (A) Shepherd MH (1971); (B) Metzger BM (1993).
[465] Metzger BM (1993).
[466] Metzger BM (1993).
[467] (A) Easton BS (1929); (B) Shepherd MH (1971).
[468] Metzger BM (1993).

North Africa and Italy as being part of I John 5:7-8.[469] Over time, the insertion spread into other Latin texts. Of importance in understanding the spread of the Johannine Comma, it was eventually incorporated into late editions of Saint Jerome's (circa 347-420 CE) Latin Vulgate version of the *Bible*, although Jerome himself did not include it in the Vulgate.[470]

With additional time, the insertion made its way into eight different Greek manuscripts, all of which appear to be translations from a late version of the Latin Vulgate. In four of these Greek manuscripts (#221, a 10th-century manuscript in the Bodleian Library at Oxford; #88, a 16th-century addition to the 14th-century Codex Regius of Naples; #429, a 16th-century manuscript at Wolfenbuttel; and #636, a 16th-century manuscript at Naples), the insertion was placed in the margin of the text and noted to be a variant reading and later addition to the original text. However, the insertion actually made its way into the actual Greek text in four manuscripts (#629, a 14th or 15th-century manuscript in the Vatican; #61, the early 16th-century Codex Montfortianus; #918, a 16th-century manuscript in Escorial, Spain; and #2318, an 18th-century manuscript, influenced by the Clementine Vulgate, at Bucharest, Rumania). As can be seen from the above, the earliest Greek manuscript to include the Johannine Comma as being part of the actual text of the *Bible* dates back only to the 14th century at the earliest.[471]

In addition, and of most importance, the Johannine Comma was included in the third edition of Erasmus' (1469-1536 CE) Greek New Testament and from there made its way into many translations into other languages.[472] The story of just how the Johannine Comma made its way

---

[469] Metzger BM (1993).
[470] (A) Koester H (1982); (B) Shepherd MH (1971); (C) Metzger BM (1993).
[471] Metzger BM (1993).
[472] Koester H (1982).

into Erasmus' Greek New Testament is told in a rather amusing manner by Robertson who uses the abbreviation "N.T." to stand for "New Testament" and "MS." to stand for "manuscript." Robertson's reference to "the Greek minuscule 61" refers to Codex Montfortianus, which traces back only to the early 16th century.

> The first Greek N.T. to be published was that of Erasmus, in 1516…When Erasmus published his first edition, he was chided by Stunica for having omitted the passage about the Trinity in I John 5:7-8. In a rash moment, Erasmus said that if the passage could be found in a single Greek MS., he would insert it. The passage was translated from the Latin Vulgate and forged into the Greek minuscule 61 of the sixteenth century (now in Dublin). [473]

When the King James Version of the Bible was created in 1611, the English translators relied on Erasmus' Greek New Testament, which was published in its first edition in 1516, and which later included the Johannine Comma addition in its third edition.[474] Thus, the Johannine Comma made its way into English. As shown previously, newer translations of the *Bible* (e.g., the Revised Standard Version, the New Revised Standard Version, the Jerusalem Version, etc.), which rely on older Greek manuscripts of I John than does the King James Version, rather unanimously omit the Johannine Comma addition. Further, almost all Biblical scholars reject the Johannine Comma as being a later interpolation into the original text of I John.

---

[473] Robertson AT (1929), p. 860-861.
[474] Robertson AT (1929).

The Trinitarian vs. Unitarian controversy was the hot topic of theological debates in the late fourth century, and the Johannine Comma attempted to tip the balance to the Trinitarian side with its insertion of several words into I John 5:7-8 that introduced a decidedly Trinitarian formulation into two verses that otherwise offered no support for the Trinitarian position. Quite clearly, the Johannine Comma is a later addition to the Biblical text and is to be rejected.[475]

THE WOMAN CAUGHT IN ADULTERY

For many Christians, the story of Jesus and the woman caught in adultery, i.e., the *Pericope Adulterae or Pericope de Adultera*, is one of the most beloved stories of Jesus to be found in the New Testament, a story that emphasizes Christ's loving compassion, mercy, and great capacity to forgive. The gist of the story is that the scribes and Pharisees bring a woman caught in the very act of adultery before Jesus. According to Leviticus 20:10-12,[476] adultery was a capital offence, and Deuteronomy 22:22-24[477] stipulated that the death sentence was to be carried out by stoning. Apparently referring to these Old Testament passages, the scribes and Pharisees noted that the Law of Moses mandated that this adulteress be stoned. Nevertheless, in an effort to trick Jesus into saying something

---

[475] (A) Black DA (1997); (B) Shepherd MH (1971).

[476] Leviticus 20:10-12 reads as follows in the King James Version. "And the man that committeth adultery with another man's wife, even he that committeth adultery with his neighbour's wife, the adulterer and the adulteress shall surely be put to death. And the man that lieth with his father's wife hath uncovered his father's nakedness: both of them shall surely be put to death; their blood shall be upon them. And if a man lie with his daughter in law, both of them shall surely be put to death: they have wrought confusion; their blood shall be upon them."

[477] Deuteronomy 22:22-24 reads as follows in the King James Version. "If a man be found lying with a woman married to an husband, then they shall both of them die, both the man that lay with the woman, and the woman: so shalt thou put away evil from Israel. If a damsel that is a virgin be betrothed unto an husband, and a man find her in the city, and lie with her; then ye shall bring them both out unto the gate of that city, and ye shall stone them with stones that they die; the damsel, because she cried not, being in the city; and the man, because he hath humbled his neighbour's wife: so thou shalt put away evil from among you."

for which they could later accuse him, they asked Jesus for his opinion as to what should be done. Reportedly, Jesus replied by stating something on the order of, "Let him who is without sin cast the first stone." Abashed, the crowd then dispersed, leaving Jesus alone with the adulterous, to whom he then asked, "Where are your accusers; has no man condemned you?" When she replied that there was no one left there who was accusing her of adultery, Jesus reportedly said, in a statement immortalized in a famous gospel hymn, "Neither do I condemn thee; go and sin no more." The entire story is to be found in the King James Version of John 7:53-8:11, which is quoted immediately below.

> And every man went unto his own house. Jesus went unto the mount of Olives. And early in the morning he came again into the temple, and all the people came unto him; and he sat down, and taught them. And the scribes and Pharisees brought unto him a woman taken in adultery; and when they had set her in the midst, they say unto him, Master, this woman was taken in adultery, in the very act. Now Moses in the law commanded us, that such should be stoned: but what sayest thou? This they said, tempting him, that they might have to accuse him. But Jesus stooped down, and with his finger wrote on the ground, as though he heard them not. So when they continued asking him, he lifted up himself, and said unto them, He that is without sin among you, let him first cast a stone at her. And again he stooped down, and wrote on the ground. And they which heard it, being convicted by their own conscience, went out one by one, beginning at the eldest, even unto the last: and Jesus was left alone, and the woman standing in the midst. When Jesus had lifted up himself, and saw none but the woman, he said unto her, Woman, where are those thine accusers? Hath no man

condemned thee? She said, No man, Lord. And Jesus said unto her, Neither do I condemn thee: go, and sin no more. (John 7:53-8:11, King James Version)

As noted previously, this is a touching story of loving compassion, mercy, and forgiveness. The only problem is that the entire passage is a later addition to the text of the Gospel of John and is not to be found in the earliest manuscripts of this gospel.[478] In fact, the *Pericope Adulterae* is not found in the oldest Greek, Syriac, Coptic, and Gothic versions of the Gospel of John,[479] and it is only after 900 CE that it begins to appear in the standard Greek text of the Gospel of John, although its presence can be found in a variant fifth-century Greek manuscript known as D,[480] a fifth or sixth-century CE text of the gospels and Acts that is also known as Bezae.[481] Further, no Greek Church Father prior to Euthymius Zigabenus in the 12th century ever mentioned the *Pericope Adulterae*, and Euthymius only mentioned it to state that accurate copies of the Gospel of John did not contain it.[482] For example, Origen (circa 185-254 CE) in his commentary on the Gospel of John went directly from 7:52 to 8:12, and Chrysostom (347-407 CE) also fails to mention it in his commentary on the Gospel of John.[483] Likewise, neither Theodore of Mopsuestia (circa 350-429 CE), or Cyril of Alexandria (circa 375-444 CE) ever mentioned it.[484] In addition, Nonnus, the fifth-century CE Greek poet, makes no mention of the *Pericope Adulterae* in his *Metabole*, a hexameter paraphrase of the Gospel of John.[485]

---

[478] (A) Marsh J (1972); (B) Garvic AE (1929); (C) Shepherd MII (1971b); (D) Fox RL (1992); (E) --- (1989).

[479] (A) Brown RE (1966); (B) Metzger BM (1993).

[480] Hills EF (1984).

[481] Reumann (1971).

[482] Metzger BM (1993).

[483] (A) Metzger BM (1993); (B) Tregelles SP (1854).

[484] Tregelles SP (1854).

[485] (A) Metzger BM (1993); (B) Tregelles SP (1854).

So how did the *Pericope Adulterae* find its way into the King James Version of the *Bible?* The story does appear in some Latin texts of the *Bible,* and Western Church Fathers, such as Ambrose (339-397 CE) and Augustine (354-430 CE), championed its cause, and Saint Jerome (circa 347-420 CE) included it in his Latin Vulgate version of the *Bible.*[486] However, several earlier Western Church Fathers apparently had no knowledge of the *Pericope Adulterae,* including Tertullian (circa 155-post 220 CE) and Cyprian (200-258 CE). Nonetheless, with its inclusion in Jerome's Latin Vulgate, the *Pericope Adulterae* became standard fare within Western Christianity and eventually made its way into the standard Greek text of the Gospel of John after 900 CE. Although Erasmus doubted the authenticity of the *Pericope Adulterae,*[487] he included it in his standard Greek New Testament, and from there it found its way into the King James Version of the *Bible.*

Most modern translations of the *Bible* omit the story in its entirety or include a footnote or margin note explaining that the story is a later insertion. As such, the American Standard Version of 1901 states: "Most of the ancient authorities omit John vii.53-viii. 11. Those which contain it vary much from each other." The Revised Standard Version of 1946 includes a marginal note that reads: "Most of the ancient authorities either omit 7.53-8.11, or insert it, with variations of the text, here or at the end of this gospel or after Luke 21.38." The Revised Standard Version of 1971 notes: "The most ancient authorities omit 7.53-8.11; other authorities add the passage here or after 7.36 or after 21.25 or after Luke 21.38, with variations of text." The New American Standard Version of 1963 states: "John 7:53-8:11 is not found in most of the old mss (manuscripts)." The New International Version of 1973 notes: "The most reli-

---

[486] (A) Brown RE (1966); (B) Tregelles SP (1854).
[487] Tregelles SP (1854).

able early manuscripts omit John 7:53-8:11." Later editions of the New International Version read: "The earliest and most reliable manuscripts and other ancient witnesses do not have John 7:53-8:11." The New Revised Standard Version includes the story within brackets, thus setting it off from the Biblical text, and offers a footnote that reads: "The most ancient authorities lack 7.53-8.11; other authorities add the passage here or after 7.36 or after 21.25 or after Luke 21.38, with variations of text; some mark the passage as doubtful." The reader's edition of the Jerusalem Version (2000) offers a footnote to the *Pericope Adulterae* that reads: "The author of this passage is not John; the oldest MSS (manuscripts) do not include it or place it elsewhere." Even the New King James Version of 1980 adds a footnote to this passage, noting that the United Bible Societies' Greek text "brackets 7:53-8:11 as not in the original text." Unfortunately, the footnote then goes on to try to save the *Pericope Adulterae* by claiming that it appears in over 900 manuscripts of the Gospel of John, while failing to note that: (1) all of the manuscripts of this gospel that contain the *Pericope Adulterae* that are written in Greek, i.e., those written in the original language of the New Testament, are of relatively late date; and (2) those manuscripts that do contain it often vary dramatically.

THE LORD'S PRAYER

Millions of Christians recite the Lord's Prayer as recorded in Matthew 6:9-13 every Sunday morning in church. For them and millions of others, the Lord's Prayer is the perfect prayer, the prayer that Jesus Christ taught his disciples to say. However, there remain significant questions as to what exactly constitutes the Lord's Prayer. This can be quickly illustrated by comparing the King James Version and New Revised Standard Version of Matthew 6:9-13.

Our Father which art in heaven, Hallowed be thy name. Thy kingdom come. Thy will be done in earth, as it is in heaven. Give us this day our daily bread. And forgive us our debts, as we forgive our debtors. And lead us not into temptation, but deliver us from evil: For thine is the kingdom, and the power, and the glory, for ever. Amen. (Matthew 6:9-13, King James Version)

Our Father in heaven, hallowed be your name. Your kingdom come. Your will be done, on earth as it is in heaven. Give us this day our daily bread. And forgive us our debts, as we also have forgiven our debtors. And do not bring us to the time of trial, but rescue us from the evil one. (Matthew 6:9-13, New Revised Standard Version)

Aside from minor differences in language, there are two significant differences between the King James Version and the New Revised Standard Version that have to do with actual content. The first significant difference has to do with the change from "lead us not into temptation" to "do not bring us to the time of trial." The Greek *eis peirasmon*, which is translated in the King James Version "into temptation," actually refers to the time of trials and tribulations in the End Times, not to the temptations of daily life.[488] As noted by one prominent *Bible* scholar:

> The prayer for deliverance from temptation and evil probably does not refer to temptation to sin, as though God would place us in the position where we would be inclined to immoral actions. Rather it is the notion found in Jewish apocalyptic writings…that just before the end of the age there would occur a time of trial and testing of God's people. This period of persecution, with the attempt to turn men aside from the way of faith

---

[488] (A) Kee HC (1971); (B) Fenton JC (1973).

and obedience, was known as the temptation or the tribulation. It is to be delivered from this situation and from the power of the Evil One (Satan) that Jesus tells the disciples to pray.[489]

The second significant difference is that the King James Version of the Gospel of Matthew's Lord's Prayer includes the familiar doxology portion ("For Thine is the kingdom, and the power, and the glory forever. Amen") of the Lord's Prayer, while the New Revised Standard Version does not. The reason for this difference is simple, straightforward, and one that has already been noted in this chapter, i.e., the New Revised Standard Version draws on much more ancient manuscripts of the *Bible* than does the King James Version. In point of fact, the doxology that was added to the Gospel of Matthew's rendition of the Lord's Prayer first appears in a somewhat shorter form ("For yours is the power and the glory forever") in the Didache,[490] an early second century CE document that is also known as the Teaching of the Twelve Apostles and that deals with church order.[491] The doxology does not appear in the oldest manuscripts of the Gospel of Matthew,[492] and it went totally unmentioned in commentaries written about the Lord's Prayer by Tertullian (circa 155-post 220 CE), Cyprian (200-258 CE), and Origen (circa 185-254 CE), strongly suggesting that it was totally unknown to them as being part of the Lord's Prayer.[493] In short, the doxology was added to the Gospel of Matthew's rendition of the Lord's Prayer by some overzealous scribe,[494] no earlier than the latter part of the second century.

---

[489] Kee HC (1971), page 617.
[490] (A) Seymour BJ (1997); (B) Coggan D (1993).
[491] Snyder GF (1997).
[492] (A) Coggan D (1993); (B) Seymour BJ (1997); (C) Davies JN (1929b).
[493] Coggan D (1993).
[494] Fenton JC (1973).

The Gospel of Luke's version of the Lord's Prayer is much shorter than the Gospel of Matthew's, and the vast majority of Biblical scholars believe that the Gospel of Luke's version is much closer to the original words of Jesus than is the Gospel of Matthew's version. What is the reason for the account in the Gospel of Matthew including so much extraneous material? Quite simply, it appears that the Gospel of Matthew incorporated into the Lord's Prayer material of a liturgical nature from the early Christian church.[495] That this is so can be illustrated by the fact that in Greek, the Gospel of Luke's version is in prose, while the Gospel of Matthew's is rhythmical.[496]

As can be seen by examining the following quotation of Luke 11:2-4 from the New Revised Standard Version and the King James Version, the King James Version includes material not found in the New Revised Standard Version. The reason for this is that the King James Version was based on later Greek manuscripts that had attempted to harmonize the Lukan version of the Lord's Prayer with the Matthean version,[497] thus corrupting the more original Lukan version.

> Father, hallowed be your name. Your kingdom come. Give us each day our daily bread. And forgive us our sins, for we ourselves forgive everyone indebted to us. And do not bring us to the time of trial. (Luke 11:2-4, New Revised Standard Version)

> Our Father which art in heaven, Hallowed be thy name. Thy kingdom come. Thy will be done, as in heaven, so in earth. Give us day by day our daily bread. And forgive us our sins; for we also forgive

---

[495] (A) Coggan D (1993); (B) Seymour BJ (1997); (C) Findlay JA (1929); (D) Davies JN (1929b); (E) Kee HC (1971); (F) Baird W (1971a).

[496] Findlay JA (1929).

[497] Coggan D (1993).

every one that is indebted to us. And lead us not into temptation; but deliver us from evil. (Luke 11:2-4, King James Version)

Before ending our discussion of the Lord's Prayer, it is important to note that Biblical scholarship has successfully identified a written "sayings" source known as Q.[498] Q was originally defined as the material that is common to the Gospels of Matthew and Luke, while being absent from the Gospel of Mark.[499] However, the 1945 discovery of the Gospel of Thomas at Nag Hammadi, Egypt, has suggested that this initial definition of Q needs to be revised. Without question, the Gospel of Thomas is a Q- related document.[500] In fact, about one third of the sayings in the Gospel of Thomas have direct parallels in the traditionally defined Q material of the Gospels of Matthew and Luke.[501] As such, Q may be better defined as: (1) material that is common to the Gospels of Matthew and Luke, while being absent from the Gospel of Mark; and (2) material that is found in the Gospels of Matthew and Thomas, Luke and Thomas, or Matthew, Luke, and Thomas, whether or not it is also found in the Gospel of Mark.[502]

The reason for the above digression into a discussion of Q and the Gospel of Thomas is that the Lord's Prayer is from Q. Given that the Lord's Prayer is from Q and that the Gospel of Thomas is a Q-related document, it is only prudent to examine the Gospel of Thomas to see if it also includes the Lord's Prayer. In doing so, it should be noted that the text of the Gospel of Thomas as we now have it is a Coptic translation of an

---

[498] (A) Robinson JM (1971a); (B) Robinson JM (1971b); (C) Koester H (1971a); (D) Mack BL (1995).

[499] (A) Filson FV (1971); (B) Kee HC (1971); (C) Baird W (1971a); (D) Burch EW (1929); (E) Leon-Dufour X (1983); (F) Koester H (1971b).

[500] (A) Koester H (1971a); (B) Robinson JM (1971b); (C) Koester H (1971b); (D) Mack BL (1995); (E) Cameron R (1982); (F) Koester H (1990).

[501] Mack BL (1995).

[502] Dirks JF (2001b).

earlier Greek text.[503] While the Coptic text traces back only to the fourth century CE,[504] the Greek original was probably composed in the mid to latter half of the first century CE.[505] With the above in mind, the following verses from the Gospel of Thomas appear to be relevant to the discussion regarding the Lord's Prayer.

> His disciples questioned Him and said to Him, "Do You want us to fast? How shall we pray? Shall we give alms? What diet shall we observe?" Jesus said, "Do not tell lies, and do not do what you hate, for all things are plain in the sight of heaven. For nothing hidden will not become manifest, and nothing covered will remain without being uncovered. (Thomas 6)[506]

The above passage portrays a radically different response from Jesus to the disciples' question about how to pray. Here, Jesus does not provide the disciples with any template for prayer. Instead, he confronts them about grudgingly performing prayers, i.e., doing what one hates, in a formulistic, ritualistic way that is devoid of any true spirituality. Quite simply, there is no Lord's Prayer to be found in the Gospel of Thomas. Does this mean that there never was any Lord's Prayer? There is no easy answer to that question. However, the Gospel of Thomas does raise questions as to the genuineness and authenticity of even the more original version of the Lord's Prayer to be found in the Gospel of Luke.

AN APPENDIX TO THE GOSPEL OF MARK

The last chapter of the Gospel of Mark begins with Mary Magdalene, Mary the mother of James, and Salome entering the tomb in which Jesus

---

[503] (A) Cameron R (1982); (B) Guillaumont A, Puech H, Quispel G, Till W, 'Abd Al-Masih Y (1959); (C) Koester H (1990); Robinson JM (1971b).

[504] (A) Cameron R (1982); (B) Pagels E (1979).

[505] (A) Cameron R (1982); (B) Koester H (1990).

[506] Cameron R (1982).

had been allegedly buried. There they were confronted by a young man who reportedly told them that Jesus had been raised from the dead and that they should tell the disciples that Jesus was raised, was going to Galilee, and would meet the disciples there. This story ends with chapter 16, verse eight. However, in the King James Version of the Gospel of Mark, the gospel goes on to include verses 9-20, which are quoted immediately below.

> Now when Jesus was risen early the first day of the week, he appeared first to Mary Magdalene, out of whom he had cast seven devils. And she went and told them that had been with him, as they mourned and wept. And they, when they had heard that he was alive, and had been seen of her, believed not. After that he appeared in another form unto two of them, as they walked, and went into the country. And they went and told it unto the residue: neither believed they them. Afterward he appeared unto the eleven as they sat at meat, and upbraided them with their unbelief and hardness of heart, because they believed not them which had seen him after he was risen. And he said unto them, Go ye unto all the world, and preach the gospel to every creature. He that believeth and is baptized shall be saved; but he that believeth not shall be damned. And these signs shall follow them that believe; In my name shall they cast out devils; they shall speak with new tongues; They shall take up serpents; and if they drink any deadly thing, it shall not hurt them; they shall lay hands on the sick, and they shall recover. So then after the Lord had spoken unto them, he was received up into heaven, and sat on the right hand of God. And they went forth, and preached everywhere, the Lord working with them, and confirming the word with signs following. Amen. (Mark 16:9-20, King James Version)

The whole of the above quoted passage from the King James Version is a later addition to the text of the Gospel of Mark.[507] In fact, the Gospel of Mark ends with verse eight, as is demonstrated by Codex Vaticanus and Codex Sinaiticus, two of the oldest and best Greek manuscripts of the Gospel of Mark.[508] Likewise, several ancient translations of the New Testament, e.g., the Sinaitic Syriac and many Armenian, Ethiopic, Old Latin, and Georgian texts, also end with the eighth verse of chapter 16.[509] In addition, such early Church Fathers as Clement of Alexandria (150-215 CE), Origen (circa 185-254 CE), Bishop Eusebius of Caesarea (circa 260-339 CE), and Saint Jerome (circa 347-420 CE) end the Gospel of Mark with verse eight or at least testify that all the best manuscripts end with verse eight.[510] Despite all of this, some copyists of the Gospel of Mark were apparently dissatisfied with the abrupt ending to this gospel with verse eight and endeavored to provide what was for them a more satisfactory conclusion. Mark 16:9-20 is illustrative of one such attempt and appears to be based upon the Gospel of Luke, the Gospel of John, possibly Acts, and non-canonical sources.[511]

As to the origin of this spurious addition to the Gospel of Mark, it can be best dated to the second century CE, and it cannot be dated any later than circa 180 CE, as Bishop Irenaeus of Lyon (130-200 or 140-210 CE) quoted it around that time as being part of the Gospel of Mark. As to the authorship of Mark 16:9-20, there is a 10th-century manuscript attributing the passage to Aristion, but the accuracy of such an attribution remains questionable.[512]

---

[507] (A) Kee HC (1997a); (B) Davies JN (1929a); (C) Pherigo LP (1971); (D) Nineham DE (1973); (E) Fox RL (1992).
[508] Kee HC (1997a).
[509] (A) Kee HC (1997a); (B) Davies JN (1929a).
[510] (A) Kee HC (1997a); (B) Nineham DE (1973).
[511] (A) Kee HC (1997a); (B) Pherigo LP (1971); (C) Nineham DE (1973).
[512] Nineham DE (1973).

An alternative addition stands alone in one manuscript and is placed between Mark 16:8 and 16:9 in several others. Known as the shorter ending of the Gospel of Mark, this passage reads as follows.

> But they reported to Peter and those with him all that they had been told. And after this Jesus himself sent out by means of them, from east to west, the sacred and imperishable proclamation of eternal salvation.[513]

Of note, Codex Washingtonianus, a fifth-century CE manuscript containing the gospels,[514] inserts yet more additional material after Mark 16:14.[515] This additional material is found in whole or in part in some other manuscripts as well and is supplied in the following footnote to Mark 16:14 in the New Revised Standard Version.

> And they excused themselves, saying, "This age of lawlessness and unbelief is under Satan, who does not allow the truth and power of God to prevail over the unclean things of the spirits. Therefore reveal your righteousness now"—thus they spoke to Christ. And Christ replied to them, "The term of years of Satan's power has been fulfilled, but other terrible things draw near. And for those who have sinned I was handed over to death, that they may return to the truth and sin no more, that they may inherit the spiritual and imperishable glory of righteousness that is in heaven."

Readers of the Revised Standard Version and New Revised Standard Version will find Mark 16:9-20 either printed only in a footnote or bracketed within the main text. In either case, the passage is marked as being of doubtful authenticity. The Jerusalem Version, while printing the

---

[513] Kee HC (1997a).
[514] Reumann J (1971).
[515] Kee HC (1997a).

passage as being the text of the Gospel of Mark, does note that many ancient manuscripts lack these verses.

THE ROCK OF THE CHURCH

Matthew 16:13-16 reports that Jesus asked his disciples who people said that he was. He was informed that some people said he was John the Baptist, Elijah, Jeremiah, or some other prophet returned from the dead. Jesus then reportedly asked his disciples who they believed he was. At that point, Simon Peter reportedly said that Jesus was the Christ, the son of the living God. Immediately following Peter's alleged statement, the following verses are recorded.

> And Jesus answered and said unto him, Blessed art thou, Simon Barjona: for flesh and blood hath not revealed it unto thee, but my Father which is in heaven. And I say also unto thee, That thou art Peter, and upon this rock I will build my church; and the gates of hell shall not prevail against it. And I will give unto thee the keys of the kingdom of heaven: and whatsoever thou shalt bind on earth shall be bound in heaven: and whatsoever thou shalt loose on earth shall be loosed in heaven. Then charged he his disciples that they should tell no man that he was Jesus the Christ. (Matthew 16:17-20, King James Version)

The problem with the immediately above quoted verses is that they simply do not exist in the Sinaitic Syriac *Bible*, a Syriac version that dates back to the fourth century and that predates most Greek versions of the *Bible*. As such, it may be concluded that the alleged words of Jesus as recorded in Matthew 16:17-20 did not exist in the ancient manuscript from which the Sinaitic Syriac was copied and that these verses represent a later addition to the text.[516]

---

[516] Robertson AT (1929).

PHILIP AND THE ETHIOPIAN EUNUCH

Acts 8:26-40 tells the story of Phillip, an early Jewish Christian, who escaped Paul's persecution of the Jerusalem Church and who was directed by God to journey south from Jerusalem to Gaza. While traveling on that wilderness road, Philip encountered an Ethiopian eunuch, a Jew who had been to Jerusalem to worship. As he traveled back home in a chariot, he was reading a passage from Isaiah.[517] Philip interrupted the eunuch to inquire as to whether the eunuch understood the passage he was reading. The eunuch replied in the negative, and he asked Philip to join him in the chariot and to explain the passage to him. Philip then began to preach to the eunuch about Jesus Christ.

> And as they went on their way, they came unto a certain water: and the eunuch said, See, here is water; what doth hinder me to be baptized? And Phillip said, If thou believest with all thine heart, thou mayest. And he answered and said, I believe that Jesus Christ is the Son of God. And he commanded the chariot to stand still: and they went down both into the water, both Phillip and the eunuch; and he baptized him. And when they were come up out of the water, the Spirit of the Lord caught away Philip, that the eunuch saw him no more: and he went on his way rejoicing. (Acts 8:36-39, King James Version)

The problem with the above quoted passage is that one verse has been added to the text that is not to be found in the most ancient manuscripts

---

[517] Reportedly, the passage was Isaiah 53:7b-8a, which in the King James Version reads as follows: "…he is brought as a lamb to the slaughter, and as a sheep before her shearers is dumb, so he openeth not his mouth. He was taken from prison and from judgment: and who shall declare his generation: and he was cut off out of the land of the living…" The same passage, quoted in the King James Version of Acts 8:32-33 reads slightly differently: "The place of the scripture which he read was this, He was led as a sheep to the slaughter; and like a lamb dumb before his shearer, so opened he not his mouth: In his humiliation his judgment was taken away: and who shall declare his generation? for his life is taken from the earth."

of this passage. The offending verse is #37, which was added to the Western text of the *Bible*.[518] This addition is not to be found in the Latin Vulgate, the fourth-century CE Codex Vaticanus, the fourth-century CE Codex Sinaiticus, and the fifth-century CE Codex Alexandrinus. The addition reads as follows.

> And Philip said, If thou believest with all thine heart, thou mayest. And he answered and said, I believe that Jesus Christ is the Son of God. (Acts 8:37, King James Version)

As can be seen, the earliest version of this passage has no statement from the eunuch proclaiming Jesus to be the "Son of God" with a capital "S." Such a statement and such a belief were not necessary to be baptized into Jewish Christianity as practiced by the Jerusalem Church and the actual disciples of Jesus. In fact, as seen in chapter two of this book, such a belief would have been contrary to the actual teachings of the Jerusalem Church.

In recognition that Acts 8:37 is a spurious addition to the text, the following English versions of the *Bible* omit this verse: Williams New Testament, Montgomery's New Testament, the Revised Standard Version, the New Revised Standard Version, the International English Version, the New American Version, Darby's Version, Weymouth's Version, and the New Living Version. Unfortunately, this obvious addition to the *Bible* continues to show up in the King James Version, the New King James Version, the American Standard Version, the Living Version, the New American Standard Version, Young's Version, Webster's Version, and the International Standard Version.

---

[518] Baird W (1971b).

CONCLUSIONS

The above examples demonstrate some of the additions to the Biblical text that can be demonstrated by reference to the oldest surviving manuscripts of the *Bible*. This immediately raises a question about what other additions there may be to the *Bible* for which we no longer have textual proof for these verses being additions. For example, many *Bible* commentators have noted the marked difference in style and content between the Prologue (chapter 1, verses 1-18) of the Gospel of John and the rest of this gospel. Much of the Prologue appears to be an early church hymn that an editor of the Gospel of John affixed to the start of this gospel and to which he then added some prose comments, i.e., verses 6-8, 12-13, 15, and 17.[519] Likewise, some commentators have suggested that the entirety of John 21 is a later addition to the original gospel.[520] These inferences are strengthened by the presence of internal evidence within John 21:24-25 that an editor did add at least some material to the original form of the gospel, as witnessed by the distinction made between "the disciple which testifieth" and the "I" who is writing these two verses.

> This is the disciple which testifieth of these things, and wrote these things: and we know that his testimony is true. And there are also many other things which Jesus did, the which, if they should be written every one, I suppose that even the world itself could not contain the books that should be written. Amen. (John 21:24-25, King James Version)

DELETIONS FROM THE ORIGINAL TEXT OF THE *BIBLE*
THE ORIGINAL ENDING TO THE GOSPEL OF MARK

Earlier in this chapter, it was shown that Mark 16:9-20 is a later addition

---

[519] Shepherd MH (1971b).
[520] Stendahl K, Sander ET (2003).

to the original text of this gospel. So did the original text actually end with 16:8? Most Biblical scholars answer in the negative. To understand this, we need to take a look at 16:8, which is quoted immediately below.

> And they went out quickly, and fled from the sepulcher; for they trembled and were amazed: neither said they any thing to any man; for they were afraid. (Mark 16:8, King James Version)

As stated in most English translations, Mark 16:8 reads as though it could have been the end of the gospel. As stated above in the King James Version, the verse expresses a complete thought and is a grammatically complete sentence. However, the situation is quite different when one examines the actual Greek text, which is quoted below, using the Roman alphabet to express the Greek letters.

> *Kai exelthousai efugon apo tou mnemeiou, eichengar autas tromos kai ekstasis. Kai oudeni ouden eipan; efobounto gar.* [521]

According to *Strong's New Testament Dictionary*, the final word, i.e., *gar*, in the above quotation means "for, because, or therefore," [522] which is clearly no way to conclude a sentence or complete thought, and which definitely implies that there is something more to come in order to complete the thought and sentence. This can best be seen by examining the last sentence of Mark 16:8 in word-for-word literal translation, as is done immediately below.

> *Kai* (And) *oudeni* (to no one) *ouden* (nothing) *eipan* (they told); *efobounto* (they were afraid) *gar* (because). [523]

One simply does not end a sentence by saying, "they were afraid because." Because why? That question was never answered if the Gospel

---

[521] --- (2001).
[522] --- (2001).
[523] --- (2001).

of Mark originally ended with verse 16:8 as we currently have it. In fact, *Bible* scholars have long noted the way 16:8 abruptly ends in mid sentence.[524]

There are four possible reasons for the incomplete thought and sentence with which 16:8 abruptly ends. (1) One possibility is that the author meant for the gospel to end this way. That, however, leaves us with a final verse that makes no grammatical or conceptual sense. As such, this hypothesis must be rejected. (2) A second possibility, although highly remote, is that the author was interrupted at this point and was never able to finish his gospel, most likely having died or been killed before he could get back to it. (3) The third possibility is that the original ending to the Gospel of Mark was simply lost at a very early time, i.e., before the Gospels of Matthew and Luke had a chance to copy from the Gospel of Mark. This could have been due to a final page of the manuscript being lost or to the end of the scroll being somehow damaged. This is the position taken by the majority of *Bible* scholars. (4) A fourth possibility, which is gaining ground with many *Bible* scholars, is that the original ending of the Gospel of Mark was deliberately destroyed. Why? Perhaps it was because the original ending portrayed Christ's disciples as not believing in his alleged resurrection, and this would have been a portrayal that the early church would not have wanted.[525]

Whether simply lost over time, accidentally destroyed, or deliberately excised from the original text, it is clear that the original ending to the Gospel of Mark is no longer with us. One can only wonder what the original text was saying.

---

[524] (A) Kee HC (1997a); (B) Nineham DE (1973); (C) Davies JN (1929a); (D) Pherigo LP (1971).
[525] Pherigo LP (1971).

THE BAPTISM OF JESUS CHRIST

All four canonical gospels of the New Testament report that Jesus was baptized by John the Baptist. Of these four accounts, the one in the Gospel of Luke is deserving of special examination.

> Now when all the people were baptized, it came to pass, that Jesus also being baptized, and praying, the heaven was opened, and the Holy Ghost descended in a bodily shape like a dove upon him, and a voice came from heaven, which said, Thou art my beloved Son; in thee I am well pleased. (Luke 3:21-22, King James Version)

"Thou art my beloved Son; in thee I am well pleased." The two most ancient textual traditions for the Gospel of Luke are the Alexandrian and the Western (D and some old Latin manuscripts).[526] In translating the above verses as it did, the King James Version is following the Alexandrian text. However, when one looks at the Western text, it appears that the Alexandrian text deleted a key phrase and substituted a different one for the original.[527] This possibility is noted in footnotes to the Revised Standard Version and the New Revised Standard Version, where verse 22 is translated as: "You are my Son, today I have begotten you." Going still further, and relying on the Western text, the New Jerusalem Version[528] offers the following translation for verses 21 and 22.

> Now it happened that when all the people had been baptized and while Jesus after his own baptism was at prayer, heaven opened, and the Holy Spirit descended on him in a physical form, like a dove. And a voice came from heaven, "You are my Son; today have I fathered you. (Luke 3:21-22, New Jerusalem Version)

---

[526] Talbert CH (1997).
[527] (A) Findlay JA (1929); (B) Baird W (1971a).
[528] --- (2001).

So which rendering of the verse is correct? Which textual tradition, Western or Alexandrian, represents the original text of Luke 3:22? The clear answer is that the Western text represents the more authentic original text. This can be seen by comparing Luke 3:22 to several other Biblical verses, including Hebrews 1:5, Hebrews 5:5, Acts 13:33, and Psalms 2:7, as well as by comparing it to the Gospel of the Ebionites, a lost gospel used by Jewish Christians in the first and second centuries CE and preserved in fragments when quoted by early Christian writers.

> For unto which of the angels said he at any time, Thou art my Son, this day have I begotten thee? And again, I will be to him a Father, and he shall be to me a Son. (Hebrews 1:5, King James Version)

> So also Christ glorified not himself to be made an high priest: but he that said unto him, Thou art my Son, today have I begotten thee. (Hebrews 5:5, King James Version)

> God hath fulfilled the same unto us their children, in that he hath raised up Jesus again; as it is also written in the second psalm, Thou art my Son, this day have I begotten thee. (Acts 13:33, King James Version)

> I will declare the decree: the Lord hath said unto me, Thou art my Son; this day have I begotten thee. (Psalms 2:7, King James Version)

> When the people were baptized, Jesus also came and was baptized by John. And as he came up from the water, the heavens were opened and he saw the Holy Spirit in the form of a dove that descended and entered into him. And a voice (sounded) from heaven that said: "Thou art my beloved son, in thee I am well

pleased." And again: "I have this day begotten thee." (Gospel of the Ebionites, as quoted by Epiphanius in *Panarian* 30.13.7-8)[529]

Why would the Alexandrian text delete the original wording of Luke 3:22, which was thankfully still preserved in the Western text? The answer has to do with Adoptionism, a movement within early Christianity that insisted that Christ's relationship to God was like that of an adopted son to his adopting father, not like a begotten son to his begetting father. Quite simply, Adoptionism, which is today viewed as a heresy by most Christian denominations, was a strong movement within early Christianity, especially among early Jewish Christian groups and especially in parts of North Africa and the Middle East. It appears that in order to counter the Adoptionist Christology, which left little, if any, room for positing a divine nature for Christ, the Alexandrian text, representing the Eastern tradition, deleted part of the original reading of Luke 3:22 in order to further a non-Adoptionist theological agenda. In short, the Biblical text was deliberately deleted in order to win a theological debate.[530]

A CRUCIAL ONE-WORD DELETION

Now at that feast the governor was wont to release unto the people a prisoner, whom they would. And they had then a notable prisoner, called Barabbas. Therefore when they were gathered together, Pilate said unto them, Whom will ye that I release unto you? Barabbas, or Jesus which is called Christ? For he knew that for envy they had delivered him...But the chief priests and elders persuaded the multitude that they should ask Barabbas, and destroy Jesus. The governor answered and said

---

[529] Epiphanius (1982), p. 105.
[530] (A) Baird W (1971a); (B) Findlay JA (1929); (C) Dirks JF(2001a).

unto them, Whether of the twain will ye that I release unto you?
They said, Barabbas. Pilate saith unto them, What shall I do then
with Jesus which is called Christ? They all say unto him, Let him
be crucified…Then released he Barabbas unto them: and when
he had scourged Jesus, he delivered him to be crucified.
(Matthew 27:15-18,20-22,26, King James Version)

The above passage from the King James Version recounts part of the
famous story of Jesus being tried before Pontius Pilate, the Roman governor of Judea. The crowd is given a choice as to which of two prisoners
Pilate will release. The crowd chooses Barabbas, who is subsequently
released, and "Jesus which is called Christ" is reportedly taken away and
crucified. However, the above passage, which is taken from relatively
late Greek texts has a crucial one-word omission in two different places.
The New Revised Standard Version, unlike the King James Version, goes
back to ancient Greek texts to supply the key missing word. However, it
is not just in ancient Greek manuscripts of the Gospel of Matthew that
one finds the missing word; it is also found in ancient Syriac manuscripts
of the Gospel of Matthew and in the writings of Origen (circa 185-254
CE).[531] As seen below in quoting from the New Revised Standard Version,
the missing word is none other than "Jesus."

At that time they had a notorious prisoner, called Jesus Barabbas.
So after they had gathered, Pilate said to them, "Whom do you
want me to release for you, Jesus Barabbas or Jesus who is called
the Messiah?" (Matthew 27:16-17, New Revised Standard
Version)

It turns out that there are two people named Jesus who are standing in
judgment before Pilate. The crowd chooses one Jesus to be released and

---

[531] (A) Fenton JC (1973); (B) Gloer WH (1997); (C) --- (2003b).

the other Jesus to be crucified. So who was who? Before beginning to answer that question, one needs to examine a couple of misleading translations to be found in the *Bible*.

MISLEADING TRANSLATIONS IN THE *BIBLE*

MULTIPLE MESSIAHS, MULTIPLE CHRISTS

It is a fundamental belief of Christianity that Jesus Christ was the messiah. However, few Christians actually understand what was meant by that concept. In order to appreciate what the word "messiah" actually means, one has to digress briefly into a journey through the Hebrew language.

The Hebrew verbal root "*mashah*" means to anoint, to consecrate through anointing, or to smear with oil or occasionally with some other substance.[532] It occurs approximately 70 times in the Hebrew Old Testament, and it usually indicates that something is being specially set apart for an office or function.[533] For example, in Genesis 28:18-19, Jacob awakens from sleep, sets upright the rock that he had used for his pillow, pours oil on the rock in consecrating it for God, and renames the place that he is at Bethel (House of God). In later referring back to this event in Genesis 31:13, the reader is told that Jacob had anointed (*mashah*) a pillar at Bethel. Likewise, the vessels used in worship at both the tabernacle and the later temple were consecrated by being anointed (*mashah*), as illustrated by the following verses, in which the current author has inserted the word "*mashah*" within parentheses each time it actually occurs.

> And thou shalt offer every day a bullock for a sin offering for
> atonement: and thou shalt cleanse the altar, when thou hast

---

[532] (A) *Strong's Old Testament Dictionary.* In --- (2001); (B) *Vine's Old Testament Dictionary.* In --- (2001).
[533] *Vine's Old Testament Dictionary.* In --- (2001).

made an atonement for it, and thou shalt anoint (*mashah*) it, to sanctify it. (Exodus 29:36, King James Version)

And thou shalt anoint (*mashah*) the tabernacle of the congregation therewith, and the ark of the testimony, and the table and all his vessels, and the candlestick and his vessels, and the altar of incense, and the altar of burnt offering with all his vessels, and the laver and his foot. And thou shalt sanctify them, that they may be most holy: whatsoever toucheth them shall be holy. (Exodus 30:26-29, King James Version)

And thou shalt take the anointing oil, and anoint (*mashah*) the tabernacle, and all that is therein, and shalt hallow it, and all the vessels thereof: and it shall be holy. And thou shalt anoint (*mashah*) the altar of the burnt offering, and all his vessels, and sanctify the altar: and it shall be an altar most holy. (Exodus 40:9-10, King James Version)

However, it was not just inanimate objects that were being anointed in the Old Testament, thus being sanctified and consecrated. People were also being anointed (*mashah*) and thus set aside for some special office. Who were these people? They were priests, prophets, and kings, with the latter group being the most commonly mentioned.[534] Thus, there are references to priests being anointed (*mashah*) in the following verses.

And for Aaron's sons thou shalt make coats, and thou shalt make for them girdles, and bonnets shalt thou make for them, for glory and for beauty. And thou shalt put them upon Aaron thy brother, and his sons with him; and shalt anoint (*mashah*) them,

---

[534] (A) *Vine's Old Testament Dictionary*. In --- (2001); (B) *Strong's Old Testament Dictionary*. In --- (2001); (C) *Easton's Bible Dictionary*. In --- (2001); (D) *International Standard Bible Encyclopedia*. In --- (2001); (E) Farmer R (1997); (F) Ellis JY (1997); (G) Sawyer JFA (1993).

and consecrate them, and sanctify them, that they may minister unto me in the priest's office. (Exodus 28:40-41, King James Version)

And thou shalt anoint (*mashah*) Aaron and his sons, and consecrate them, that they may minister unto me in the priest's office. (Exodus 30:30, King James Version)

Likewise, the kings of ancient Israel were anointed (*mashah*), as illustrated in the following verses, the first of which references David being anointed king, the second Solomon, and the third Jehu. The third verse also documents that prophets were anointed (*mashah*) to their prophetic office.

And Samuel said unto Jesse, Are here all thy children? And he said, There remaineth yet the youngest, and, behold, he keepeth the sheep. And Samuel said unto Jesse, Send and fetch him: for we will not sit down till he come hither. And he sent, and brought him in. Now he was ruddy, and withal of a beautiful countenance, and goodly to look to. And the Lord said, Arise, anoint (*mashah*) him: for this is he. Then Samuel took the horn of oil, and anointed (*mashah*) him in the midst of his brethren: and the Spirit of the Lord came upon David from that day forward… (I Samuel 16:11-13, King James Version)

And let Zadoc the priest and Nathan the prophet anoint (*mashah*) him (Solomon) there king over Israel: and blow ye with the trumpet, and say, God save king Solomon. (I Kings 1:34, King James Version)

And Jehu the son of Nimshi shalt thou anoint (*mashah*) to be king over Israel: and Elisha the son of Shaphat of Abelmeholah shalt thou anoint (*mashah*) to be prophet in thy room. (I Kings, 19:16, King James Version)

Having established that the Old Testament states that one anoints
(*mashah*) the kings, prophets, and priests of Israel, one turns to the
Hebrew word "*mashiah*" (the anointed[535]), which is derived from the
verbal root "*mashah*."[536] In Greek, the Hebrew word "*mashiah*" is transliterated as "*messias*," which is how it appears in the King James Version of
John 1:41 and 4:25,[537] and it is from this that we get the anglicized word
"messiah." The Hebrew word "*mashiah*" occurs 39 times in the Hebrew
scriptures.[538] In its substantive form, the use of the word "*mashiah*" is
typically restricted in the Hebrew scriptures to kings ("the Lord's
anointed"); however, as a plural of the substantive, it is used in reference
to the patriarchs ("mine anointed ones"), and as an adjective, it is used to
describe priests ("the anointed priests").[539] As one can thus see, the title
"messiah" is hardly unique to Jesus. In fact, the Protestant Old Testament
is practically overflowing with different messiahs.

(1) Abraham, Isaac, and Jacob were *mashiahs*, i.e., messiahs.

Saying, Touch not mine anointed (messiahs, i.e., in this case, by
the context of verses 13-21, the patriarchs Abraham, Isaac, and
Jacob), and do my prophets no harm. (I Chronicles 16:22, King
James Version)

Which covenant he made with Abraham, and his oath unto Isaac;
and confirmed the same unto Jacob for a law...He suffered no
man to do them wrong: yea, he reproved kings for their sakes;

---

[535] (A) Farmer R (1997); (B) Ellis JY (1997); (C) Sawyer JFA (1993); (D) *Strong's Old Testament Dictionary*. In --- (2001); E) *Vine's Old Testament Dictionary*. In --- (2001).

[536] (A) Ellis JY (1997); (B) *Strong's Old Testament Dictionary*. In --- (2001); (C) *Vine's Old Testament Dictionary*. In --- (2001).

[537] *International Standard Bible Encyclopedia*. In --- (2001).

[538] (A) Ellis JY (1997); (B) Farmer R (1997); (C) *Easton's Bible Dictionary*. In --- (2001).

[539] *International Standard Bible Encyclopedia*. In --- (2001).

Saying, Touch not mine anointed (messiahs), and do my prophets no harm (Psalms 105:9-10, 14-15, King James Version)

(2) King Saul was a messiah.

And it came to pass afterward, that David's heart smote him, because he had cut off Saul's skirt. And he said unto his men, The Lord forbid that I should do this thing unto my master, the Lord's anointed (messiah), to stretch forth mine hand against him, seeing he is the anointed (messiah) of the Lord...And David said to Saul, Wherefore hearest thou men's words, saying, Behold, David seeketh thy hurt? Behold, this day thine eyes have seen how that the Lord had delivered thee to day into mine hand in the cave: and some bade me kill thee: but mine eye spared thee; and I said, I will not put forth mine hand against my lord; for he is the Lord's anointed (messiah). (I Samuel 24: 5-6, 9-10, King James Version)

(3) King David was a messiah.

And when king David came to Bahurim, behold, thence came out a man of the family of the house of Saul, whose name was Shimei, the son of Gera: he came forth, and cursed still as he came. And he cast stones at David, and at all the servants of king David...But Abishai the son of Zeruiah answered and said, Shall not Shimei be put to death for this, because he cursed the Lord's anointed (messiah). (II Samuel 16:5-6; 19:21, King James Version)

Now these be the last words of David. David the son of Jesse said, and the man who was raised up on high, the anointed (messiah) of the God of Jacob, and the sweet psalmist of Israel, said, The Spirit of the Lord spake by me, and his word was in my tongue. (II Samuel 23:1-2, King James Version)

(4) King Solomon was a messiah.

For Solomon ...spread forth his hands towards heaven, And said...O Lord God, turn not away the face of thine anointed (messiah)... (II Chronicles 6:13-14, 42, King James Version)

(5) King Zedekiah of Judah, who was imprisoned ("taken in their pits") in Babylon, was a messiah.

Then he put out the eyes of Zedekiah; and the king of Babylon bound him in chains, and carried him to Babylon, and put him in prison till the day of his death...The breath of our nostrils, the anointed (messiah) of the Lord, was taken in their pits, of whom we said, Under his shadow we shall live among the heathen. (Jeremiah 52:11 and Lamentations 4:20, King James Version)

(6) The priests of Israel were messiahs.

These are the names of the sons of Aaron: Nadab the firstborn, and Abihu, Eleazar, and Ithamar; these are the names of the sons of Aaron, the anointed (messiah) priests, whom he ordained to minister as priests. (Numbers 3:2-3, New Revised Standard Version)

If it is the anointed (messiah) priest who sins, thus bringing guilt on the people, he shall offer for the sin that he has committed a bull of the herd without blemish as a sin offering to the Lord...The anointed (messiah) priest shall take some of the blood of the bull and bring it into the tent of meeting...The anointed (messiah) priest shall bring some of the blood of the bull into the tent of meeting...And so the priest, anointed (messiah) from among Aaron's descendants as a successor, shall prepare it. (Leviticus 4:3, 5, 16 and 6:22, New Revised Standard Version)

(7) It is even the case that one non-Israelite, King Cyrus of Persia, is directly called the messiah of God.

Thus saith the Lord to his anointed (messiah), to Cyrus, whose right hand I have holden, to subdue nations before him; and I will loose the loins of kings, to open before him the two leaved gates; and the gates shall not be shut... (Isaiah 45:1, King James Version)

Clearly, the *Bible* speaks of multiple messiahs and demonstrates that the concept of messiah was not uniquely applied to Jesus. In fact, during the period between the Old Testament and the New Testament, such Jewish writings as the Testament of Levi 18 and Testament of Reuben 6 (both part of the Testaments of the Twelve Patriarchs) and Appendix A 2:19-20 to the Manual of Discipline (part of the Dead Sea Scrolls) suggested that the Jews were awaiting two messiahs, one a priestly messiah from the line of Aaron, and the other a kingly messiah from the line of David.[540]

Just as the word "messiah" was not uniquely applied to Jesus, neither was the term "Christ." As mentioned previously, when *mashiah* was transliterated from Hebrew into Greek, it became *messias*. However, when *mashiah* is actually translated into Greek, it becomes *christos*.[541] The word "Christ" is merely the anglicized version of the Greek word "*christos*." Therefore, in each of the above cases where we find some Old Testament person being called messiah, we simultaneously could be calling him Christ!

---

[540] Farmer R (1997).
[541] (A) *Strong's Old Testament Dictionary*. In --- (2001); (B) *Vine's Old Testament Dictionary*. In --- (2001). (C) Ellis JY (1997); (E) Sawyer JFA (1993); (F) Leon-Dufour X (1993).

The translators of the *Bible* have not mistranslated anything when it comes to *mashah, mashiah, messias,* and *christos*. However, they clearly have not always handled these terms the same way. Sometimes they translate all the way into English and use the term "anointed." At other times, such as when referring to Jesus, they fail to translate the term into English, thus creating the illusion of some unique title being given to Jesus. While that doesn't constitute a mistranslation, it is misleading.

Given the above understanding of the word "messiah," just exactly what was meant when Pontius Pilate asked the crowd his question as he sat in judgment over Jesus?

> At that time they had a notorious prisoner, called Jesus Barabbas. So after they had gathered, Pilate said to them, "Whom do you want me to release for you, Jesus Barabbas or Jesus who is called the Messiah?" (Matthew 27:16-17, New Revised Standard Version)

Just who was "Jesus who is called the Messiah?" As has been seen, those who were anointed, i.e., were messiahs, were kings, prophets, and priests, especially the high priest.[542] From Josephus' listing of the high priests of Israel, we know this Jesus was not the high priest.[543] That appears to leave only prophets and kings as possible offices held or claimed by this Jesus who, according to the *Bible*, was crucified. Which one was it—prophet or king?

The canonical gospels rather unanimously answer that question for us by stating that the charge for which this Jesus was crucified was used as a

---

[542] (A) Farmer R (1997); (B) Leviticus 4:3.
[543] Josephus F (1988).

taunt by the Roman soldiers who tortured him and was also written above his head on the cross.

> Then the soldiers of the governor took Jesus into the common hall, and gathered unto him the whole band of soldiers. And they stripped him, and put on him a scarlet robe. And when they had platted a crown of thorns, they put it upon his head, and a reed in his right hand: and they bowed the knee before him, and mocked him, saying, Hail, King of the Jews!...And they crucified him...And set up over his head his accusation written, THIS IS JESUS THE KING OF THE JEWS. (Matthew 27:27-29, 35, 37, King James Version)

> And the soldiers led him away into the hall, called Praetorium; and they call together the whole band. And they clothed him with purple, and platted a crown of thorns, and put it about his head, and began to salute him, Hail, King of the Jews!...And it was the third hour, and they crucified him. And the superscription of his accusation was written over, THE KING OF THE JEWS. (Mark 15:16-18, 25-26, King James Version)

> And when they were come to the place, which is called Calvary, there they crucified him...And the soldiers also mocked him, coming to him, and offering him vinegar, and saying, If thou be the king of the Jews, save thyself. And a superscription also was written over him in letters of Greek, and Latin, and Hebrew, THIS IS THE KING OF THE JEWS. (Luke 23:33, 36-38, King James Version)

> And Pilate wrote a title, and put it on the cross. And the writing was, JESUS OF NAZARETH THE KING OF THE JEWS. This title then read many of the Jews: for the place where Jesus

was crucified was nigh to the city: and it was written in Hebrew, and Greek, and Latin. Then said the chief priests of the Jews to Pilate, Write not, The King of the Jews; but that he said, I am King of the Jews. Pilate answered, What I have written I have written. (John 19:19-22, King James Version)

The above verses make very clear that the Jesus who was crucified was executed for claiming to be the king of the Jews, a capital offense against the Roman Empire. Had this Jesus led an insurrection against Rome? Had he used military force to try to overthrow the Roman authority in Palestine? Such events were not uncommon in first-century Palestine, and it may very well be that he had attempted armed rebellion against Rome. After all, he did claim to be the king of the Jews, a sovereign ruler independent of Rome.

BARABBAS

Having now dealt with the "Jesus who is called the Messiah" of Matthew 27:17 and 22, one turns to the "Jesus Barabbas" of Matthew 27:16-17. The issue here is that the word "Barabbas" is not a name in the conventional sense. Rather, Barabbas is a two-word patronymic,[544] i.e., a statement that someone is the son of so-and-so. In reality, Jesus Barabbas should be written Jesus bar Abbas, where "*bar*" is the Aramaic word for "son of." This can be readily seen by looking at the King James Version of Matthew 16:17, where Peter is called "Simon Barjona," and comparing it to the New Revised Standard Version, where Peter is called "Simon son of Jonah."[545]

---

[544] (A) Gloer WH (1997); (B) Leon-Dufour X (1983); (C) Fenton JC (1973); (D) Pherigo LP (1971).
[545] Pherigo LP(1971).

However, even at this point, the term has not been dealt with sufficiently. This is because the word "*Abbas*" is not a name. It is, instead, an Aramaic noun that still needs to be translated. When the entire term is translated from the Aramaic, it becomes "Jesus, the son of the father"[546] or "Jesus, the son of the Father."[547]

Is it little wonder that the *Bible* translators have failed to translate "Barabbas" as it should be translated?! The text of Matthew 27:11-23 actually suggests that a Jesus who was claiming to be the king of the Jews was crucified but that Jesus, the son of the Father, was released and set free. By not translating "Barabbas," the translators have given us a misleading translation at best.

THE NAME "JESUS"

Within most English translations of the *Bible*, the name "Jesus" is treated as being rather unique. However, this is far from actually being the case. There are many people named Jesus running around in the *Bible*, but by a verbal sleight-of-hand, this fact is obscured. "Jesus" is merely the anglicized version of the Greek name "Iesous," which in turn is the Greek rendering of the Hebrew "Yeshua" and "Yhoshua,"[548] which elsewhere in the *Bible* are usually given as "Joshua."[549]

Once one realizes that the name "Jesus" is elsewhere in the *Bible* usually rendered as the name "Joshua," one finds many people named Jesus/Joshua. There is Joshua (Jesus) the son of Nun, the successor to

---

[546] (A) Gloer WH (1997); (B) Shaw G (1993); (C) Fenton JC (1973); (D) Leon-Dufour X (1983).
[547] (A) Pherigo LP (1971); (B) Dirks JF (2001c).
[548] (A) Kee HC (1971); (B) Leon-Dufour X (1983).
[549] (A) Leon-Dufour X (1983); (B) Dirks JF (2001c).

Moses.[550] There are also Joshua (Jesus) of Beth-shemesh,[551] Joshua (Jesus) the governor of a city,[552] the high priest Joshua (Jesus) the son of Jehozadak,[553] and Joshua (Jesus) the son of Eliezer.[554] Furthermore, of the 28 high priests of Judaism from the time of Herod the Great (circa 73 BCE-4 BCE) to the destruction of the Temple in 70 CE, four were named Jesus, including Jesus who was the son of Phabet or Phiabi, Jesus who was the son of Sec or Sei, Jesus who was the son of Damneus, and Jesus who was the son of Gamaliel.[555]

Given the sum total of the above, it should be quite clear that Jesus was hardly a unique name. Unfortunately, the manner in which the *Bible* translators have handled the names Jesus, Joshua, Yeshua, Iesous, and Yhoshua can easily lead readers to assume quite erroneously that "Jesus" was somehow a unique name applied to a unique person.

SON OF GOD

English translations of the canonical gospels frequently refer to Jesus as "Son of God" or "God's Son," with the "S" in "Son" always being capitalized.[556] However, the original Greek text of the New Testament books does not distinguish between capital and lower case letters. Thus, the translation could just as easily and just as accurately be made "son of

---

[550] (A) Exodus 33:11; (B) Numbers 11:28; 14:30, 38; 26:25; 27:18; 32:12, 28; 34:17; (C) Deuteronomy 1:38; 31:23; 32:44; 34:9; (D) Joshua 1:1; 2:1, 23; 6:6; 14:1; 17:4; 19:49, 51; 21:1; 24:29; (E) Judges 2:8; (F) I Kings 16:34; (G) I Chronicles 7:27.

[551] I Samuel 6:14, 18.

[552] II Kings 23:8.

[553] (A) Haggai 1:1, 12, 14; 2:2, 4; (B) Zechariah 3:1, 3, 6, 8-9; 6:11.

[554] Luke 3:29.

[555] (A) Josephus F (1988); (B) Schonfield JH (1967).

[556] For example: (A) Matthew 4:3, 6; 8:29; 14:33; 16:16; 26:63; 27:40, 54; (B) Mark 1:1; 3:11; 5:7; 15:39; (C) Luke 1:32, 35; 4:3, 9, 41; 8:28; 22:70; (D) John 1:34, 49; 3:18; 5:25; 10:36; 11:4, 27; 19:7; 20:31.

God" and "God's son." By employing a capital "S" in the English translations, the *Bible* translators are introducing a theological viewpoint, i.e., the supposed uniqueness of Jesus as "Son of God," that is not inherent in the original Greek text.

In point of fact, numerous people throughout the *Bible* are referred to as being the sons or children of God. For example, the Israelites as a whole, and especially the sub-tribe of Ephraim, are referred to as being the sons and children of God.[557] Israelite kings such as David[558] and Solomon[559] were called the sons of God. Faithful Israelites were also called the sons of God.[560] In short, the phrase "son of God" was a metaphoric title that was applied to any righteous man. However, the translators do not capitalize the "s" in "son" when referring to those people. By capitalizing the "S" in "Son" for Jesus but not for others, the translators are misleading the reader when it comes to the original Greek text of the New Testament, implying a uniqueness to Christ's "sonship" that is not warranted by the actual words being translated.

SUMMARY

In none of the above examples can it be accurately stated that the verses in question have been actually mistranslated into English. The translations are technically correct as far as they go. However, the translations or lack thereof can easily mislead the reader into drawing conclusions that are not supported by the actual Biblical text.

---

[557] (A) Exodus 4:22; (B) Hosea 11:1-3, 10-11; (C) Jeremiah 31:9, 20.
[558] Psalms 2:7; 89:26-27.
[559] II Samuel 7:13-14.
[560] Deuteronomy 14:1.

CONCLUSIONS

As should be clear by now, English translations of the *Bible* are often corrupted by later additions to the text, by omissions from the text, and by misleading translations. With regard to additions to and omissions from the text, the King James Version, relying as it does on relatively late Greek manuscripts, is one of the worst offenders. In contrast, the New Revised Standard Version, which frequently goes back to the earliest available manuscripts, is a much better choice for readers who want to know what was originally written. Unfortunately, all current English versions continue to suffer from some misleading translations, either by commission or by omission.

CHAPTER 6

JESUS IN JEWISH AND ISLAMIC TRADITIONS

INTRODUCTION

MOST CHRISTIANS ARE AT LEAST somewhat conversant with the story of Jesus as portrayed in the New Testament gospels. Typically these same Christians are, however, totally unaware that the story of Jesus is also presented in both Jewish and Islamic traditions. More specifically, many of the Jewish traditions regarding Jesus may be found in the *Babylonian Talmud*, while the Islamic traditions are found in both the *Qur'an* and the sayings of Prophet Muhammad. In what follows, both the Jewish Talmudic and the Islamic perspectives of Jesus are presented. However, as most Christians are probably unfamiliar with the *Babylonian Talmud*, a brief background on this book is offered before considering its portrait of Jesus.

THE JEWISH *TALMUD*

INTRODUCTION

Within Judaism, the *Talmud*, i.e., "study" or "learning," is often stated to be second in religious authority only to the official Jewish canon of scripture, i.e., the *Tanakh*. However, it might be cogently argued that the *Talmud* is of primary religious authority for Orthodox Judaism, as Orthodox Judaism maintains that it is only through the *Talmud* that the *Tanakh* may be properly interpreted and understood. In that regard, it is important to note that the *massekhtot* (i.e., tractate) entitled Sanhedrin of the *sedarim* (i.e., order) entitled Neziqin of the Mishnah, which is part of the *Talmud*, specifically states that: "the punishment of him who transgresses the decision of the scribes is more rigorous than for that which is plainly written in the scriptures." If the punishment for violating the scribes, i.e., what was written down to comprise the *Talmud*, is to be greater than that for violating the *Tanakh*, it would certainly appear that the *Talmud* is of primary religious authority, while the *Tanakh* is of secondary authority. Given this emphasis on the *Talmud*, it is important to realize that the *Talmud* is not a unitary, literary construct. Not only are there two different versions of the *Talmud* , i.e., the Yerushalmi (Jerusalem) or Palestinian and the Bavli or Babylonian, but each version of the *Talmud* is comprised of two separate literary compositions, i.e., the Mishnah and the Gemara, each of which can be subdivided into numerous constituent parts. A proper understanding of the contents and formation of the *Talmud*, a term which is sometimes restricted by some writers to just the Gemara, is best and most easily achieved by first considering the Mishnah, and then presenting the Gemara.[561]

THE MISHNAH

Judaism frequently makes the distinction between the written law of Moses and the oral law of Moses. Within the Orthodox Judaic tradition, both sets of laws, i.e., written and oral, are believed to have been part of the revelation from God to Moses, which revelation was given to him on Mt. Sinai during the Israelite sojourn from Egypt. According to the Orthodox Judaic tradition, Moses wrote down one part of this revelation, and this written narrative allegedly conforms

---

[561] (A)Dimitrovsky HZ, Silberman LH, et al. (2003); (B) --- (2003h); (C) Epstein I (1966); (D) Werblowsky RJ (1967); (E) Silberman LH (1971); (F) Goldin J (1964); (G) Hardon JA (1968); H) Schafer P (2007).

to the majority of the Torah, i.e., "teaching," but often incorrectly translated as "law." [562]

However, according to traditional Orthodox Judaic belief, part of this revelation was not written down by Moses, but was only orally transmitted by him. This oral tradition was then passed down generation by generation from the time of Moses until finally starting to be put down in written form by no later than the first century CE, i.e., approximately 1,500 years after Moses. This oral law, allegedly conforming to that part of the revelation to Moses that he did not write down, constitutes the Mishnah, i.e., "repeated study." [563]

Despite the above stated, traditional account of the origin of the Mishnah, the historical reality of its evolution and development is somewhat more prosaic and begins late in the fifth or early in the fourth century BCE. The key actor in that unfolding drama was Ezra, an Israelite scribe. Circa 397 BCE, Ezra returned to Jerusalem from exile and captivity in Babylonia, bringing with him a copy of "the Law," i.e., the Torah. [564] Thus armed with the Torah, Ezra began to instruct the Israelite inhabitants of Palestine concerning religious statutes, requirements, and ordinances. [565] It is from this moment that one can begin to date the transformation of the religion of the ancient Israelites into the religion of Judaism, with Judaism having maintained an evolutionary and developmental course ever since.

Ezra's study of the Torah was continued in an intensive manner by the *soferim*, i.e., scribes, who followed him. In turn, the *soferim* began to

---

[562] (A) Dimitrovsky HZ, Silberman LH, et al. (2003); (B) --- (2003h); (C) Epstein I (1966); (D) Werblowsky RJ (1967); (E) Silberman LH (1971).
[563] (A) Dimitrovsky HZ, Silberman LH, et al. (2003); (B) --- (2003h); (C) Epstein I (1966); (D) Werblowsky RJ (1967); (E) Silberman LH (1971).
[564] Duncan GB (1971a).
[565] Dimitrovsky HZ, Silberman LH, et al. (2003).

develop and maintain an oral commentary on and exegesis of the Torah. Around the beginning of the second century BCE, the role of the *soferim* was basically replaced by a body of religious scholars or judges, which was headed by a pair of preeminent scholars, who were known as the *zugot*. The role of the *zugot* would continue until late in the first century BCE, when their function gradually began to be superseded by that of the *tannaim*, i.e., rabbinical scholars of the Pharisaic tradition. A key aspect of the evolution of this commentary and exegesis, which was begun by the *soferim* and was continued by the *zugot* and by the Pharisaic rabbis, was the continuing interpretation and reinterpretation of the Torah, in order to meet and adapt to shifting contingencies, new events, chronological developments, and a changing world scene. By at least the first century CE, these oral traditions regarding the interpretation of the Torah began to be set down in various discrete and independent written statements, and the so-called oral law began its written existence.[566]

The next step in the evolution leading up to the Mishnah focuses on Judah ha-Nasi (circa 135-220 CE). Judah ha-Nasi was one of the last of the *tannaim* and served as president of the Jewish Sanhedrin. Originally more of a court or judicial body, by the time of Judah ha-Nasi, the Sanhedrin had evolved into more of a legislative body. Judah ha-Nasi's genealogical credentials as a Judaic scholar were impeccable, as he was the son of Simeon, who had also served as president of the Sanhedrin and who was the son of Gamaliel II, who had also served as the president of the Sanhedrin. Gamaliel II was in descent from Gamaliel I, the great rabbinical scholar of the Pharisees, who had also served as president of the Sanhedrin. Finally, it should be noted that Gamaliel I was in descent from Hillel, who with Shammai constituted the last pair of *zugot*, and who is often held to have been the greatest of the

---

[566] Dimitrovsky HZ, Silberman LH, et al. (2003).

Pharasaic rabbis.[567]

Utilizing various written tracts and oral traditions concerning the oral law, Judah ha-Nasi began to edit and compile the oral law into one written compendium. Tradition holds that he spent approximately 50 years editing and compiling this work, which was probably not completed by him until early in the third century CE, and which then underwent a series of revisions and modifications by his various students and followers. However, for all practical intents and purposes, the edited compilation of Judah ha-Nasi is the Mishnah, and it can be reliably dated to the third century CE.[568]

CONTENTS OF THE MISHNAH. The same Mishnah is found in both the *Babylonian Talmud* and the *Palestinian Talmud*, and it consists of six *sedarim*, i.e. "orders", which can be further subdivided into 63 *massekhtot*, i.e. "tractates," that can be still further subdivided into *peraqim*, i.e. "chapters." The first of the *sedarim* is Zera'im, i.e., "seeds", which consists of 11 *massekhot*. Except for the first of the *massekhtot*, which is entitled Berakhot, i.e. "blessings", and which deals with the Judaic laws governing daily prayers, the *massekhtot* of the Zera'im primarily deal with religious law as it pertains to agricultural issues. The second of the *sedarim* is Mo'ed, i.e., "season" or "festival," which consists of 12 tractates that deal with religious laws applying to various special days of the year, e.g., the Sabbath, holidays, and fast days. The third of the *sedarim* is Nashim, i.e. "women," which consists of seven *massekhtot* that deal with laws concerning betrothal, marriage, relations between husband and wife, adultery, and divorce. However, as Nazirite vows of asceticism and other vows may affect the marital state, Nashim includes one tractate, i.e., Nedarim, on vows, and one tractate, i.e., Nazir, on the

---

[567] (A) Epstein I (1966); (B) --- (2003i); (C) --- (2003j); (D) --- (2003k); (E) Dimitrovsky HZ, Silberman LH, et al. (2003).
[568] (A) Dimitrovsky HZ, Silberman LH, et al. (2003); (B) --- (2003h); (C) Epstein I (1966); (D) --- (2003i).

Nazirite state of asceticism. The fourth of the *sedarim* is Neziqin, i.e., "damages," which consists of 10 tractates that focus on laws concerning criminal and civil damages, various business relations, usury, inheritance, court proceedings, physical punishment, etc. The fifth of the *sedarim* is Qodashim, i.e., "sacred things," which consists of 11 tractates, which concern Judaic religious law as applied to the temple, sacrifices, offerings, and donations. The last of the *sedarim* is Tohorot, i.e., "purifications," which consists of 12 tractates that govern and legislate issues of ritual purity and impurity for persons, things, and foods.[569]

THE GEMARA

The Mishnah of Judah ha-Nasi and his students and followers had provided a third-century CE commentary on the Torah, through which the Torah had to be interpreted. It was basically maintained by Judaism that the Torah, i.e., the written law, of circa 400 BCE could only be understood and applied through the reworking, reinterpretation, and adaptation provided by the centuries long compilation of oral tradition, i.e., oral law. This oral law did not find its culmination in the Mishnah of Judah ha-Nasi until the early third century CE, i.e., approximately 1,700+ years after Moses. However, the process of adapting the written law and of modifying its natural interpretation, in order to meet the changing circumstances of an evolving and progressing world, did not end with the Mishnah. To use modern parlance, the ink had barely had time to dry on the final copy of the Mishnah before the rabbis began a running commentary on the Mishnah, began to add to the oral tradition, and thus began yet a further elaboration and adaptation of the Torah. This process was to culminate in the Gemara, of which two distinct versions exist.

---

[569] (A) Dimitrovsky HZ, Silberman LH, et al. (2003); (B) Epstein I (1966).

The origin of the Gemara, i.e., "completion," can be traced to three followers of Judah ha-Nasi: (1) Johanan bar Nappaha, who established a
rabbinical academy at Tiberias in Palestine; (2) Rav (Abba Arika), who
established a rabbinical academy at Sura in Babylonia; and (3) Samuel
bar Abba, who established a rabbinical academy at Nehardea in
Babylonia. These three academies, as well as additional ones in Palestine
(at Sepphoris, Caesarea, and Lydda) and in Babylonia (at Pumbedita,
Mahoza, and Naresh), became the centers of learning of the *amoraim*,
i.e., "interpreters." It was the *amoraim* who began the task of developing
a commentary on the Mishnah, i.e., developing a commentary on the
commentary of the Torah, which later became known as the Gemara.
Although there was some crossover and communication between the
Palestinian and Babylonian academies, and although *amoraim* might
have journeyed from one set of academies to the other, the resulting
commentaries from Palestine and Babylonia were and are two distinct
sets of religious writing, even though there are impressive similarities
between the Palestinian Gemara and the Babylonian Gemara.[570]

The differences between the Palestinian and Babylonian Gemara can be
succinctly summarized as follows. (1) The Palestinian version was written
in the Western Aramaic dialect, while the Babylonian version was written
in the Eastern Aramaic dialect. (2) The Palestinian version was never
completed and deals with only four of the *sedarim* of the Mishnah, while
the Babylonian version offers commentary and exegesis on all six of the
sedarim of the Mishnah and on 37 of the 63 tractates of the Mishnah.
(3) Even where the Palestinian version addresses one of the *sedarim*, the
commentary is often much shorter than that found in the Babylonian
version, and it is sometimes incomplete. (4) The Palestinian version tends

---

[570] Dimitrovsky HZ, Silberman LH, et al. (2003).

to be a more literal interpretation of the Mishnah, while the commentary of the Babylonian version often goes further afield in its interpretation. (5) As Babylonia was under Persian rule at the time of the *amoraim*, the Babylonian version sometimes shows the contaminating influence of Persian law, while the Palestinian version avoids this obvious confound. (6) Work ended on the Palestinian version around the start of the fifth century CE, while the Babylonian version was not completed until around the start of the sixth century CE.[571]

In contrast to the Mishnah, which stuck fairly closely to issues of Judaic law and was thus primarily *halakhic* in nature, the Gemara was more frequently influenced by *haggadic* themes, i.e., homilies, folklore, and myth, as reflected in its occasional inclusion of Midrashic literature. Of the two Gemara, the Babylonian is generally considered to be the more authoritative.[572]

SUMMARY

As can be seen from the above, the *Talmud* represents both: (1) a commentary on and adaptation of the *Tanakh*, i.e., the Mishnah; and (2) a commentary on and adaptation of the commentary on and adaptation of the *Tanakh*, i.e., the Gemara. Despite the fact that Orthodox Judaism considers the *Talmud* to be second in authority only to the written law, i.e., the Torah in the narrow sense or the *Tanakh* in the wider sense, by this time in the discussion, many non-Jewish readers may be considering the *Talmud,* and especially the Gemara, to have gotten pretty far afield from the original scriptural basis of Judaism. Such readers will be reassured to discover that many groups throughout the history of Judaism have felt the same way.[573]

---

[571] Dimitrovsky HZ, Silberman LH, et al. (2003).
[572] (A) Dimitrovsky HZ, Silberman LH, et al.: (2003); (B) Epstein I (1966).
[573] Dimitrovsky HZ, Silberman LH, et al. (2003).

In that regard, it is noted that the Karaite (originally known as Ananites, after their founder Anan) sect of Judaism, which arose in eighth-century CE Babylonia, utterly rejected the *Talmud* as being a rabbinical fabrication and invention. (Fragments of the Damascus Document of the Dead Sea Scrolls and of Ecclesiasticus of the Old Testament Apocrypha were discovered in a Kairite synagogue in Cairo at the end of the 19th century CE. Of note, the Kairite sect continues as a small group even today.) Likewise, the mystic sects of medieval Judaism rejected the *Talmud* as being a device that kept the uninitiated from discovering the underlying, concealed, and mystical meaning of the Torah. Still further, the messianic sects of 17th and 18th-century CE Judaism rejected the *Talmud*. Finally, it should be noted that the 19th-century CE Jewish enlightenment movement, which gave birth to Reform Judaism, rejected the *Talmud* as being an anachronistic fabrication of the rabbis, as being overly legalistic, and as having so reinterpreted the *Tanakh* scriptures as to have distorted their otherwise clear and obvious meaning.[574]

JESUS IN THE *BABYLONIAN TALMUD*

DIFFERENT MANUSCRIPT VERSIONS

It is important to note that many of the most ancient manuscripts of the *Babylonian Talmud* either were lost over time or were destroyed by fire or altered as a result of the anti-Talmudic policies of the Roman Catholic Church. For example, in 1242 in Paris, the Church ordered that the *Talmud* be burned. Later in the 13th century, the Church began censoring the *Talmud*, either erasing or blackening out passages that were deemed to be offensive to Christian doctrines and beliefs. In the face of such persecution, even Jewish printers began censoring the *Talmud* out of fear that anti-Christian statements within the *Talmud* might jeopardize the publication of the *Talmud* and other Jewish books.

---

[574] (A) Dimitrovsky HZ, Silberman LH, et al. (2003); (B) Stegemann H (1998).

Needless to say, many of the *Babylonian Talmud's* passages related to Jesus suffered the fate of being censored. As such, it is sometimes necessary to piece together a passage from across several different manuscripts of the *Babylonian Talmud*, as one manuscript may delete one thing and another manuscript might delete something else.[575]

Given the above situation, in what follows, a quoted passage from the *Babylonian Talmud* may at times be a patchwork from across different manuscripts that date back to the 12th through 19th centuries. Creating such a patchwork, where part of a passage is from one manuscript and another part of the same passage is from another manuscript, is occasionally necessary in order to convey the full meaning of the passage. Such cases will always be identified as being a "composite passage."[576]

BIRTH AND FAMILY OF JESUS

While the New Testament gospels claim that Jesus' mother was Mary, that Jesus was the result of a virgin birth, and that Joseph was Mary's husband, the *Babylonian Talmud* offers a very different story regarding Jesus' family and birth. Piecing together scattered Talmudic references to Jesus, one is informed that: (1) Mary (Miriam) was a promiscuous woman of ill-repute; (2) Mary was married to a Jew named Stada (aka Satra, Stara, and Sateda), although one passage lists her husband as having been a Jew named Pappos ben Yehuda (Pappos the son of Judah) and lists Mary as being called Stada; (3) Mary had an adulterous affair with a Roman soldier named Pandera (aka Pantera); and (4) Jesus was the illegitimate offspring of Mary and Pandera, being thus referred to in the *Babylonian Talmud* both as Ben Stada (after his mother's husband) and

---

[575] Schafer P (2007).
[576] All of the composite passages of the *Babylonian Talmud* that are used in this chapter are based upon the current author's editing of translations found in Schafer P (2007) and Neusner J (2005).

Ben Pandera (after his biological father). Of note, Jesus is also called the son of Pandera in passages of the Tosefta (Tractate Hullin 2:22 and 2:24; the Tosefta is an early Jewish commentary much like the Mishnah) and the *Jerusalem Talmud* (Tractate Shabbat and Tractate Avodah Zarah).[577]

"(Was he, i.e., Jesus,) the son of Stada (and not on the contrary) the son of Pandera?"

Said Rav Hisda: "The husband was Stada, (and) the cohabiter/lover was Pandera."

"(But was not) the husband (of Mary) Pappos the son of Judah and rather his (Jesus') mother (was called) Stada, (and) he is Jesus the Nazarene?"

"His mother was Miriam (Mary), (the woman) who let (her) women's hair grow long. This is as they say about her in Pumbeditha: 'This one was unfaithful to her husband.'" (Tractate Shabbat 104b, composite version)

As can be seen from the above passage, which is pieced together from four different manuscripts[578] of Tractate Shabbat of the *Babylonian Talmud*, the portrayal of Jesus and his family is radically different from that found in the New Testament gospels and is sure to be considered outrageously slanderous by most believing Christians. Furthermore, while most modern Christian readers may miss the reference, the statement that Mary let her hair grow long and had unfastened hair was within the culture of first-millennial Judaism a damning indictment that a woman was promiscuous.[579] That this was so can be seen by the fact that

---

[577] Schafer P (2007).

[578] The four manuscripts are as follows: (1) Munich 95, written in 1342 CE in Paris; (2) Vatican 108, written in the 13th or 14th century CE; (3) Oxford 23, written in the 14th or 15th century CE; and (4) the Vilna printed edition of 1880-1886 CE. Schafer P (2007).

[579] Schafer P (2007).

a woman with long hair was compared to the demonic Lilith, the succubus who haunted men at night and who killed infants and young children.

> She grows her hair long, like Lilith; she pisses sitting down, like an animal; and she serves as a pillow for her husband. (Tractate 'Erubin 100b, Neusner translation)

Peter Shafer, the Perelman Professor of Judaic Studies at Princeton University, has suggested that the lone reference to Mary being called Stada in Tractate Shabbat is probably a play on words, in which Stada is not suggested as Mary's name, but as an epithet that derives from the Hebrew/Aramaic root *sata/sete'*, which means to go astray or to be unfaithful. Thus, the questioner who calls Mary by the epithet Stada is simply casting aspersions on her sexual character rather than offering up an alternative name for her. Furthermore, the reference to Pappos the son of Judah being the husband of Mary probably comes from a separate passage of the *Babylonian Talmud*, in which a certain Pappos the son of Judah was said by Rabbi Meir to lock up his wife whenever he left the house, presumably because he could not trust her sexual fidelity to him.[580]

> R. Meir would say, "Just as there are different tastes in food, so there are different tastes in women. You can have a man who, if a fly falls into his cup, tosses out the contents and won't drink what's there. This is the type of Pappos b. Judah, who would lock up his wife when he went out." (Tractate Gittin 90a, Neusner translation)

It should be noted that the above portrayal of Jesus' family and birth is not confined to the *Babylonian Talmud*. As early as the second century,

---

[580] Schafer P (2007).

Jews were portraying Mary as a wanton woman and Jesus as the illegitimate offspring of Mary's out-of-wedlock affair with Pandera, the Roman soldier. For example, in his *Alethes Logos*, Celsus, a pagan philosopher of the second century CE, wrote the Jewish position in a passage that has been preserved by Origen (circa 185-254 CE) in his *Contra Celsum*, which was written circa 248 CE.

> ...he (Jesus) came from a Jewish village and from a poor country woman who earned her living by spinning. He (the Jew) says that she was driven out by her husband, who was a carpenter by trade, as she was convicted of adultery. Then he says that after she had been driven out by her husband and while she was wandering about in a disgraceful way she secretly gave birth to Jesus ...the mother of Jesus is described as having been turned out by the carpenter who was betrothed to her, as she had been convicted of adultery and had a child by a certain soldier named Panthera.[581]

JESUS' MISSION AND MINISTRY

With regard to the mission and ministry of Jesus, contemporary Christianity typically maintains that Jesus had a divinely sanctioned and universal ministry to the world at large. In contrast, Judaism denies any divine mission and ministry associated with Jesus, and the *Babylonian Talmud* explicitly states in two different passages that Jesus was a bad son or disciple and that he publicly burned his food. With regard to the charge that Jesus publicly burned his food, Schafer suggests that this is a euphemism indicating some sexual impropriety on the part of Jesus.[582] In contrast, Rabbi Neusner suggests that the phrase means teaching something heretical.[583]

---

[581] Origen (1953), p. 28-32.
[582] Schafer P (2007).
[583] Neusner J (2005).

Rav Hisda said in the name of Rabbi Jeremiah the son of Abba: "What is meant by the verse (i.e., Psalms 91:10): No evil will befall you; no plague will come near your tent?"

"'No evil will befall you' means that the evil impulse shall have no power over you! 'No plague will come near your tent' means that when you return from a journey, you will not find your wife in doubt as to whether she is menstruating (and thus, per Jewish law, off limits for sexual intercourse). Another interpretation: 'No evil will befall you' means that bad dreams and bad thoughts will never frighten you. 'No plague will come near your tent' means that you will not have a son or a disciple who publicly burns his food like Jesus the Nazarene." (Tractate Sanhedrin 103a, composite version)[584]

When rabbis took their leave of the house of Rabbi Hisda, and some say, from the house of Rabbi Samuel bar Nahmani, this is what they said to him: "'We are instructed, we are well laden' (Psalms 144:14)."

"We are instructed, we are well laden" (Psalms 144:14): Rab and Samuel, and some say it was Rabbi Yohanan and Rabbi Eleazar. One said, "'We are instructed' in Torah and 'we are well-laden' with religious duties." The other said, "'We are instructed' in Torah and in religious duties, and 'we are well laden' in suffering."

"There is no breach" (Psalms 144:14): May our class not be like the class of David, from which Ahitophel went forth. "And no going forth" (Psalms 144:14): May our class not be like the class

---

[584] The explicit identification of the bad son/disciple with Jesus is made in the following manuscripts of the *Babylonian Talmud*: Herzog 1 (post 1565 CE), Munich 95 (circa 1342 CE), Firenze II.1.8-9 (circa 1177 CE), Karlsruhe 2 (13th century CE), and Barco. Schafer P (2007).

of Saul, from which Doeg the Edomite went forth. "And no outcry" (Psalms 144:14): May our class not be like the class of Elisha, from which Gehazi went forth. "In our broad places" (Psalms 144:14): May we have no son or disciple who publicly burns his food like Jesus the Nazarene. (Tractate Berakhot 17a-b, composite version [585])

A second passage from the *Babylonian Talmud*, this time from Tractate Sanhedrin, accuses Jesus of having been a wicked student of Rabbi Joshua the son of Perahyah. According to this story, Jesus was prone to letting his mind wander to issues regarding the attractiveness of certain females. As a result, Rabbi Joshua excommunicated Jesus and sent him away. Thereafter, Jesus began to practice sorcery and magic, and he began to practice idolatry by worshiping a brick.

> What of Rabbi Joshua the son of Perahyah? — When King Yannai slew our rabbis, Rabbi Joshua the son of Perahyah (and Jesus) fled to Alexandria of Egypt. On the resumption of peace, Shimon the son of Shetah sent (the following message) to him: "From Jerusalem, the Holy City, to you, Alexandria of Egypt, my sister. My husband dwells within you, and I am desolate." He arose, went, and found himself in a certain inn, where great honor was shown him. "How beautiful is this *Akhsanya*?" (*Akhsanya* means both inn and innkeeper. Rabbi Joshua used it in the first sense, while Jesus' response demonstrates that he understood it as referring to a female innkeeper.) Thereupon Jesus observed, "Rabbi, her eyes are narrow." "Wretch," he rebuked

---

[585] The statement that it is Jesus who is the bad son/disciple is found in the following manuscripts: Oxford 23 (14th or 15th century CE), Munich 95 (circa 1342 CE), Firenze II.1.7 (circa 1177 CE), and Paris 671 (15th century CE). Schafer P (2007).

him, "do you thus engage yourself (with such a thought)." He (Rabbi Joshua) sounded four hundred trumpet blasts and excommunicated him (Jesus). He (Jesus) came before him many times pleading, "Receive me!" But he (Rabbi Joshua) would pay no heed to him. One day, he (Rabbi Joshua) was reciting the Shema (Deuteronomy 6:4[586]) when Jesus came before him. He intended to receive him and made a sign to him. He (Jesus), thinking that it was to repel him, went, put up a brick, and worshipped it. "Repent," said he (Rabbi Joshua) to him (Jesus). He (Jesus) replied, "I have thus learned from you: 'He who sins and causes others to sin is deprived of the means of repentance.'" And a Master has said, "Jesus the Nazarene goes out to be stoned because he practiced magic and led Israel astray." (Tractate Sanhedrin 107b, composite version[587])

There is yet another passage in the *Babylonian Talmud* accusing Jesus of practicing witchcraft and sorcery. According to Tractate Shabbat, Jesus, here referred to as Ben Stada, i.e., the son of Stada/Sateda, learned the black arts in Egypt, wrote or tattooed the magical incantations on his skin, and then brought the Egyptian witchcraft that he had learned back to Israel. Back in Israel, Jesus reportedly enlisted five disciples, whose names, with the single exception of Mattai = Matthew, do not correspond with any New Testament list of Jesus' disciples.

Said Rabbi Eliezer to them, "But didn't Ben Stada (Jesus) bring witchcraft from Egypt by writing/tattooing the formulas on his

---

[586] Deuteronomy 6:4 reads as follows: "Hear, O Israel: The Lord our God is one Lord..." (King James Version)
[587] The disciple of Rabbi Joshua is specifically identified as being Jesus in the following manuscripts: Herzog 1 (post 1565 CE), Firenze II.1.8-9 (circa 1177 CE), Barco, and Vilna (1880-1886 CE). Schafer P (2007).

skin?" They said to him, "He was a singular fool, and we don't derive proof of propositions on the basis of the actions of idiots." (Tractate Shabbat 104b, composite version)

Our rabbis taught that Jesus the Nazarene had five disciples: Mattai, Naqqai, Netzer, Buni, and Todah. (Tractate Sanhedrin 43a-b, composite version.[588])

END OF JESUS' MINISTRY

While contemporary Sunday school lessons maintain that Jesus was crucified by the Roman authorities in Palestine, the *Babylonian Talmud* presents a radically different version of events. According to the following Talmudic passage, Jewish authorities sentenced Jesus to be stoned to death for the crimes of practicing sorcery and of enticing Israel to apostasy and idolatry.[589] In accordance with Talmudic law,[590] these authorities then sent a herald around the country for 40 days, with the herald publicly asking for any exonerating evidence. When no one offered any defense for Jesus, he was then stoned to death on a Sabbath eve that also happened to be the eve of Passover. Upon his death, in a humiliation reserved for those who practiced the worst of offenses, his corpse was then hung on a tree in public display of the punishment that he had received for his crimes.

...it was taught: On the eve of the Passover Jesus was hanged. For forty days before the execution took place, a herald went forth and cried, "Jesus the Nazarene is going forth to be stoned

---

[588] The name of Jesus is specifically mentioned in the following manuscripts: Herzog 1 (post 1565 CE), Firenze II.1.8-9 (circa 1177 CE), and Karlsruhe 2 (13th century CE). Schafer P (2007).

[589] Leviticus 20:27 reads as follows: "A man also a woman that hath a familiar spirit, or that is a wizard, shall surely be put to death: they shall stone them with stones: their blood shall be upon them." (King James Version)

[590] Schafer P (2007).

because he has practiced sorcery and seduced Israel to apostasy. Anyone who can say anything in his favor, let him come forward and plead on his behalf." But since nothing was brought forward in his favor, he was hanged on Sabbath eve and the eve of the Passover! Ulla retorted: "Do you suppose that he was one for whom a defense could be made? Was he not someone who enticed Israel to idolatry, concerning whom Scripture says, 'Show him no compassion, and do not shield him' (Deuteronomy. 13:9)? With Jesus the Nazarene, however, it was different, for he was connected with the government (or royalty, i.e., he was influential)." (Tractate Sanhedrin 43a, composite version[591])

The story that Jesus was killed by stoning, not by crucifixion, is also mentioned in the *Jerusalem Talmud* in Tractate Sanhedrin 25c-d and in Tractate Yevamot 15d. In addition, Tractate Sanhedrin 67a of the *Babylonian Talmud* maintains that Jesus' corpse was publicly hung on a tree at Lydda, not at Jerusalem,[592] suggesting that Lydda would have been the location of Jesus' alleged stoning.

JESUS IN THE HEREAFTER

Given the above portrayal of Jesus as the illegitimate offspring of an adulterous Mary and a Roman soldier named Pandera, as someone who practiced sorcery and idolatry, and as someone who attempted to lead Israel into apostasy and idolatry, it should come as no surprise to the reader to discover that the *Babylonian Talmud* presents a particularly slanderous depiction of Jesus in the afterlife. As noted in several manuscripts of Tractate Gittin, Jesus is said to be confined to boiling excrement in hell.

---

[591] The name of Jesus is specifically mentioned in Firenze II.1.8-9 (circa 1177 CE), Karlsruhe 2 (13th century CE), and Herzog 1 (post 1565 CE). Schafer P (2007).
[592] Schafer P (2007).

Onqelos the son of Qalonimos was the son of the sister of Titus. He wanted to convert to Judaism. He went and raised Titus from the dead through witchcraft. He asked him, "Who is important in that world (i.e., in the world of the dead)?"

He (Titus) said to him, "Israel."

He (Onqelos) asked, "So what about joining them?"

He (Titus) said to him, "Their (religious) requirements are many, and you won't be able to carry them out. Go and attack them in that world (i.e., of the living), and you will be on top, for it is written, 'Her adversaries are the chief; her enemies prosper' (Lamentations. 1: 5) – whoever distresses Israel is made head."

He (Onqelos) said to him, "So what is the punishment meted out to you (in hell)?"

He (Titus) said to him, "It is precisely what I decreed on myself. Everyday they collect my ashes, and they pass sentence on me, and I am burned, and my ashes are spread over the seven seas."

He (Onqelos) went and called up Balaam[593] from his grave by witchcraft. He asked him, "Who is important in that world?"

He (Balaam) said to him, "Israel."

(Onqelos) "So what about joining them?"

He (Balaam) said to him, "'You shall not seek their peace nor their prosperity all your days forever' (Deuteronomy 23: 7)."[594]

He (Onqelos) asked him, "So what is the punishment meted out to you?"

---

[593] The Biblical story of Balaam is told in Numbers 22:5-24:25 and 31:8.

[594] In the various versions of the Christian *Bible*, this verse is Deuteronomy 23:6 instead of 23:7.

He (Balaam) answered him, "With boiling semen."

He (Onqelos) went and with witchcraft raised up Jesus the Nazarene out of his grave. He said to him, "Who is important in that world?"

He (Jesus) said to him, "Israel."

(Onqelos) "So what about joining them?"

He (Jesus) said to him, "Seek their welfare, but don't seek evil for them. Whoever touches them is as though he touched the apple of His (God's) eye."

He (Onqelos) said to him, "So what is the punishment meted out to you?"

He (Jesus) said to him, "With boiling shit."

For the master has said, "Whoever ridicules the teachings of sages is punished by boiling shit." Come and notice the difference between Israelite sinners and the prophets of the gentile nations. (Tractate Gittin, composite version [595])

THE *QUR'AN* AND *AHADITH*

Islam stands on two foundational pillars. The first is the *Qur'an*, the book that Muslims believe contain the actual words of God as delivered by the angel Gabriel to Prophet Muhammad between the years 610 and 632 CE. The second is the *sunnah* of Prophet Muhammad, i.e., what Prophet Muhammad actually said and did with regard to religion. A closely related concept to the *sunnah* is the *ahadith* (singular = *hadith*), i.e., what other people reported that Prophet Muhammad said and did with regard to

---

[595] Although some versions of the *Babylonian Talmud* replace Jesus with "sinners of Israel," Jesus is specifically named in the following manuscripts: Vatican 130 (circa 1381 CE), Vatican 140 (14th century CE), and Munich 95 (circa 1342 CE). Schafer P (2007).

religion. These *ahadith* were collected, analyzed, and recorded in written form over the first few centuries after Prophet Muhammad, and they serve as a window through which to view the *sunnah* of Prophet Muhammad. However, a distinction needs to be kept between *sunnah* and *ahadith*. The former is what Prophet Muhammad actually said and did, while the latter consists of attributions regarding what he said and did. Some of those attributions may be accurate, and some may not. Within Islamic studies as taught in an Islamic setting, an entire academic discipline exists that is devoted to sorting through the various *ahadith* and to determining which ones are authentic and which ones are not. It is through analysis and investigation of the *ahadith* that Islamic scholars determine what actually was the *sunnah* of Prophet Muhammad.

Within Sunni Islam, which comprises about 85% of all Muslims, there are six principle collections of *ahadith* that are considered authoritative and that are referred to collectively as Al-Kutub Al-Sittah, i.e., "the six books." These are the collections of Al-Bukhari, Muslim, Abu Dawud, Al-Tirmidhi, Al-Nisa'i, and Ibn Majah. Other prominent *ahadith* collections valued by Sunni Muslims include those of Ibn Hanbal, Malik, Al-Nawawi, etc. Shia Muslims have their own collections of *ahadith*, e.g., *Al-Kafi* of Imam Ja'far Al-Sadiq and *Nahjul Balagha* of Imam 'Ali ibn Abu Talib. In contrast to the Sunni *ahadith* that trace back to Prophet Muhammad, the Shia collections typically record the statements of one of their recognized Imams,[596] i.e., descendants of Prophet Muhammad who are recognized by the Shia as being their religious leaders.

JESUS IN THE *QUR'AN* AND *AHADITH*

BIRTH AND FAMILY OF JESUS

Unlike the Talmudic portrayal of Mary as a promiscuous and wanton

---

[596] Depending upon the Shia sect, either five, seven, or 12 Imams are recognized.

adulterous, the *Qur'an* maintains that Mary was dedicated to God even before she was born and was at least partially raised by Zachariah, the father of John the Baptist. Throughout, the *Qur'an* repeatedly proclaims that Mary was an example of piousness and probity, was especially purified and favored by God, and was chosen by God above all the women on earth.

> A woman of the family of Amran prayed, "My Lord, I dedicate my unborn child to Your service. So accept this from me, for You're the Hearing and the Knowing." After she gave birth, she cried, "Oh my Lord, I've delivered a girl!" God knew better (the value of that child) she bore. "A male is not the same as a female," she said, "and so I will call her Mary, and I commend her and her children to Your protection against Satan, the Outcast."

> Her Lord accepted (the child) graciously, and she grew up healthy and well under the sponsorship of Zachariah to whom she was assigned (as a dependent). Whenever he would enter her room, he would find her provided with food. "Mary," he would ask, "where did all this (food) come from?" "It's from God," she would reply, "and God provides to whomever He wants without any limit."…

> The angels (appeared) to Mary and said, "Mary! God has chosen you and purified you. He's chosen you above the women of all nations, so be compliant to your Lord, prostrate yourself, and bow down with those who bow (before God)." (*Qur'an* 3:35-37 & 42-43, Emerick translation)[597]

And (Mary), the one who had maintained her virginity - We

---

[597] The story of Mary being provided with food by angels is no doubt unfamiliar to the vast majority of Christians, as it is never taught in Sunday school. However, this story is paralleled in the Protevangelion of James, an apocryphal Christian gospel. The relevant verse, i.e., 8:2, reads as follows. "But Mary continued in the temple as a dove educated there, and received her food from the hand of an angel." (---, 1926)

breathed Our spirit into her and made her and her son a sign for all the worlds. (*Qur'an* 21:91, Emerick translation)

(Yet another example) is that of Mary, daughter of (the house of) Amran, who guarded her chastity. We breathed Our spirit into her (womb), and she accepted the truth of her Lord's words and scriptures, for she was among the compliant. (*Qur'an* 61:12, Emerick translation)

Having reached the age of childbearing, the *Qur'an* states that Mary received an angelic visitation. Her angelic visitors informed Mary that she would be giving birth to Jesus. At first, Mary protested that she could not give birth because she was still a virgin whom no man "had touched." The angel then reassured her that a virgin birth only required God's stated command, "Be," and then it would assuredly happen. This story is told twice in the *Qur'an*, and both passages are presented below.

When the angels (again returned to Mary after some time had passed), they said, "Mary! God gives you the good news of a word from Him. He's going to be called the Messiah, Jesus, the son of Mary. He'll be honored in this world, as well as in the next, where he'll be among those nearest (to God). He will speak to people in childhood and also when he's grown, and he's going to be one of the morally righteous."

"But my Lord!" she cried out. "How can I have a son when no man has touched me?"

"And so it is that God creates whatever He wants," the angels replied. "When He decides something, He only has to say, 'Be' and it is." (*Qur'an* 3:45-48, Emerick translation)

Mention in the Book (the story of) Mary when she withdrew from her family to a place in the east. She erected a curtain (to screen herself) off from (her family), and then We sent Our angel to her, who appeared like a mortal man in all respects.

"I seek the protection of the Compassionate from you!" she cried out (when she saw the stranger approaching). "If you're mindful (of God, then you'll leave me alone)!"

"Truly, I am a messenger from your Lord," he answered, "(sent to tell) you about the gift of a pure boy."

"But how can I have a son," she asked (in surprise), "when no man has ever touched me, and I'm not a loose woman?"

"And so it will be," he answered, "for your Lord says, 'That's easy for Me.' (Your son) will be appointed as a sign for people, as well as a (source of) mercy from Us, and thus it's been decided!"

Then she conceived him and withdrew with him to a far off place (outside the city). The labor pains soon drove her to the trunk of a palm tree, and she cried out, "Oh! If only I had died before this and become something forgotten or lost to sight!"

"Don't be distressed!" a voice called out from under her. "Your Lord has provided a spring for you. Now shake the palm tree towards you, and it will shower ripe dates upon you. So eat, drink and rest your eye, and if you happen to see any man, tell him, 'I've vowed a fast for the Compassionate, and I won't talk to any person at all today.'" (*Qur'an* 19:16-26, Emerick translation)

Having given birth to Jesus, the *Qur'an* continues its account of Mary and the infant Jesus. According to this Qur'anic passage, Mary and the infant Jesus returned to Mary's own people, where she was immediately accused of sexual impropriety. Mary offered not a word in her own defense against these slanderous accusations. Instead, she merely pointed to her infant, and then the infant Jesus miraculously spoke to defend his mother from charges remarkably similar to those noted previously in Talmudic accounts.

> In time, she went back to her people, carrying (the baby, but when they saw her) they cried out, "Mary! You've come to us with something bizarre! Sister of Aaron! Your father wasn't a bad man, and your mother wasn't a loose woman!"
>
> (Mary was speechless and frightened), and she merely pointed to the baby. (Her family looked surprised) and asked, "How can we talk to a baby in a cradle?"
>
> (Then the baby Jesus spoke out), saying, "I am a servant of God. He's given me (knowledge of) the scripture and made me a prophet. He's placed blessings upon me wherever I may be and has made me prayerful and charitable for as long as I live. (He also) made me gentle towards my mother, being neither aggressive nor rude. So peace be upon me the day that I was born, the day that I die and the day that I'll be raised to life again." (*Qur'an* 19:27-33, Emerick translation)[598, 599]

As can be seen from the above Qur'anic passages, Islam, like Christianity, maintains that Jesus was born from a virgin. However, for Islam, the vir-

---

[598] The story of Jesus speaking in infancy is, once again, unknown to most Christians, as it is never taught in Sunday school. However, Jesus speaking while still in the cradle is mentioned in The First Gospel of the Infancy of Jesus Christ, an apocryphal Christian gospel. The relevant verses, i.e., 1:1-2, read as follows. "The following accounts we found in the book of Joseph the high-priest, called by some Caiaphas: He relates that Jesus spake even when he was in the cradle..." (---, 1926).

[599] Within Islam, the reference to the day that Jesus dies and is raised up again is understood to refer to Jesus' death at the end of his coming messianic rule in the End Times.

gin birth of Jesus is an act of divine creation. It is not an act of "divine begetting" or of "eternal generation" from God, as Christianity typically professes. In that regard, the following Qur'anic verses state the Islamic understanding of the virgin birth, while denying the Christian position on the virgin birth.

The example of Jesus in the sight of God is like that of Adam. He created him from dust, saying, "Be," and he was. (*Qur'an* 3:59, Emerick translation)

Those who say that God is Jesus, the Messiah, the son of Mary, are covering over (the real truth). Say to them, "Who has the power to hold back God if He wanted to destroy the Messiah, the son of Mary, his mother and everyone else on earth? To God belongs the control of the heavens and the earth and everything in between. He creates whatever He wants, for God has power over all things."… Those who say that God is the Messiah, the son of Mary – they're covering over (the truth)! The Messiah, himself, said, "Children of Israel! Serve God, the One Who is my Lord and your Lord."…The Messiah, the son of Mary, was no more than a messenger, and many messengers passed away before him. His mother was an honest woman—they both had to eat food (like any other mortal human being). (*Qur'an* 5:17, 72, & 75, Emerick translation)

Jesus, the son of Mary, was a messenger from God and His (creative) word bestowed upon (the virgin) Mary and a spirit sent from Him. So believe in God and His messengers (who were mortal men). Don't say, "Trinity." Don't do it, as that would be best for you. Truly, God is just one God, glory be to Him! He's (far above) having a child! He owns everything in the heavens and on the earth, and God is quite enough to take care of matters (for Himself)! (*Qur'an* 4:171, Emerick translation)

This was Jesus, the son of Mary, and that's an exposition of the truth about which they're arguing. It's not right (to say) that God has taken a son. All glory be to Him! Whenever He decides something, all He has to do is say, "Be," and it is! (*Qur'an* 19:34-35, Emerick translation)

JESUS' MISSION AND MINISTRY

While the Talmudic portrayal of Jesus is one of an apostate and idolater and one who practiced the black arts of sorcery and witchcraft, the *Qur'an* asserts that Jesus was a prophet and messenger of God who came with a divinely appointed mission and ministry. Within the *Qur'an*, it is stated that God taught Jesus scripture and filled him with wisdom. Additionally, the *Qur'an* maintains that God inspired Jesus with the gospel, appointed him to be His messenger to the Children of Israel,[600] and supported him with the Holy Spirit.[601] The following passages illustrate this Qur'anic presentation of Jesus.

He (God) will teach him (Jesus) scripture and fill him with wisdom (by teaching him) the Torah and the Gospel. (Thereafter He's going to appoint) him as a messenger to the Children of Israel. (*Qur'an* 3:48-49, Emerick translation)

---

[600] Unlike the contemporary Christian concept that Jesus' ministry was universal, i.e., to the whole world, the Islamic teaching is that Jesus was a messenger to Israel and that his mission and ministry were limited to Israel. (See Matthew 10:5-6 and 15:21-28 for Biblical support for the Islamic position.)

[601] While Trinitarian Christianity maintains that the Holy Spirit is one of three "persons" within the one "substance" of the godhead, the Islamic position is that the Holy Spirit is simply another name for the angel Gabriel.

We gave scripture to Moses and raised up many messengers after him, and We gave clear evidence to Jesus, the Son of Mary, and strengthened him with the Holy Spirit. (*Qur'an* 2:87, Emerick translation)

Jesus, the son of Mary, was a messenger from God and His (creative) word bestowed upon (the virgin) Mary and a spirit sent from Him. So believe in God and His messengers (who were mortal men). (*Qur'an* 4:171, Emerick translation)

Then say to them, "We believe in God and in what He sent down to us and to Abraham, Ishmael, Isaac, Jacob and the tribes (of Israel). (We believe in the message) given to Moses and Jesus and in (the messages) given to all the other prophets from their Lord. We regard each of them as equally authentic, and we surrender ourselves to God." (*Qur'an* 2:136, Emerick translation)

We revealed the Torah, and it contained both guidance and enlightenment (within its pages). The prophets (of old), who surrendered (themselves to God's command), used it to judge among the Jews, and the rabbis and legal scholars (also used it to render their judgments, as well). (They were charged with safeguarding and living by) the portion of God's Book that was entrusted to them, and they witnessed to their duty…We sent Jesus, the son of Mary, following in their footsteps, to affirm the (truth of the) Torah that had come before him, and We gave him the Gospel, in which there was both guidance and enlightenment, as an affirmation of the Torah that had come before him. (The Gospel) was a source of guidance and also admonition for those who were mindful (of God). (*Qur'an* 5:44 & 46, Emerick translation)

Jesus came with clear evidence (of the truth). He said (to his people), "I've come to you with wisdom, so I can resolve those issues that cause you to differ. Therefore, be mindful of God and obey me. Truly, God is my Lord and your Lord, so serve Him alone, for that's a straight path." (However, after Jesus was gone from the world), sects arose over differences among them. So ruin upon those who do wrong, (for they're going to suffer) from the punishment of a dreadful day. (*Qur'an* 43: 63-65, Emerick translation)

The New Testament gospels are full of stories of Jesus performing a variety of miracles. As previously seen, Judaism's Talmudic references to Jesus denigrate these miracles as mere sorcery, magic, and witch-craft. In contrast to these Talmudic claims, the *Qur'an* repeatedly asserts that Jesus did perform a number of miracles and that these miracles were a divine gift from God to Jesus. In particular, *Qur'an* 5:110-111 specifically rebuts the Talmudic statement that Jesus' mir-acles were the result of magic, attributing such a statement to those who lack faith.

Of those messengers, We've favored some above others; God spoke directly to one (of them), while others were raised to a higher rank. To Jesus, the son of Mary, We gave miracles, reinforcing him with the Holy Spirit. (*Qur'an* 2:253, Emerick translation)

(As a youth, Jesus) told (his people), "I've come to you with a sign from your Lord. I'm going to breathe life into a lifeless clay bird that I'll create by God's command, and I'll heal the blind and the lepers and bring the dead to life, all by God's command. I'll tell you what you consume (and waste of the world), as well as what you store away (of good deeds for Judgment Day). (Know that) in all of these things is a great sign if you really have faith. I've also come to verify the truth of the Torah that was revealed before me and to make lawful some things that were forbidden to you before. I'm coming to you with proof from your Lord, so be mindful of God and obey me. Truly, God is my Lord and your Lord, so serve Him. That's a straight way (of life)." (*Qur'an* 3:49-51, Emerick translation)

God will then say, "Jesus, son of Mary! Recall My favors upon you and your mother. I supported you with the Holy Spirit. (I allowed) you to speak to people in infancy, as well as when you were fully grown. I taught you the scripture and gave you wisdom, along with the Torah and the Gospel. You made a bird out of clay by My leave that you breathed to life, and it became a (real) bird by My leave. You healed the blind and the lepers by My leave, and you revived the dead by My leave. I prevented the Children of Israel (from harming) you while you were showing them the clear evidence, though the faithless among them said, 'This is nothing more than some kind of magic.' I also inspired the disciples to believe in Me and in My messenger, and they said (to you), 'We believe, and you be (our) witness that we're surrendered (to God's will).'" (*Qur'an* 5:110-111, Emerick translation)

In the immediately preceding quotations of *Qur'an* 3:49-51 and 5:110-111, reference is made to a specific miracle, i.e., turning some clay birds into living birds, which Jesus performed during his childhood. This specific miracle is likely to be something not previously encountered by most Christians and is certainly not a story that is typically taught in Sunday school. However, two different apocryphal Christian gospels mention this same event.[602]

As seen in the fourth chapter of this book, the New Testament states that Jesus had 12 primary disciples, although the various New Testament lists of the names of these 12 are in occasional disagreement. In contrast, a previously quoted Talmudic passage states that Jesus had only five disciples, with the names of four of them being totally different from anything found in the New Testament. Within the *Qur'an*, while Jesus' disciples are mentioned in several passages, the number and names of the disciples are not given.

> When Jesus (began his mission and) noticed the disbelief (of his people), he (looked for helpers), saying, "Who will help me (call the people) to God?" (Then a group of) disciples (started to follow him), saying, "We'll help (you call people) to God, for we believe in God, and you can be our witness that we're truly surrendered (to His will). Our Lord, We believe in what You've

---

[602] (A) The First Gospel of the Infancy of Jesus Christ 15:1-2 & 4-6 read as follows. "And when the Lord Jesus was seven years of age, he was on a certain day with other boys his companions about the same age. Who when they were at play made clay into several shapes, namely, asses, oxen, birds, and other figures…Then the Lord Jesus said to the boys, I will command these figures which I have made to walk. And immediately they moved, and when he commanded them to return, they returned. He had also made the figures of birds and sparrows, which, when he commanded to fly, did fly, and when he commanded to stand still, did stand still; and if he gave them meat and drink, they did eat and drink." (---, 1926). (B) Thomas' Gospel of the Infancy of Jesus Christ 1:2, 4, & 8-10 reads as follows. "When the child Jesus was five years of age and there had been a shower of rain, which was now over, Jesus was playing with other Hebrew boys by a running stream; and the water running over the banks stood in little lakes…Then he took from the bank of the stream some soft clay, and formed out of it twelve sparrows; and there were other boys playing with him…Then Jesus clapping together the palms of his hands, called to the sparrows, and said to them: Go, fly away; and while ye live remember me. So the sparrows fled away, making a noise. The Jews, seeing this, were astonished, and went away, and told their chief persons what a strange miracle they had seen wrought by Jesus." (---, 1926).

revealed, and we follow this messenger, so record us among those who bear witness." (*Qur'an* 3:52-53, Emerick translation)

All you who believe! Be disciples in the cause of God, even as Jesus, the son of Mary, called for disciples, saying, "Who will help me (to call the people to) God?" Then the disciples (joined him and) declared, "We shall help you (call the people to) God." It just so happened that some of the Children of Israel believed, while others rejected, but We reinforced the believers against their enemies, and they ultimately prevailed. (*Qur'an* 61:14, Emerick translation)

Once the disciples said, (in a moment of doubt), "Jesus, son of Mary! Can your Lord send down upon us a banquet table from heaven?"

"Be mindful of God," Jesus answered, "if you're really (true) believers."

They replied, "We only want to eat from it to satisfy (the doubts) in our hearts, so we can know (for certain) that you're truthful and also to witness a miracle for ourselves."

Jesus, the son of Mary, prayed, "O God, our Lord! Send down upon us a banquet table from the sky so there will be a joyous occasion for the first and the last of us, and also as a sign from You. Provide for us, because You're the best provider."

"I will send it down to you," God said, "but if any of you cover over (your ability to have faith) after this, then I'll punish him like I haven't punished anyone else in all the worlds!" (*Qur'an* 5:112-115, Emerick translation)

The story of the banquet table coming down from heaven has no direct parallel in the New Testament. However, Yahiya Emerick, a prolific Muslim author and a noted Islamic educator and Qur'anic commentator, offers the following possibilities for consideration.

> Some commentators believe this refers to the famed Last Supper in which Jesus and his disciples sat down to share a sumptuous meal together. Others say it refers to a different time when a table came down from the sky with seven fishes and seven loaves of bread and that some of the disciples stole food from it, saying it might not descend to feed them the next day. Thus, the table immediately ascended…It could also refer to the miracle of the loaves and fishes in which the disciples asked Jesus how they were to feed a multitude of thousands with only a few fish and loaves. Then Jesus handed out the food and the supply was never exhausted. (See Mark 6:33-44.) Finally, it could have been a situation like that of his mother Mary whom her uncle Zachariah always found supplied with food, possibly by a well-wisher who was moved by God to give it to her. Jesus prayed for the food and a well-wisher provided for them. In this case, it could, in fact, refer to the Last Supper, though God knows better. (See Mark 14:12-17.) Other commentators say that the Disciples were asking for a festive banquet table so they could turn that day into an annual feast day, such as the Jews had other feast days.[603]

END OF JESUS' MINISTRY

The usual Christian tradition is that Jesus' mission and ministry ended in crucifixion, which was then followed by Jesus' resurrection on the third day. In contrast, the Talmudic Jesus is stoned to death for apostasy, idolatry, and the practice of witchcraft. The *Qur'an* presents yet a third end-

---

[603] Emerick Y (2000), p. 201.

ing to Jesus' ministry. In the *Qur'an*, Jesus is neither stoned nor crucified. Instead, God saves him from death, and Jesus ascends into heaven.

(Furthermore, they're in such a state because) they suppressed (God's truth), made unfounded accusations against Mary, and boasted, "We killed Jesus, the Messiah, the son of Mary." However, they didn't kill him, nor did they crucify him, but it was made to appear to them that they did. Those who argue about it are full of doubts and have no (concrete) information. On the contrary, they only follow theories, for they certainly didn't kill him.

Certainly not! God raised (Jesus) up to Himself, for God is powerful and wise. (*Qur'an* 4:156-158, Emerick translation)

(After his people rejected him,) God said, "Jesus, I'm going to take you completely and lift you up to Myself. I will purify (your reputation which has been tarnished) by those who reject (the truth). I will make those who follow you superior to those who suppress (their awareness of the truth), even until the Day of Resurrection. Then all of you will come back to Me, and I'll judge between you in those matters in which you differed." (*Qur'an* 3:55, Emerick translation)

JESUS IN THE END TIMES AND THE HEREAFTER

The story of Jesus in the Islamic tradition does not end with his ascension into heaven. Both the *Qur'an* and the sayings of Prophet Muhammad attest that Jesus will have a prominent role in the End Times and on the Day of Judgment. For example, numerous sayings of Prophet Muhammad maintain that Jesus will return to earth in the End Times, will slay the Antichrist, and will establish a messianic rule that will last for either seven or 40 years. In what follows, several of these sayings are presented.

Abu Hurairah reported the Prophet…as saying: "There is no prophet between me and him, i.e., Jesus. He will descend (to the earth). When you see him, recognize him: a man of medium height, reddish fair, wearing two light yellow garments, looking as if drops were falling down from his head, though it will not be wet. He will fight the people for the cause of Islam. He will break the cross, kill swine, and abolish *jizyah* (i.e., a tax paid by non-Muslims living in a Muslim state[604]). God will perish all religions except Islam. He (Jesus) will destroy the Antichrist and will live on the earth for forty years, and then he will die. The Muslims will pray over him. (*Abu Dawud, hadith* #4310)[605]

Narrated Abu Hurairah: "God's Messenger said, 'By Him in Whose hands my soul is, the son of Mary will shortly descend among you people as a just ruler and will break the cross and kill the pig and abolish the *jizyah*…Then there will be abundance of money, and nobody will accept charitable gifts.'" (*Al-Bukhari,* volume #3, *hadith* #425, see also *Al-Bukhari,* volume #3, *hadith* #656 and *Al-Bukhari,* volume #4, *hadith* #657)[606]

Narrated Abu Hurairah: "God's Messenger said, 'How will you be when the son of Mary descends among you, and he will judge people by the law of the *Qur'an* and not by the law of the gospel. (*Al-Bukhari,* volume #4, *hadith* #658)[607]

---

[604] Muslims must pay *zakat,* an obligatory charity tax. Non-Muslims living in a Muslim state do not pay *zakat,* but instead pay *jizyah* for the services and protection rendered to them by the Muslim state. Of note, the *jizyah* paid by non-Muslims can be less than the *zakat* paid by Muslims.

[605] The quoted *hadith* is the present author's editing of the translation provided in Hasan A (1990).

[606] The quoted *hadith* is the present author's editing of the translation provided in Khan MM (---).

[607] The quoted *hadith* is the present author's editing of the translation provided in Khan MM (---).

Jabir b. 'Abdullah reported: "I heard (Prophet Muhammad)…say: 'A section of my people will not cease struggling for the truth and will prevail till the Day of Resurrection.' He said: 'Jesus, son of Mary, would then descend, and their commander would invite him to come and lead them in prayer, but he would say: 'No, some among you are commanders over some. This is the honor from God for this community.'" (*Muslim, hadith #293*) [608]

Hudhaifa b. Usaid Ghifari reported: "(Prophet Muhammad)…came to us all of a sudden as we were (busy in a discussion). He said: 'What are you discussing?' They said: 'We are discussing about the Last Hour.' Thereupon he said: 'It will not come until you see ten signs,' and (in this connection) he made a mention of the…Antichrist…(and) the descent of Jesus, son of Mary…" (*Muslim, hadith #6931*, see also *Muslim, ahadith #6932-6934*) [609]

An-Nawwas b. Sam'an reported that Prophet Muhammad made mention of the Antichrist…he said…"It will be at this very time that God will send Christ, the son of Mary, and he will descend at the white minaret in the eastern side of Damascus, wearing two garments lightly dyed with saffron, and placing his hands on the wings of two angels…He (Jesus) then searches for him (the Antichrist) until he catches hold of him at the gate of Ludd and kills him. Then a people whom God has protected will come to Jesus, son of Mary, and he will wipe their faces and inform them of their ranks in Paradise…and then God will send Gog and Magog, and they will swarm down from every slope. The first of them will pass the lake of Tiberias (i.e., the Sea of Galilee) and

---

[608] The quoted *hadith* is the present author's editing of the translation provided in Siddiqi 'AH (---).

[609] The quoted *hadith* is the present author's editing of the translation provided in Siddiqi 'AH (---).

drink out of it. And when the last of them passes, he will say: 'There was once water there.' Jesus and his companions will then be besieged here (at Tur, and they will be so pressed) that the head of the ox will be dearer to them than one hundred dinars. And God's Messenger Jesus and his companions will supplicate to God...(and God will then destroy Gog and Magog)...(Then Jesus' messianic reign will be established, and) the earth will be told to bring forth its fruit and restore its blessing. As a result thereof, there would grow (such a big) pomegranate that a group of people will be able to eat it and seek shelter under its skin, and the milk cow will give so much milk that a whole party will be able to drink it. And the milk camel will give such (a large quantity) of milk that the whole tribe will be able to drink out of that, and the milk sheep will give so much milk that the whole family will be able to drink out of that...(at the end of Jesus' messianic reign) God will send a pleasant wind that sooths (people) even under their armpits, and (God) will take the life of every Muslim, and only the wicked will survive and will commit adultery like asses, and the Last Hour will come to them. (*Muslim, hadith #7015*, see also *Muslim, hadith #7016*)[610]

'Abdullah b. 'Amr reported...that (Prophet Muhammad)...said: "The Antichrist will appear in my Muslim nation, and he will stay (in the world) for 40"—I cannot say whether he meant 40 days, 40 months, or 40 years—"and God will then send Jesus, the son of Mary, who...will chase him (the Antichrist) and kill him. Then people will live for seven years wherein there will be no rancor between any two people..." (*Muslim, hadith #7023*)[611]

---

[610] The quoted *hadith* is the present author's editing of the translation provided in Siddiqi 'AH (---).

[611] The quoted *hadith* is the present author's editing of the translation provided in Siddiqi 'AH (---).

Several of the above quoted sayings of Prophet Muhammad make mention of Jesus' messianic reign as being a time of absolute peace and plenty. As many Christians interpret Isaiah 11:6-9 as being a beautiful description of this messianic reign,[612] it is interesting to note that descriptors that are remarkably parallel to Isaiah 11:6-9 are used to detail Jesus' messianic reign in the following saying of Prophet Muhammad.

> During Jesus' reign, such security will exist that a camel will graze with the lion and the beast of prey with cows and sheep. Children will play with snakes, and none harm the other. (*Musnad* of Ahmad ibn Hanbal 406:2)[613]

The *Qur'an* also states that the return of Jesus will be one of the signs of the End Times regarding the coming Day of Judgment. Moreover, the *Qur'an* emphasizes that Jesus will be a witness for or against people on the Day of Judgment.

> (Jesus) is a portent of the Hour, so have no doubt about (its arrival). (*Qur'an* 43:61, Emerick translation)

> Each of the Followers of Earlier Revelation must believe in (Jesus) before they die, for on the Day of Assembly, (Jesus) will be a witness against them. (*Qur'an* 4:159, Emerick translation)

> God will say (on Judgment Day): "Jesus, son of Mary! Did you tell people, 'Worship me and my mother as gods in place of God'?"

---

[612] Isaiah 11:6-9 reads as follows. "The wolf also shall dwell with the lamb, and the leopard shall lie down with the kid; and the calf and the young lion and the fatling together; and a little child shall lead them. And the cow and the bear shall feed; their young ones shall lie down together: and the lion shall eat straw like the ox. And the sucking child shall play on the hole of the asp, and the weaned child shall put his hand on the cockatrice' den. They shall not hurt nor destroy in all my holy mountain: for the earth shall be full of the knowledge of the Lord, as the waters cover the sea." (King James Version)

[613] As quoted in Bin Bayyah 'A (2003).

"Glory be to you!" he'll reply. "I could never have said what I had no right (to say), and if I ever said something like that, then You would've known about it. You know what's in my heart, while I don't know what's in Yours, and You know all hidden mysteries. I never said anything to them except what You commanded me to say: 'Worship God, my Lord and your Lord.' I was their witness while I lived among them. When You took me up (to heaven), You became their Watcher, and You're a witness over all things. If You choose to punish them, well, they're Your servants (to treat as You please), though if You choose to forgive them, (then of course You can because) You're the Powerful and the Wise." (*Qur'an* 5:116-118, Emerick translation)

While the *Babylonian Talmud* assigns Jesus to suffer throughout all eternity in boiling excrement in hell, the *Qur'an* states that Jesus will be honored in the next world and will be among those nearest to God.

He's going to be called the Messiah, Jesus, the son of Mary. He'll be honored in this world, as well as in the next, where he'll be among those nearest (to God). (*Qur'an* 3:45, Emerick translation)

SUMMARY AND CONCLUSIONS

Three different pictures of Jesus emerge from contemporary Christianity, from the *Babylonian Talmud,* and from the *Qur'an* and sayings of Prophet Muhammad. In general, the Islamic and contemporary Christian portrayals of Jesus have much in common, although disagreeing about such issues as Jesus' nature and whether or not Jesus was crucified. However, both Christian and Islamic sources agree that Jesus was born of a virgin, was given a divine mission and ministry by God, ascended into heaven, will reappear in the End

Times, and will spend eternity in heaven. In marked contrast, the Talmudic Jesus is born of a promiscuous and adulterous woman, is the result of an adulterous affair with a Roman soldier named Pandera, was an apostate who practiced witchcraft and idolatry, attempted to lead Israel astray, was killed by stoning, had his corpse hung on a tree for public viewing, and will spend eternity in boiling excrement in hell.

Figure # 8

A COMPARISON OF THE CONTEMPORARY CHRISTIAN, TALMUDIC, AND ISLAMIC PORTRAYALS OF JESUS

ISSUE	CHRISTIAN	TALMUDIC	ISLAMIC
Mary	a virgin & chosen by God	promiscuous, an adulteress	a virgin, pious, virtuous, & chosen by God
Jesus' birth	from a virgin, begotten by God	illegitimate	from a virgin, created by God
Jesus' father	God	Pandera, a Roman	none
Jesus' nature	human & divine	human	human, God's prophet
Jesus' mission	divine miracles,	witchcraft, sorcery, apostasy, idolatry, & leads Israel astray	miracles by God's leave, message from God to Israel
Jesus' end	crucified, resurrected, and ascended to heaven	stoned to death, corpse hung on a tree	not killed, ascended to heaven
End Times	Jesus returns, slays the Antichrist, & establishes messianic rule	no role for Jesus	Jesus returns, slays the Antichrist, & establishes messianic rule
Hereafter	Jesus in heaven	Jesus in boiling excrement in hell	Jesus in heaven

CHAPTER 7

THE MYTH OF
THE CHRISTIAN FOUNDATIONS
OF AMERICA

INTRODUCTION

A PROMINENT MYTH HAS EMERGED over the last century that America was founded as a Christian nation whose genesis was based and whose continuing existence is grounded upon Christian and Biblical principles. This myth has currently gained widespread acceptance among many Christians in America, especially among those who can be classified as adhering to evangelical, fundamentalist, charismatic, and Pentecostal persuasions. Regularly propagated by those televangelists and clergymen of the extreme Christian Right who seem to be constitutionally incapable of separating politics and religion, the end result of this myth is to imply that all those who are not Christians are somehow less than truly American.

In reality, America was not founded as a Christian nation, and its origins were not based upon Christian and Biblical principles. Despite the many stories of various Christian sects, e.g., Puritans, Quakers, Mennonites, Baptists, Huguenots, etc., coming to America in the 17th through early 19th centuries in order to escape religious persecution in Europe, it can be argued that Christianity was a minority religion in America at the time of this country's founding and that it was a minority religion among this country's most famous Founding Fathers.

In order to expose the myth of America being founded as a Christian nation, one has only to examine four variables: (1) the religious beliefs and practices of most Americans during the origins of this country; (2) the religious beliefs and practices of the Founding Fathers; (3) early state constitutions and declarations of rights; and (4) the official documents (the Declaration of Independence, the United States Constitution, and the 1797 Treaty of Tripoli) of the United States of America.

THE RELIGION OF THE GENERAL PUBLIC

If the United States had been founded as a Christian nation, it would stand to reason that the vast majority of early Americans were Christians. In reality, however, Christianity was probably a minority religion in the early United States, and the religious orientation of America's general population at the time of the founding of the United States could hardly be considered Christian. During the colonial period, the most optimistic estimates suggest that only about 15% of the majority white population had membership in any given Christian church,[614] giving America a lower percentage of church members than of any Christian nation of Europe.[615] Hofstadter provides more somber estimates, placing the percentage of whites having Christian church membership during the colonial period at 15% in New England, about 07% in the middle colonies, and fewer still in the South.[616] Christian membership among the black slaves would have been even less, as between 20 and 30% of the slaves imported to America from Africa were Muslims[617] and most of the rest adhered to native African religions, which were usually animistic in nature. Further, Christian church membership in the white population actually decreased during the first 20 years of American independence, falling to a low of about 10%[618] or even as low as 07%.[619]

---

[614] Butler J (1979).
[615] Hofstadter R (1974).
[616] Miltzer M (1990).
[617] Dirks JF (2006).
[618] (A) Butler J (1979); (B) Handy RT (1977).
[619] Hofstadter R (1974).

The minimal place of Christianity in early America can also be illustrated by looking at the number of churches that were present. By around 1750, there were less than 1,500 churches of all denominations scattered across the 13 American colonies. More specifically, the Church of England (Anglican) had less than 300 parishes, and these few churches suffered from poor attendance. Within the colony of Georgia, there were only three Anglican parishes.[620]

Figures such as those reported in the above two paragraphs certainly give lie to the claim that the American colonies and early United States constituted a Christian nation. In support of that conclusion, one can quote Joseph Ottolenghe, a Christian missionary, who wrote to John Waring on November 19, 1753, to lament that the people of Georgia had "but very little more knowledge of a Savior than the aboriginal natives (American Indians)."[621]

Some might still want to argue that the religious fervor associated with the Great Awakening (circa 1720-1750) and the Second Great Awakening (circa 1795-1835) supports the contention that the American populace was decidedly Christian and that America was founded as a Christian nation. However, those who would advance such an argument must surely realize that there could never have been a great outbreak of Christian revivalism if the vast majority of Americans were not non-Christian. One simply cannot "awaken" those who are already awake. The very fact that these two revival movements even occurred speaks to the inevitable conclusion that America was not a majority Christian nation.

If only 07 to 15% of the white population belonged to a Christian church

---

[620] Gaustad ES (1987).
[621] Gaustad ES (1987), p. 16.

and if church membership was even lower among enslaved Africans and African Americans, then what was the religious orientation of the general population at America's founding? The answer is twofold.

Deism, not Christianity, appears to have been the religion of choice for America's educated elite in the late 18th century. Growing out of the European Enlightenment, Deism maintained that religion must derive from natural reason and offered itself as a rational alternative to Christianity. Deists typically maintained two basic beliefs. Firstly, they believed in the existence of God. However, the God of the Deists was an impersonal Creator Who established a rational universe and then left it and mankind to function on their own. Secondly, Deists believed in a life after death in which rewards and punishments would be doled out according to the type of life an individual had led, thus negating such Christian concepts as salvation through faith and through vicarious atonement via the alleged crucifixion of Jesus Christ.[622]

Given their emphasis on rationality and human reason, Deists sought to establish a simple, primitive monotheism far removed from traditional Christianity. For example, Deists typically denied the supernatural and mystical in human affairs. As such, the miracles recorded in the *Bible* were repudiated by Deists. Likewise, Deists scoffed at such Christian doctrines as the divinity of Jesus Christ and the concept of the Trinity. Further, Deists believed that a certain body of religious knowledge is inherent in every individual and that such knowledge could be accessed and actualized through man's use of his own natural reasoning abilities, without any recourse to divine revelation, holy scripture, or the teachings of any church. In fact, many Deists went so far as to question whether divine revelation was even possible.[623]

---

[622] (A) Manuel FE (2003); (B) Kagan D, Ozment S, Turner FM (1991).
[623] (A) Manuel FE (2003); (B) Kagan D, Ozment S, Turner FM (1991).

While Deism was the prevalent religious orientation of early America's educated elite, the more poorly educated majority of early Americans appear to have subscribed primarily to a belief in what can best be described as an animistic folk magic, although one incorporating some minimally Christian themes. Divination by means of seer stones and divining rods, fortune telling, palmistry, folk cures, various and sundry superstitions, spirits guarding hidden treasures that would elude diggers of treasure by mysteriously sinking further into the earth if the proper incantations and rituals were not followed, astrology, soothsaying, and various other magical practices appear to have constituted the primary religious practices and beliefs of the common man. In short, at the time of the founding of the American republic, the majority of Americans were "unchurched" believers in and/or practitioners of magical incantations and spells, divination, fortune telling, folk cures, and superstition.[624]

THE RELIGION OF THE FOUNDING FATHERS

As will be seen in what follows, many of this country's most prominent Founding Fathers were not practicing Christians. For example, Adler[625] has noted that none of the first six presidents of the United States was an orthodox Christian. Further, none of the first seven presidents belonged to a church at the time of being elected to the presidency.[626] Neither George Washington, John Adams, Thomas Jefferson, James Madison, James Monroe, John Quincy Adams, nor Andrew Jackson maintained formal church membership upon being elected to the highest office of the land. In elaborating on the non-Christian religious orientation of our early presidents, the Reverend Bird Wilson, an Episcopal priest, stated

---

[624] (A) Williams PW (1980); (B) Quinn DM (1987).
[625] Adler M (1968).
[626] Pfeffer L (1975).

from the pulpit in October of 1831 that none of the presidents up until then had been a practitioner, i.e., "a professor," of Christianity. "(A)mong all our presidents from Washington downward, not one was a professor of religion, at least not of more than Unitarianism,"[627] i.e., a denial of the concept of the Trinity and of Jesus Christ being anything more than a metaphorical son of God. In reality, many of the Founding Fathers were Deists and harbored frankly anti-Christian sentiments.

GEORGE WASHINGTON

Commanding general of the Continental Army and our first president, George Washington's place of preeminence among America's Founding Fathers is assured. Yet, historians are commonly agreed that Washington was not a practicing Christian. Rather, he was a Deist, as were the many educated Americans of his day who were influenced by the European Enlightenment. In concluding that Washington was a Deist, not a Christian, historians frequently point to the following considerations.

- Throughout all of Washington's voluminous correspondence, the name of Jesus Christ is nowhere to be found, not even to the extent of alluding to the moral and ethical teachings of Jesus.[628]
- Washington did not believe in the divinity and resurrection of Jesus or in Christ's atonement for humanity's sins.[629]
- In his first inaugural address, Washington neither mentioned nor used the word "God." Rather, he used such typically Deist terms as "the invisible hand which conducts the affairs of men" and "the benign parent of the human race." In fact, Washington hardly ever used the word "God," preferring such Deist

---

[627] Boller PF (1963), p. 15.
[628] Boller PF (1963).
[629] Boller PF (1963).

terminology as "Providence," "Grand Architect," "Higher Cause," "Great Author," and the terms noted above. That Washington's Providence was an impersonal Deist concept can be shown by the fact that he used pronouns of all three genders, i.e., he, she, and it, in referring to Providence.[630]

• Washington's diaries indicate that he seldom attended church on his own.[631]

• Throughout his life, Washington consistently refused to participate in the Christian sacrament of Holy Communion.[632] Even when accompanying his wife Martha to church, Washington refused the sacraments. If Martha participated in taking Holy Communion, Washington would exist the sanctuary and wait for her there.[633]

• After Washington's death, Dr. Abercrombie, a friend of Washington's, was asked about Washington's religion by a Dr. Wilson. Dr. Abercrombie replied, "Sir, Washington was a Deist."[634]

• In a journal entry dated February of 1800, Thomas Jefferson wrote the following regarding Washington. "I know...that Gouverneur Morris, who pretended to be in his (Washington's) secrets and believed himself to be so, has often told me that Genl. Washington believed no more of that system (Christianity) than he himself did."[635]

Considerations such as the above have rather consistently lead historians to conclude that Washington was a Deist, not a Christian. Paul F. Boller offered the following conclusion in his book *George Washington and Religion*:

---

[630] (A) Flexner JT (1972); (B) Gaustad ES (1987).
[631] Walker J (1997).
[632] (A) Boller PF (1963); (B) Schwartz B (1987).
[633] Schwartz B (1987).
[634] Walker J (1997) p. 2.
[635] Boller PF (1963) p. 85.

(Washington) was really a typical eighteenth-century Deist, not a Christian, in his religious outlook…Washington, on the evidence which we have examined, can hardly be considered a Christian… [636]

Likewise, James Thomas Flexner noted in *George Washington: Anguish and Farewell (1793-1799)* that:

Washington's religious belief was that of the Enlightenment: Deism.[637]

Still further, in his *George Washington: The Making of an American Symbol,* Barry Schwartz concluded:

George Washington's practice of Christianity was limited and super-ficial because he was not himself a Christian. In the enlightened tradition of his day, he was a devout Deist—just as many clergymen who knew him suspected.[638]

JOHN ADAMS

John Adams was a major figure in both the First Continental Congress (1774) and Second Continental Congress (1775-1777). In that capacity, it was Adams who nominated George Washington to be the commander of the Continental Army, selected Thomas Jefferson to author the first draft of the Declaration of Independence, and helped edit that first draft. He subse-quently authored the Massachusetts Constitution (1780), and was the first American ambassador to the Court of Saint James (1785-1788), the first vice president of the United States (1789-1797), and the second president of the United States (1787-1801). It is, indeed, hard to imagine a more prominent and influential member of the Founding Fathers.[639]

---

[636] Boller PF (1963) p. 85.
[637] Flexner JT (1972) p. 490.
[638] Schwartz B (1987) p. 175.
[639] Ellis JJ (2003).

Like others of the Founding Fathers, Adams was not an orthodox Christian, although he did believe in God and in the concepts of morality, and immortality. Rather than being a doctrinal Christian, he was an early Unitarian who denied such standard Christian concepts as the Trinity, the divinity of Jesus Christ, eternal damnation, Original Sin, and vicarious atonement for sin.[640]

In private letters to Thomas Jefferson, Adams vented some of his anti-Christian thoughts.

> I almost shudder at the thought of alluding to the most fatal example of the abuses of grief which the history of mankind has preserved—the Cross. Consider what calamities that engine of grief has produced.[641]

> The substance and essence of Christianity, as I understand it, is eternal and unchangeable, and will bear examination forever, but it has been mixed with extraneous ingredients, which I think will not bear examination, and they ought to be separated. [642]

Additional insight into the religious beliefs of John Adams can be gleaned from his letter of May 30, 1821, to Stephen Sewall, in which among other things Adams suggested that Muslims (the primary inhabitants of Turkey) send English translations of the *Qur'an* to the United States, that Hindus (the primary inhabitants of India) send English translations of their books of scripture to the United States, and that Buddhists, Confucians, and Taoists (the primary inhabitants of China) send English translations of their scripture to the United States.

---

[640] (A) Walker J (1997), (B) Gaustad ES (1987).
[641] Walker J (1997) p. 2.
[642] Koch A (1965) p. 234.

...Bible Societies have been invented by deeper Politicians still to divert mankind from the study and pursuit of their Natural Rights. I wish Societies were formed in India, China, and Turkey to send us gratis translations of their Sacred Books.[643]

On more than one occasion, Adams flatly denied that the United States was founded as a Christian nation or was based on Christian principles. As will be seen subsequently, as president of the United States, he signed the 1797 Treaty of Tripoli, which flatly stated that "the Government of the United States of America is not, in any sense, founded on the Christian religion." Further, in writing about the American Constitution, Adams directly stated that the United States was founded on principles of nature and human reason, not on any religious considerations. The following quotation from Adams, with italics added by the present author for emphasis, illustrates these points.

The United States of America have exhibited, perhaps, the first example of governments *erected on the simple principles of nature...It will never be pretended that any persons employed in that service had interviews with the gods, or were in any degree under the influence of Heaven*, more than those at work upon ships or houses, or laboring in merchandise or agriculture; it will forever be acknowledged that *these governments were contrived merely by the use of reason and the senses...*Thirteen governments (the original 13 states) *thus founded on the natural authority of the people alone, without a pretence of miracle or mystery...*[644]

The italicized phrases in the above quotation, which emphasize human reason and the natural authority of the people alone, and which disavow

---

[643] Gaustad ES (1987) p. 95.
[644] (A) Koch A (1965), p. 248; (B) Walker J (1997), p. 2.

the influence of heaven, miracle, or mystery, are certainly consistent with maintaining a Deist foundation for the United States, but hardly for a Christian origin.

THOMAS JEFFERSON

Thomas Jefferson was a delegate to the Second Continental Congress, where he was the principal author of the Declaration of Independence. In 1779, he was elected governor of Virginia. In December of 1782, he returned to the Continental Congress. Two years later, he became America's minister to France, a position that he held until 1789. Back in the United States, he became America's first secretary of state (1789-1794), second vice president (1797-1801), and third president (1801-1809). As can be seen, Jefferson's credentials as a prominent Founding Father are quite impressive.

Jefferson's personal religious orientation was that of a Deist and a Unitarian. In fact, during his successful presidential campaign against John Adams, Jefferson was accused by his opponents of being an atheist, infidel, and archdemon who opposed revelation and undermined Christian morals. As if to give substance to the charges of his critics, he refused to proclaim a national day of fasting during his presidency.[645]

Not only was Jefferson a non-Christian, his thinking was often actively anti-Christian, especially when he accused Christianity of having perverted and contaminated the pure, simple, and rational monotheism of Deism and the laudable moral teachings of Jesus.[646] For Jefferson, Paul (Saul of Tarsus) was the first significant corruptor of the superb moral philosophy of Jesus, and in his 1810 letter to Samuel Kercheval, he stated that:

---

[645] Gaustad ES (1987).
[646] Gaustad ES (1987).

But a short time elapsed after the death of the great reformer (Jesus Christ) of the Jewish religion, before his principles were departed from by those who professed to be his special servants, and perverted into an engine for enslaving mankind, and aggrandizing their oppressors in Church and State. [647]

Three years later, he penned the following remarks in a letter to Baron von Humboldt:

History I believe furnishes no example of a priest-ridden people maintaining a free civil government. This marks the lowest grade of ignorance, of which their political as well as religious leaders will always avail themselves for their own purpose. [648]

As yet another example of Jefferson's anti-Christian sentiments, one has only to note his language regarding the Christian clergy in an 1814 letter to Horatio Spofford:

In every country and every age, the priest has been hostile to liberty. He is always in alliance with the despot, abetting his abuses in return for protection to his own. It is easier to acquire wealth and power by this combination than by deserving them, and to affect this, they have perverted the purest religion ever preached to man into mystery and jargon, unintelligible to all mankind. [649]

Still further, on January 29, 1815, Jefferson wrote to Charles Clay that "this loathsome combination of church and state," had for centuries turned human beings in Europe into "dupes and drudges." [650] Finally, one

---

[647] Seldes G (1983), p. 370.
[648] Seldes G (1983), p. 370.
[649] Seldes G (1983), p. 371.
[650] Gaustad ES (1987), p. 47.

notes that Jefferson claimed that Christianity had become perverted "into an engine for enslaving mankind."[651]

Jefferson was particularly vitriolic when considering some of the most cherished doctrines and concepts of Christianity. For example, he considered Christianity's concept of God to be nothing more than a "hocus-pocus phantasm of a god."[652] In discussing the Christian concept of the Trinity in a letter of July 19, 1822, to Benjamin Waterhouse, Jefferson referred to the concept of the Trinity as being "mere Abracadabra" and noted that "I should as soon undertake to bring the crazy skulls of Bedlam to sound understanding, as to inculcate reason into that of an Athanasian (Trinitarian)."[653] A year earlier, he had written to Timothy Pickering on February 27, 1821, to complain about the "incomprehensible jargon of Trinitarian arithmetic."[654] On December 8, 1822, Jefferson wrote to James Smith, confidently but erroneously predicting the end of Trinitarian Christianity in America: "I confidently expect that the present generation will see Unitarianism become the general religion of the United States."[655] He had earlier that year expressed the same sentiments in another letter: "I trust that there is not a young man now living in the U.S. who will not die an Unitarian."[656] Jefferson's scorn at traditional Christian doctrine was not, however, confined to his rejection of the concept of the Trinity. In a letter to John Adams written on April 11, 1823, Jefferson also rejected the concept of Christ's virgin birth:

> And the day will come when the mystical generation of Jesus, by the supreme being as his father in the womb of a Virgin Mary,

---

[651] Gaustad ES (1987), p. 47.
[652] (A) Quinn DM (1987), p. 8, (B) Gaustad ES (1987), p. 105.
[653] Gaustad ES (1987), p. 104.
[654] Gaustad ES (1987), p 104.
[655] Gaustad ES (1987), p. 105.
[656] Gaustad ES (1987), p. 105.

will be classed with the fable of the generation of Minerva in the brain of Jupiter…But we may hope that the dawn of reason and freedom of thought in these United States will do away (with) all this artificial scaffolding.[657]

With regard to the *Bible*, Jefferson was, to say the least, hostile and cynical. He wrote that the gospels were filled with "much untruth, charlatanism, and imposture,"[658] and he edited his own version of the gospels, in which all miracles and references to the divinity and resurrection of Jesus were summarily deleted.[659] Commenting on Revelation, the last book in the Protestant and Roman Catholic *Bible*, in a January 17, 1825, letter to Alexander Smyth, Jefferson labeled it:

> …merely the ravings of a maniac, no more worthy, nor capable of explanation than the incoherencies of our own nightly dreams…what has no meaning admits no explanation.[660]

Jefferson was constantly vigilant in defending America as a secular nation and from being labeled as a Christian nation. For example, he specifically rejected the notion that British common law, upon which much of American law was based, had a Christian origin. In his letter to Thomas Cooper of February 10, 1814, Jefferson stated that: "(W)e may safely affirm…that Christianity neither is, nor ever was, a part of the common law."[661]

Finally, it should be noted that when Jefferson established the University of Virginia, he made it a point to exclude theology from the academic curriculum.

---

[657] Gaustad ES (1986), p. 287.
[658] Quinn DM (1987), p. 8.
[659] (A) Quinn DM (1987); (B) Gaustad ES (1987).
[660] Gaustad ES (1986), p. 287.
[661] Walker J (1997), p. 6.

In summary, Jefferson was a Deist and freethinker whose emphasis on his own personal reasoning consistently trumped the teachings and dictates of organized religion, including that of Christianity. As he stated in a letter to Ezra Stiles Ely on June 25, 1819: "You say you are a Calvinist. I am not. I am of a sect by myself, as far as I know."[662] Many years earlier, he had advised Peter Carr in a letter dated August 10, 1787, to: "Question with boldness even the existence of a god."[663]

JAMES MADISON

James Madison was elected to Virginia's 1776 Revolutionary Convention, which subsequently evolved into that state's legislature. Defeated for reelection in 1778, Madison then served two years on the governor's council. In March of 1780, he became one of Virginia's representatives to the Continental Congress. In 1784, he returned to the Virginia legislature. Three years later, in 1787, he represented Virginia at the Constitutional Convention where he was one of the major authors of the United States Constitution and earned the informal title of "Father of the Constitution." Not content to have been one of the main guiding spirits behind the Constitution, Madison campaigned tirelessly for its adoption by the 13 colonies, in part by writing at least 29 out of the 85 Federalist Papers, a series of newspaper articles that became the standard commentary on the Constitution. (The other Federalist Papers were written by Alexander Hamilton and John Jay.) Elected to the newly formed United States House of Representatives in 1789, Madison sponsored the first 10 amendments to the Constitution, i.e., the Bill of Rights. Madison left Congress in 1797 due to his objections to a treaty with England. He subsequently served as the United States Secretary of State (1801-1809) and as America's fourth president (1809-1817).

[662] (A) Walker J (1997), p. 2; (B) Gaustad ES (1987), p. 108.
[663] Walker J (1997), p. 2.

Clearly one of this nation's most important Founding Fathers, Madison was a Deist whose avoidance of traditional Christianity began as early as 1769, when he entered the College of New Jersey, subsequently to become Princeton University, which he selected because of its hostility to the episcopacy. During his second tour in the Virginia legislature, Madison helped to defeat a bill that would have given support to "teachers of the Christian religion." Madison continued his distance from Christianity throughout his entire life, never once joining any Christian church, and opposing the appointment of congressional and military chaplains. The closest Madison would come to traditional Christianity was in expressing some preference for Unitarianism, a religious movement that denied the Christian church's concept of the divinity of Jesus Christ. [664]

Madison's antipathy towards traditional Christianity is well evidenced in his writings. For example, in his *Memorial and Remonstrance against Religious Assessments*, written in 1785, Madison stated that:

> During almost fifteen centuries has the legal establishment of Christianity been on trial. What have been its fruits? More or less in all places, pride and indolence in the Clergy, ignorance and servility in the laity, in both, superstition, bigotry and persecution…What influence in fact have ecclesiastical establishments had on Civil Society? In some instances they have been seen to erect a spiritual tyranny on the ruins of the Civil authority; in many instances they have been seen upholding the thrones of political tyranny: in no instance have they been the guardians of the liberties of the people. Rulers who wish to subvert the public liberty may have found an established Clergy convenient auxiliaries. A just Government, instituted to secure and perpetuate it, needs them not. [665]

---

[664] --- (2003).
[665] (A) Gaustad ES (1987), p. 145-146; (B) Walker J (1997), p. 3.

As a second example of Madison's feelings regarding organized religion, consider the wording found in his letter of April 1, 1774, to William Bradford. "Religious bondage shackles and debilitates the mind and unfits it for every noble enterprise, every expanded prospect." [666]

JOHN QUINCY ADAMS

The son of our second president, John Quincy Adams had one of the most celebrated diplomatic careers of any of our Founding Fathers. In 1781, at the tender age of 14, he served for one year as the private secretary to Francis Dana, the United States envoy to Russia. He then left the diplomatic service for several years, during which time he attended and graduated from Harvard College, studied law, and then passed the bar exam in 1790. In May of 1794, he returned to the diplomatic corps, being appointed as the United States minister to the Netherlands by President Washington. Two years later, Washington appointed him as minister to Portugal. Shortly thereafter, John Adams, having become the second president of the United States, appointed his son to be minister to Prussia (Germany), a position the son held until 1800. In 1802, John Quincy Adams was elected to the Massachusetts Senate. One year later, in 1803, the Adams was elected to the United States Senate, a position he held until 1808. In 1809, Adams was appointed by President Madison as the United States minister to Russia, where he served until 1815, and in which position he helped negotiate the end of the War of 1812 between Great Britain and the United States. In 1815, he became the United States minister to Great Britain, a position he held until becoming the United States Secretary of State in 1817. In the latter position, Adams formulated what has since become known as the Monroe

---

[666] Gaustad ES (1987), p. 37.

Doctrine, which remains a cornerstone of American foreign policy to this day. From 1824 to 1829, Adams served as the sixth president of the United States. Losing the presidency to Andrew Jackson in 1829, Adams continued his public service as a member of the United States House of Representatives from Massachusetts from 1831 until his death in 1848. During these later years, Adams worked unsuccessfully to abolish slavery, introducing a constitutional amendment that would have provided that: every child born in the United States after July 4, 1842, would be free and that no new state, with the single exception of Florida, could allow slavery.[667]

As previously noted, John Quincy Adams had no formal church membership upon being elected to the presidency. His religious beliefs appear to have been those of a Unitarian who denied the traditional Christian doctrine of the Trinity. Moreover, so adamantly did he maintain the separation of church and state that he refused to be sworn into the office of the presidency by swearing with his hand on a *Bible*. Instead, Adams was sworn in with his hand on a book of United States law.[668] That's more than a pretty clear indication that Adams rejected the proposition that the United States was founded as a Christian nation.

BENJAMIN FRANKLIN

Benjamin Franklin was the clerk of the Pennsylvania legislature from 1736 to 1751, and he was also postmaster of Philadelphia from 1737 to 1753. Beginning in 1753, Franklin became deputy postmaster general, being in charge of mail in all the northern colonies. In 1764, he was sent

---

[667] Bemis SF (2003).
[668] Romero F (2009).

to London to represent Pennsylvania to the British crown. Remaining in London until 1775, Franklin supplemented his representation of Pennsylvania to Great Britain by beginning to represent Georgia in 1768, New Jersey in 1769, and Massachusetts in 1770. He returned to America in 1775, where he immediately became a representative from Pennsylvania to the Second Continental Congress. In that capacity, he helped Thomas Jefferson draft the Declaration of Independence and served on a committee that established the American postal system. In September of 1776, Congress sent Franklin to France as one of three commissioners who negotiated French aid to the American Revolution. He remained in France as America's representative to that country until being replaced by Thomas Jefferson in 1784. Returning to America in 1785, he was a member of the Constitutional Convention of 1787, where he helped frame the United States Constitution. Given the sum total of the above, his reputation as one of America's Founding Fathers is certainly well assured.

Franklin's religious orientation is described succinctly in his posthumously published autobiography.

> My parents had given me betimes religious impressions, and I received from my infancy a pious education in the principles of Calvinism. But scarcely was I arrived at fifteen years of age, when, after having doubted in turn of different tenets, according as I found them combated in different books that I read, I began to doubt of Revelation itself...Some books against Deism fell into my hands...It happened that they wrought an effect on me quite contrary to what was intended by them; for the arguments of the Deists, which were quoted to be refuted, appeared to me

much stronger than the refutations; in short, I soon became a thorough Deist.[669]

Dr. Priestley, an intimate friend of Franklin, confirmed that Franklin was not a Christian, being instead a Deist. Writing in his autobiography, Priestly also noted that Franklin was quite active in getting others to disbelieve in Christianity. Priestly's comments on Franklin's religious beliefs are quoted immediately below.

> It is much to be lamented that a man of Franklin's general good character and great influence should have been an unbeliever in Christianity, and also have done as much as he did to make others unbelievers. [670]

In commenting on the hypocrisy that he found in Christianity, Franklin succinctly noted that "(s)erving God is doing good to man, but praying is thought an easier service and therefore is more generally chosen."[671] With regard to his own Deist creed, Franklin wrote as follows.

> Here is my Creed. I believe in one God, Creator of the Universe: That he governs the World by his Providence. That he ought to be worshipped. That the most acceptable Service we can render to him, is doing good to his other Children. That the Soul of Man is immortal, and will be treated with Justice in another Life, respect(ing) its Conduct in this. These I take to be the fundamental Principles of all sound Religion, and I regard them as you do, in whatever Sect I meet with them.[672]

---

[669] Walker J (1997), p. 3.
[670] Walker J (1997), p. 3.
[671] Gaustad ES (1987), p. 61.
[672] Gaustad ES (1987), p. 61.

THOMAS PAINE

Thomas Paine was British by birth, being born and raised in England. Immigrating to America at the urging of Benjamin Franklin in 1774, Paine quickly became one of the prime movers in America's quest for independence. On January 10, 1776, he published his 50-page pamphlet *Common Sense*, which sold more than 500,000 copies in just a few months. As noted by Philip S. Foner, "More than any other single publication, 'Common Sense' paved the way for the Declaration of Independence, unanimously ratified July 4, 1776."[673] During the Revolutionary War, Paine was aide-de-camp to General Nathanael Greene of the Continental Army. On December 19, 1776, Paine published his paper entitled "The American Crisis: Number 1." The paper opened with the immortal words: "These are the times that try men's souls." So important was the paper in helping American morale in those early dark days of the American Revolution that George Washington had the paper read to all his assembled troops at Valley Forge. One year later, in 1777, Paine was appointed secretary to the Committee for Foreign Affairs by the Continental Congress, a post he held until 1779. On November 2, 1779, Paine became the clerk of the General Assembly of Pennsylvania

Paine wrote quite openly of his non-Christian and Deist beliefs in his *The Age of Reason*, which was originally published in 1795.

> I do not believe in the creed professed by the Jewish church, by the Roman church, by the Greek church, by the Protestant church, nor by any church that I know of. My own mind is my church.[674]

---

[673] Foner PS (2003).
[674] Walker J (1997), p. 3.

However, Paine did not stop with simply affirming Deism and disassociating himself from Christianity. He went on in *The Age of Reason* to attack both Christianity as an organized religion and the *Bible*.

All national institutions of churches, whether Jewish, Christian or Turkish, appear to me no other than human inventions, set up to terrify and enslave mankind, and monopolize power and profit.[675]

Whenever we read the obscene stories, the voluptuous debaucheries, the cruel and torturous executions, the unrelenting vindictiveness, with which more than half the Bible is filled, it would be more consistent that we called it the word of a demon, than the word of God. It is a history of wickedness, that has served to corrupt and brutalize mankind…Take away from Genesis the belief that Moses was the author, on which only the strange belief that it is the word of God has stood, and there remains nothing of Genesis but an anonymous book of stories, fables, and traditionary or invented absurdities, or of downright lies…The most detestable wickedness, the most horrid cruelties, and the greatest miseries that have afflicted the human race have had their origin in this thing called revelation, or revealed religion. It has been the most dishonorable belief against the character of the Divinity, the most destructive to morality and the peace and happiness of man, that ever was propagated since man began to exist.[676]

Of all the systems of religion that ever were invented, there is no more derogatory to the Almighty, more unedifying to men, more repugnant to reason, and more contradictory to itself than this thing called Christianity.[677]

---

[675] Paine T (1977), p. 134-135.
[676] Paine T (1988), p. 494.
[677] Walker J (1997), p. 4.

ETHAN ALLEN

Organizer of the Green Mountain Boys, Ethan Allen was a Brevet Colonel during the American Revolutionary War. In that capacity, he led the troops that captured the British fort at Ticonderoga, New York. Subsequently, he was taken captive as a prisoner of war in an attempt to capture Montreal, Canada, from the British.

Allen was a militant Deist and virulently anti-Christian. In 1784, he published his *Reason: The Only Oracle of Man,* which was a rambling denunciation of revealed religion. So anti-Christian was the manuscript that Allen originally had difficulty finding publishers, who feared that inflamed Christians would hang them if they published the book.[678]

SUMMARY

George Washington, John Adams, Thomas Jefferson, James Madison, Benjamin Franklin, Thomas Paine, and Ethan Allen were all important contributors to the founding of America, and all may share the appellation of Founding Father. In addition, they all rejected traditional Christianity. While Adams and Madison expressed some Unitarian sympathies, as a group, all of the aforementioned may be classified as Deists. Their common creed was that human reason consistently trumps the *Bible* and the teachings of the traditional Christian churches. Some of them, such as Jefferson, Franklin, Paine, and Allen, were positively anti-Christian in their views and writings. In short, any fair consideration of the Founding Fathers would have to conclude that America was not founded as a Christian nation and was not founded on Christian or Biblical principles and beliefs. The Founding Fathers appealed to reason, not Christianity or the *Bible,* in helping to forge our nation.

---

[678] Hoyt EP (1976).

EARLY STATE CONSTITUTIONS

GENERAL CONSIDERATIONS

The early constitutions and declaration of rights of the individual states offered a hodge-podge of positions with regard to the relationship between state government and Christianity. While some of these documents supported special rights for Christians, restricted government posts to Christians, or even established Christianity as the state religion, such favoritism towards Christianity was not uniform and unanimous across these documents. Further, early state constitutions often displayed dramatically conflicting wording and concepts regarding religion, sometimes within a single document.

At one extreme, South Carolina's 1778 constitution went so far as officially to define the state religion as Protestantism. In contrast, Delaware (1776 and 1792), Georgia (1798), Kentucky (1792), New Jersey (1776), North Carolina (1776), and Tennessee (1796) prohibited the establishment of any state religion.[679]

Several states (Delaware 1776, Georgia 1777, Massachusetts 1780, New Hampshire 1784, North Carolina 1776, South Carolina 1778, and Vermont 1777) banned non-Christians from holding state and/or legislative offices and in some cases also banned non-Protestant Christians. The wording of Delaware's 1792 constitution appeared to restrict offices to Deists, Christians, Muslims, and Jews. However, at least seven states (Delaware 1776 and 1792, Georgia 1777, Kentucky 1792, New York 1777, North Carolina 1776, South Carolina 1778, and Tennessee 1796) denied state and/or legislative offices to the Christian clergy. Three states (Georgia 1789 and 1798, Virginia 1786, and Tennessee 1796) allowed

---

[679] Gaustad ES (1987).

public office to be held by any adult male citizen, regardless of religious orientation. One state (Delaware 1792) allowed any adult male citizen to hold public office so long as that person was not a Christian minister. One state (Pennsylvania 1790), restricted the state legislature to monotheists, a requirement favoring Deists, Christians, Jews, and Muslims.[680]

Finally, it should be noted that Delaware (1792), Georgia (1777 and 1798), Kentucky (1792), New Hampshire (1784), New Jersey (1776), New York (1777), North Carolina (1776), Pennsylvania (1776), Tennessee (1776), Vermont (1777), Virginia (1776 and 1786) guaranteed their inhabitants complete freedom of religious choice and practice. South Carolina, the one state to establish Christianity, actually only Protestant Christianity, as the state religion, nonetheless guaranteed freedom of religion to all monotheists who acknowledged a "future state of rewards and punishments," thus guaranteeing freedom of religion to Deists, Jews, and Muslims.[681]

Clearly, there was no uniformity across the different states with regard to the role of Christianity in state government. If the United States really were founded as a Christian nation, why didn't every one of the early state constitutions establish Christianity as the state religion? Why did so many states prohibit the establishment of a state religion? Why did so many states ban the Christian clergy from serving in the state legislature?

While expressly Christian sentiments and provisions were present in some of the early state documents, such examples of favoritism towards Christianity were all rescinded within a matter of years.

[680] Gaustad ES (1987).
[681] Gaustad ES (1987).

THE SPECIAL CASE OF VIRGINIA

Section 10 of the 1776 Virginia Declaration of Rights guaranteed freedom of religion and stipulated that religion "can be directed only by reason and conviction,"[682] thus seeming to undermine the concept of divine revelation in a manner consistent with Deism. The same section then proceeded to state that it was "the mutual duty of all to practice Christian forbearance, love, and charity towards each other,"[683] a statement so restricted to Christian ethics, as opposed to theology, as to be consistent with the beliefs of most Deists. Section 10 was in force until being replaced by the Statute of Virginia for Religious Freedom in 1786.

The Statute of Virginia for Religious Freedom was authored by Thomas Jefferson in 1777, was introduced to the Virginia legislature in 1779, and became state law on January 16, 1786. Jefferson was so proud of this bill that he listed it as one of his three greatest accomplishments in his self-written epitaph, the other two accomplishments being his authorship of the Declaration of Independence and his founding of the University of Virginia. The bill is a remarkable statement in support of each individual's right to freedom of choice in religion.

> Be it enacted by the General Assembly, That no man shall be compelled to frequent or support any religious worship, place, or ministry whatsoever, nor shall be enforced, restrained, molested, or burthened in his body or goods, nor shall otherwise suffer on account of his religious opinions or beliefs; but that all men shall be free to profess, and by argument to maintain, their opinion in matters of religion, and that the same shall in no wise diminish, enlarge, or affect their civil capacities.[684]

---

[682] Gaustad ES (1987), p. 174.
[683] Gaustad ES (1987), p. 174.
[684] Gaustad ES (1987), p. 151.

While the above statement concerning religious freedom is both laudable and enlightened, it is one portion of the preamble of the statute that has the most to offer in debunking the myth that America was founded as a Christian nation. The relevant passage from the preamble, with italics added by the present author, is quoted immediately below.

> ...a departure from the plan of the Holy author of our religion, who being Lord both of body and mind, yet chose not to propagate it by coercions on either, as was in his Almighty power to do, *but to extend it by its influence on reason alone...* [685]

There are two points that need to be made with regard to the above quotation. Firstly, the passage refers to "the Holy author of our religion," a totally impersonal and abstract phrase that appears to be more consistent with Deism than with Christianity. Secondly, Jefferson's original draft included the words italicized above, which were amended out of the bill before it was passed. These italicized words allude to people accepting or rejecting any given religion based upon "reason alone," a sentiment totally in line with Deism. It is to "reason alone," not to revelation, to which the Deist turns.

However, what is most important about the preamble is what is not said. Before final passage of the bill, there was an amendment offered to insert the words "Jesus Christ" before the phrase "the Holy author of our religion." The proposed wording of the amendment was certainly Christian in its origin. Nonetheless, the amendment was overwhelmingly defeated in the state legislature. While not going along with Jefferson's concept that "reason alone" is the vehicle by which mankind can know God, which would have negated the concept of divine revelation, the

---

[685] (A) Gaustad ES (1987), p. 149; (B) Gaustad ES (1986), p. 259.

legislature of Virginia ended up using Jefferson's abstract Deist language of "the Holy author of our religion" and rejecting the explicit Christian implications of inserting the words "Jesus Christ." Jefferson later wrote about the defeat of the proposed amendment.

> Where the preamble declares, that coercion is a departure from the plan of the holy author of our religion, an amendment was proposed by inserting the words "Jesus Christ," so that it should read, "a departure from the plan of Jesus Christ, the holy author of our religion;" the insertion was rejected by a great majority, in proof that they meant to comprehend, within the mantle of its protection, the Jew and the Gentile, the Christian and the Mohammedan, the Hindoo and infidel of every denomination.[686]

THE DECLARATION OF INDEPENDENCE

On June 11, 1776, the Continental Congress appointed a committee of five men to draft America's Declaration of Independence. Three of these men have been previously presented in these pages, i.e., Thomas Jefferson, John Adams, and Benjamin Franklin, none of whom was a traditional Christian. The other two were Roger Sherman and Robert R. Livingston. The committee met and assigned the task of drafting the Declaration of Independence to Thomas Jefferson. The committee then slightly modified Jefferson's draft before presenting it to the Continental Congress. On July 1, 1776, nine state delegations voted for separation from Great Britain. The next day, July 2, 1776, the Declaration of Independence was unanimously passed by 12 of the state delegations. The 13th state, New York, abstained because the delegation had not yet received authority to vote for separation. On July 15, 1776, the New York delegation, having received the necessary authorization from its state, also

[686] Seldes G (1983), p. 363.

voted for independence. Beginning on August 2, 1776, the representatives to the Continental Congress began signing the Declaration of Independence, with the last signature being that of Thomas McKean of Delaware in 1777.

In examining the Declaration of Independence, one finds absolutely no reference to Jesus Christ and only three references to a deity. In all three cases, the words chosen reflect the abstract and impersonal concept of God propounded by Deists, not the personal concept of God advocated by Christianity. The phrases in question are "the Laws of Nature and of Nature's God," "they are endowed by their Creator," and "the Supreme Judge of the world." By emphasizing the "Laws of Nature and of Nature's God" and "their Creator," the Declaration of Independence follows the Deist belief that God created the universe and natural laws and then left the universe to run according to those laws without divine intervention, until such time as there will be a final judgment conducted by "the Supreme Judge of the world." Further, the Declaration of Independence does not declare American independence in the name of God, but "in the Name, and by Authority of the good People of these Colonies."

THE UNITED STATES CONSTITUTION

Unlike the Declaration of Independence with its Deistic allusions to God, the United States Constitution is a decidedly secular document. Neither the words "Jesus Christ" nor any allusion to God, however conceptualized, appears in the Constitution per se or in the Bill of Rights. Further, there are only two references to religion to be found in the Constitution and its first 10 amendments, and both of those clearly exclude the Constitution from being a Christian document and America from being a Christian nation. The first appears in Article VI, section 3: "...no religious test shall ever be required as a qualification to any office or public trust under the United States." The second is found in the First Amendment: "Congress shall make no law respecting the establishment of religion..."

THE 1797 TREATY OF TRIPOLI

The Treaty of Peace and Friendship between the United States and the Bey and Subjects of Tripoli of Barbary was authored in 1796 while George Washington was still the president by Joel Barlow, a former military chaplain who later converted to Deism. It was subsequently approved by both President John Adams, who took office in 1797, and the United States Secretary of State, Timothy Pickering. On June 7, 1797, the treaty was unanimously ratified by the United States Senate. Among the 23 senators present and voting to ratify the treaty were Bingham, Bloodworth, Blount, Bradford, Brown, Cocke, Foster, Goodhue, Hillhouse, Howard, Langdon, Latimer, Laurance, Livermore, Martin, Pain, Read, Rutherfurd, Theodore Sedgwick of Massachusetts, Stockton, Josiah Tattnall of Georgia, Isaac Tichenor of Vermont, and Tracy. The treaty was signed into law by President John Adams on June 10, 1797. It remained in effect until 1805, at which time it was renegotiated. [687]

Usually known by the abbreviated title of the 1797 Treaty of Tripoli, this document is especially remarkable for its 11th article, which reads as follows:

> Art. 11. As the Government of the United States of America is
> not, in any sense, founded on the Christian religion; as it has
> in itself no character of enmity against the laws, religion, or
> tranquility of Mussulmen; and, as the said States never entered

[687] (A) Buckner E (1997); (B) Peters T (1996).

into any way, or act of hostility against any Mahometan nation, it is declared by the parties, that no pretext arising from religious opinions, shall ever produce an interruption of the harmony existing between the two countries.

In signing the treaty into law, President John Adams issued the following signing statement:

Now be it known, That I John Adams, President of the United States of America, having seen and considered the said Treaty do, by and with the advice and consent of the Senate, accept, ratify, and confirm the same, and every clause and article thereof. And to the End that the said Treaty may be observed and performed with good Faith on the part of the United States, I have ordered the premises to be made public; And I do hereby enjoin and require all persons bearing office civil or military within the United States, and all other citizens or inhabitants thereof, faithfully to observe and fulfill the said Treaty and every clause and article thereof.[688]

It must be emphasized that President Adams specifically enjoined all Americans "faithfully to observe and fulfill the said Treaty and every clause and article thereof," including Article #11, which specifically states that "the Government of the United States of America is not, in any sense, founded on the Christian religion." Given President Adam's exhortation, it would appear to be positively un-American to maintain that the United States was "in any sense, founded on the Christian religion!"

However, the un-American nature of maintaining that the United States was a Christian nation or founded on the Christian religion can be made

---

[688] Buckner E (1997), p. 2-3.

even more explicit by referring to Article VI, Section 2 of the United States Constitution.

> This Constitution, and the laws of the United States which shall be made in pursuance thereof; and all treaties made, or which shall be made, under the authority of the United States, shall be the supreme law of the land; and the judges in every State shall be bound thereby, anything in the Constitution or laws of any State to the contrary notwithstanding.

Given the Constitution's definitive statement that "all treaties made...shall be the supreme law of the land," it can be seen that Article 11 of the 1797 Treaty of Tripoli with its pointed statement that "the Government of the United States of America is not, in any sense, founded on the Christian religion" was the supreme law of the United States between 1797 and 1805, the years in which the treaty was in effect. As noted earlier, to maintain that the United States was founded as a Christian nation is simply un-American.

MISCELLANEOUS CONSIDERATIONS

There are perhaps two other considerations that are relevant to our current discussion. First of all, it was not until 1864 that the United States began to print "In God We Trust" on U.S. coins. This addition was apparently prompted by an increased religious devotion during the midst of the Civil War. However, it was not until the 1950s that "In God We Trust" began to appear regularly on paper currency. Secondly, it was not until 1954 that the words "under God" were added to the Pledge of Allegiance. From 1892, when it was first authored, until June of 1954, the Pledge of Allegiance existed without any mention of God. [689]

---

[689] (A) Walker J (1997); (B) Yeoman RS (1984).

SUMMARY AND CONCLUSIONS

The myth that America was founded as a Christian nation based upon Christian and Biblical principles probably owes much to the much repeated stories of Christian groups fleeing to America from religious persecution in Europe. After all, what elementary school student has not been indoctrinated with the stories of the Puritans and their exodus from Europe to Massachusetts? However, one must stop to ask a simple question: "From what countries were these persecuted Christians fleeing?" The answer in every case is that they were fleeing from religious persecution by the Christian nations of Europe, nations where one or another branch of Christianity was the state religion—the Puritans from the Anglican Church in England, the Huguenots from Catholic France, the Quakers from the Anglican Church and the Puritans in England and then later on from the Puritans in New England, etc. (Yes, the Puritans were persecutors of the Quakers. For example, during the 17th century, Puritans in Massachusetts dealt with Quakers by cropping their ears and burning their tongues. When that was not sufficient to dissuade Quakers from their beliefs, they were either exiled or hanged.[690]) In short, those early Americans who were Christians and who fled from Europe because of religious persecution were fleeing from persecution by their fellow Christians.

It is, unfortunately, seldom mentioned in our elementary and secondary school history books that colonial America was a fairly cosmopolitan place when it came to religion. For example, both Jews and Muslims were early settlers of America, both in many cases settling in America to escape religious persecution at the hands of Christian Europe.[691] The fact that

---

[690] Gaustad ES (1987).
[691] Dirks JF (2006).

many different religious groups were represented in colonial America and the early United States was alluded to in a statement written in 1784 by George Washington in a letter to Tench Tilghman, in which Washington was attempting to find a carpenter and a bricklayer to employ at Mount Vernon.

> If they are good workmen, they may be of Asia, Africa, or Europe. They may be Mohometans, Jews or Christians of any Sect, or they may be Atheists.[692]

Washington's reference to be willing to hire Muslims, Jews, and atheists clearly indicates that he was well aware of their presence in the United States as early as 1784, the year in which he wrote his letter. In fact, both Jews and Muslims had been present in America in good numbers for many years before Washington's letter.

If America was not built upon Christianity and the *Bible*, then to what do we owe our country's origins? The answer is that America's democratic foundation was built upon the legacy of natural reason and rationality established by the Enlightenment and Deism, two European movements that were typically antithetical to all organized religions, including Christianity. In truth, the United States was established as a secular nation, based on moral and political principles derived from human reason, not from Christianity or the *Bible*. As Helmut Koester, the John H. Morison Research Professor of Divinity and Winn Research Professor of Ecclesiastical History at Harvard Divinity School, has noted:

> Like other signers of the Declaration of Independence, the Constitution, and the Bill of Rights, (Thomas) Jefferson was an

---

[692] Boller PF (1963), p. 118.

avowed Deist. It was enlightened Deism that inspired the separation of church and state in the American Constitution...The more recent claim that the American Constitution was based upon conservative Christian principles is pure legend. Enlightenment and Deism were the fathers of the American Constitution.[693]

---

[693] Koester H (2007a), p. 195.

BIBLIOGRAPHY

Al-Azdi SA (Abu Dawud): *Kitab Al-Sunan*. In Hasan A (trans.): *Sunan Abu Dawud*. New Delhi, Kitab Bhavan, 1990.

Ackroyd PR: The Book of Isaiah. In Laymon CM (ed.): *The Interpreter's One-Volume Commentary on the Bible*. Nashville, Abingdon Press, 1971.

Adler M (ed.): Chapter 22: Religion and religious groups in America: In *The Annals of America: Great Issues in American Life, Vol. II*. Chicago, Encyclopaedia Britannica, 1968.

Al-Bukhari MI: *Kitab Al-Jami' Al-Sahih*. In Khan MM (trans): *The Translation of the Meanings of Sahih Al-Bukhari*. Madinah, ---, undated.

Al-Qushayri MH (Muslim): *Al-Jami' Al-Sahih*. In Siddiqi 'AH (trans.): *Sahih Muslim*. ---, ---, 1971.

Anderson H: The Book of Job. In Laymon CM (ed.): *The Interpreter's One-Volume Commentary on the Bible*. Nashville, Abingdon Press, 1971.

Armstrong K: *A History of God: The 4,000-Year Quest of Judaism, Christianity and Islam*. New York, Ballantine Books, 1994.

Armstrong K: *Holy War: The Crusades and their Impact on Today's World*. New York, Anchor Books, 2001.

Asimov I: *Asimov's Guide to the Bible: Volume I. The Old Testament*. New York, Avon Books, 1968.

Asimov I: *Asimov's Guide to the Bible: Volume II. The New Testament*. New York, Avon Books, 1969.

Avalos HI: Goliath. In Metzger BM, Coogan MD (eds.): *The Oxford Companion to the Bible*. New York, Oxford University Press, 1993.

Baird W: The Gospel According to Luke. In Laymon CM (ed.): *The Interpreter's One-Volume Commentary on the Bible*. Nashville, Abingdon Press, 1971a.

Baird W: The Acts of the Apostles. In Laymon CM (ed.): *The Interpreter's One-Volume Commentary on the Bible*. Nashville, Abingdon Press, 1971b.

Bauer W: *Orthodoxy and Heresy in Earliest Christianity*. Philadelphia, Fortress Press, 1971.

Baur FC: *Church History of the First Three Centuries*. London, Williams and Norgate, 1878.

Beckwith R: *The Old Testament Canon of the New Testament Church and its Background in Early Judaism*. Grand Rapids, William B. Eerdmans Publishing Company, 1985.

Beegle DM: Moses. In --- (ed.): *Encyclopaedia Britannica 2003*. ---, Encyclopaedia Britannica, 2003.

Bemis SF: John Quincy Adams. In --- (ed.): *Encyclopaedia Britannica 2003*. ---, Encyclopaedia Britannica, 2003.
Bennett RA: Africa. In Metzger BM, Coogan MD (eds.): *The Oxford Companion to the Bible*. New York, Oxford University Press, 1993.

Bin Bayyah 'A: Despair not of God's grace. *Seasons: Bi-annual Journal of Zaytuna Institute* 1: (1) 5-8, 2003.

Black DA: Trinity. In Mills WE (ed.): *Mercer Dictionary of the Bible.* Macon, Mercer University Press, 1997.

Boller PF: *George Washington and Religion.* Dallas, Southern Methodist University Press, 1963.

Box GH, Oesterley WO: The Book of Sirach. In Charles RH (ed.): *The Apocrypha and Pseudepigrapha of the Old Testament in English: Volume I. Apocrypha.* Oxford, Clarendon Press, 1971.

Brown RE: *The Gospel According to John (i-xii).* Garden City, Doubleday, 1966.

Brownlee WH: The Book of Ezekiel. In Laymon CM (ed.): *The Interpreter's One-Volume Commentary on the Bible.* Nashville, Abingdon Press, 1971.

Bucker E: Does the 1796-97 Treaty with Tripoli matter to church/state separation? Speech given to the Humanists of Georgia on June 22, 1997, and at the 1997 Lake Hypatia Independence Day Celebration. In www.stephenjaygould,org/ctrl/buckner_tripoli.html. 1997.

Bullard RA: Texts/Manuscripts/Versions. In Mills WE (ed.): *Mercer Dictionary of the Bible.* Macon, Mercer University Press, 1997.

Bultmann R: Significance of the historical Jesus for the theology of Paul. In Bultmann R: *Faith and Understanding: Collected Essays.* New York, Harper and Row, 1969.

Burch EW: The structure of the synoptic gospels. In Eiselen FC, Lewis E, Downey DG (eds.): *The Abingdon Bible Commentary.* New York, Abingdon-Cokesbury Press, 1929.

Burks RE: Atonement/Expiation in the New Testament. In Mills WE (ed.): *Mercer Dictionary of the Bible*. Macon, Mercer University Press, 1997.

Butler J: Magic, astrology, and the early American religious heritage, 1600-1760. *American Historical Review* 84, 317-346, 1979.

Cadbury HJ: The language of the New Testament. In Eiselen FC, Lewis E, Downey DG (eds.): *The Abingdon Bible Commentary*. New York, Abingdon-Cokesbury Press, 1929.

Caird GB: *Saint Luke*. Baltimore, Penguin Books, 1972.

Cameron R: *The Other Gospels: Non-Canonical Gospel Texts*. Philadelphia, Westminster Press, 1982.

Cate RL: Samuel, Books of First and Second. In Mills WE (ed.): *Mercer Dictionary of the Bible*. Macon, Mercer University Press, 1997.
Chadwick H: Origen. In --- (ed.): *Encyclopaedia Britannica 2003*. ---, Encyclopaedia Britannica, 2003.

Charles RH: The book of Jubilees. In Charles RH (ed.): *The Apocrypha and Pseudepigrapha of the Old Testament in English: Volume II. Pseudepigrapha*. Oxford, Clarendon Press, 1969.

Coggan D: Lord's Prayer. In Metzger BM, Coogan MD (eds.): *The Oxford Companion to the Bible*. New York, Oxford University Press, 1993.

Coogan MD: Thomas. In Metzger BM, Coogan MD (eds.): *The Oxford Companion to the Bible*. New York, Oxford University Press, 1993.

Cook MA: I Esdras. In Charles RH (ed.): *The Apocrypha and Pseudepigrapha of the Old Testament in English: Volume I. Apocrypha.* Oxford, Clarendon Press, 1971.

Cowley RW: The Biblical Canon of the Ethiopian Orthodox Church Today. In *Ostkirchliche Studien* 23: 318-323, 1974.

Culpepper RA: John, Gospel and Letters of. In Mills WE (ed.): *Mercer Dictionary of the Bible.* Macon, Mercer University Press, 1997.

Danielou J, Marrou H: *The Christian Centuries: Volume One: The First Six Hundred Years.* New York, McGraw-Hill Book Company, 1964.

Davies JN. Mark. In Eiselen FC, Lewis E, Downey DG (eds.): *The Abingdon Bible Commentary.* New York, Abingdon-Cokesbury Press, 1929a
Davies JN. Matthew. In Eiselen FC, Lewis E, Downey DG (eds.): *The Abingdon Bible Commentary.* New York, Abingdon-Cokesbury Press, 1929b.

Denton RC: The Proverbs. In Laymon CM (ed.): *The Interpreter's One-Volume Commentary on the Bible.* Nashville, Abingdon Press, 1971a.

Denton RC: The Song of Solomon. In Laymon CM (ed.): *The Interpreter's One-Volume Commentary on the Bible.* Nashville, Abingdon Press, 1971b.

Dimitrovsky HZ, Silberman LH, et al.: Judaism: The Judaic tradition: The literature of Judaism. In --- (ed.): *Encyclopaedia Britannica 2003.*

---, Encyclopaedia Britannica, 2003.

Dirks JF: The Baptism of Jesus: The Origin of the "Sonship" of Jesus. In Dirks JF: *The Cross and the Crescent.* Beltsville, Amana Publications, 2001a.

Dirks JF: The Books of Revelation and Scripture: A Comparison of Judaism, Christianity, and Islam. In Dirks JF: *The Cross and the Crescent.* Beltsville, Amana Publications, 2001b.

Dirks JF: The Crucifixion: A Question of Identity. In Dirks JF: *The Cross and the Crescent.* Beltsville, Amana Publications, 2001c.

Dirks JF: *Muslims in American History: A Forgotten Legacy.* Beltsville, Amana Publications, 2006.

Drane JW: Paul. In Metzger BM, Coogan MD (eds.): *The Oxford Companion to the Bible.* New York, Oxford University Press, 1993.

Duncan GB: Chronology. In Laymon CM (ed.): *The Interpreter's One-Volume Commentary on the Bible.* Nashville, Abingdon Press, 1971a.

Duncan GB: Measures and money. In Laymon CM (ed.): *The Interpreter's One-Volume Commentary on the Bible.* Nashville, Abingdon Press, 1971b.

Dupont-Sommer A: *Les Ecrits esseniens decouverts pre de la mer Morte.* In Vermes G (trans.): *The Essene Writings from Qumran.* Cleveland, The World Publishing Company, 1967.

Easton BS: The Epistles of John. In Eiselen FC, Lewis E, Downey DG (eds.): *The Abingdon Bible Commentary.* New York, Abingdon-Cokesbury Press, 1929.

Eisenman R: *James the Brother of Jesus.* New York, Penguin Books, 1997.

Eisenman R: *The New Testament Code—The Cup of the Lord, the Damascus Covenant, and the Blood of Christ.* London, Watkins Publishing, 2006.

Ellis JJ: John Adams. In --- (ed.): *Encyclopaedia Britannica 2003.* ---, Encyclopaedia Britannica, 2003.

Ellis JY: Messiah/Messianism. In Mills WE (ed.): *Mercer Dictionary of the Bible.* Macon, Mercer University Press, 1997.
Emerick Y: *The Meaning of the Holy Qur'an in Today's English—Extended Study Edition.* New York, IFNA, 2000.

Emerick Y: *A Journey through the Holy Qur'an.* New York, IFNA, 2009.

Epiphanius: Panarion 30.13.7-8. In Cameron R: *The Other Gospels: Non-Canonical Gospel Texts.* Philadelphia, Westminster Press, 1982.

Epstein I: *Judaism.* Baltimore, Penguin Books, 1966.

Eusebius: *Ecclesiastical History.* In Maier PL (trans.): *Eusebius: The Church History: A New Translation with Commentary.* Grand Rapids, Kregel Publications, 1999.

Farmer R: Messiah/Christ. In Mills WE (ed.): *Mercer Dictionary of the Bible.* Macon, Mercer University Press, 1997.

Fenton JC: *Saint Matthew.* Baltimore, Pelican Books, 1973.

Ferguson E: Canon Muratori: Date and Provenance. *Studia Patristica* 18: 677-683, 1982.

Filson FV: The literary relations among the gospels. In Laymon CM (ed.): *The Interpreter's One-Volume Commentary on the Bible.* Nashville, Abingdon Press, 1971.

Findlay JA: Luke. In Eiselen FC, Lewis E, Downey DG (eds.): *The Abingdon Bible Commentary.* New York, Abingdon-Cokesbury Press, 1929.

Fitzmyer JA: Luke, The Gospel According to. In Metzger BM, Coogan MD (eds.): *The Oxford Companion to the Bible.* New York, Oxford University Press, 1993.

Flexner JT: *George Washington: Anguish and Farewell (1793-1799).* Boston, Little, Brown and Company, 1972.

Foner PS: Thomas Paine. In --- (ed.): *Encyclopaedia Britannica 2003.* ---, Encyclopaedia Britannica, 2003.

Fox RL: *The Unauthorized Version: Truth and Fiction in the Bible.* New York, Alfred A. Knopf, 1992.

Fredericksen L: Biblical Literature: Nevi'im (the Prophets): Kings: Background and Solomon's Reign. In --- (ed.): *Encyclopaedia Britannica 2003.* ---, Encyclopaedia Britannica, 2003.

Fritsch CT: The first book of the Chronicles. In Laymon CM (ed.): *The Interpreter's One-Volume Commentary on the Bible.* Nashville, Abingdon Press, 1971.

Gardner JL: *Reader's Digest Atlas of the Bible.* Pleasantville, Reader's Digest Association, Inc., 1983.

Garland DE: Mark, Gospel of. In Mills WE (ed.): *Mercer Dictionary of the Bible.* Macon, Mercer University Press, 1997.

Garvie AE: John. In Eiselen FC, Lewis E, Downey DG (eds.): *The Abingdon Bible Commentary.* New York, Abingdon-Cokesbury Press, 1929. Gaustad ES (ed.): *A Documentary History of Religion in America.* Grand Rapids, William B. Eerdmans Publishing Company, 1982.

Gaustad ES: Religion. In Peterson MD (ed.): *Thomas Jefferson: A Reference Biography.* New York, Charles Scribner's Sons, 1986.

Gaustad ES: *Faith of Our Fathers: Religion and the New Nation.* San Francisco, Harper & Row, 1987.

Gloer WH: Barabbas. In Mills WE (ed.): *Mercer Dictionary of the Bible.* Macon, Mercer University Press, 1997.

Goldin J: *The Living Talmud: The Wisdom of the Fathers.* New York, New American Library, 1964.

Gottwald NK: The book of Deuteronomy. In Laymon CM (ed.): *The Interpreter's One-Volume Commentary on the Bible.* Nashville, Abingdon Press, 1971.

Gray J: The book of Exodus. In Laymon CM (ed.): *The Interpreter's One-Volume Commentary on the Bible.* Nashville, Abingdon Press, 1971.

Grobel K: The languages of the Bible. In Laymon CM (ed.): *The Interpreter's One-Volume Commentary on the Bible.* Nashville, Abingdon Press, 1971.

Guillaumont A, Puech H, Quispel G, Till W, 'Abd Al-Masih Y: *The Gospel According to Thomas.* New York, Harper & Row, 1959.

Guthrie HH: The Book of Numbers. In Laymon CM (ed.): *The Interpreter's One-Volume Commentary on the Bible.* Nashville, Abingdon Press, 1971a.

Guthrie HH: The Book of Ecclesiastes. In Laymon CM (ed.): *The Interpreter's One-Volume Commentary on the Bible.* Nashville, Abingdon Press, 1971b.

Hamilton W: *The Modern Reader's Guide to Matthew and Luke.* New York, Association Press, 1959.

Handy RT: *A History of the Churches in U.S. and Canada.* New York, Oxford University Press, 1977.

Hardon JA: *Religions of the World: Volume I.* Garden City, Image Books, 1968.

Hardy ER: Gregory of Nazianzus, Saint. In --- (ed.): *Encyclopaedia Britannica 2003.* ---, Encyclopaedia Britannica, 2003a.

Hardy ER: Gregory of Nyssa, Saint. In --- (ed.): *Encyclopaedia Britannica 2003.* ---, Encyclopaedia Britannica, 2003b.

Hasan A: *Sunan Abu Dawud: Volumes 1-3.* New Delhi, Kitab Bhavan, 1990.

Hayes JH: Old Testament. In Mills WE (ed.): *Mercer Dictionary of the Bible.* Macon, Mercer University Press, 1997.

Hebert G: *The Old Testament from Within.* London, Oxford University Press, 1965.

Hedrick CW: Thomas, Gospel of. In Mills WE (ed.): *Mercer Dictionary of the Bible.* Macon, Mercer University Press, 1997.

Hills EF: *The King James Version Defended.* Des Moines, Christian Research Press, 1984.

Hinson EG: Canon. In Mills WE (ed.): *Mercer Dictionary of the Bible.* Macon, Mercer University Press, 1997.

Hirsch EG, Levi GB: Elhanan. In --- (ed.): *Jewish Encyclopedia.* Jewish Encyclopedia.com, 2002.

Hofstadter R: *Anti-Intellectualism in American Life.* New York, Alfred A. Knopf, 1974.

Hooker MD: Mark, The Gospel According to. In Metzger BM, Coogan MD (eds.): *The Oxford Companion to the Bible.* New York, Oxford University Press, 1993.

Hoyt EP: *The Damnedest Yankees: Ethan Allen and His Clan.* Brattlesboro, The Stephen Greene Press, 1976.

Humphreys F: Thomas. In Mills WE (ed.): *Mercer Dictionary of the Bible.* Macon, Mercer University Press, 1997.

Hyatt JP: The compiling of Israel's story. In Laymon CM (ed.): *The Interpreter's One-Volume Commentary on the Bible.* Nashville, Abingdon Press, 1971.

Jefford CN: Laodicea. In Mills WE (ed.): *Mercer Dictionary of the Bible.* Macon, Mercer University Press, 1997.

Jonas H: *The Gnostic Religion.* Boston, Beacon Press, 1967.

Jones FS: *An Ancient Jewish Christian Source on the History of Christianity—Pseudo-Clementine Recognitions 1.27-71.* Atlanta, Scholars Press, 1995.

Josephus F: *Jewish Antiquities.* In Maier PL (trans.): *Josephus: The Essential Writings: A Condensation of Jewish Antiquities and The Jewish War.* Grand Rapids, Kregel Publications, 1988.
Josephus F: *Jewish Antiquities.* In Whiston W (trans.): *The New Complete*

Works of Josephus. Grand Rapids, Kregel Publications, 1999.

Kagan D, Ozment S, Turner FM: *The Western Heritage: Fourth Edition.* New York, Macmillan Publishing Company, 1991.

Kee HC: The Gospel According to Matthew. In Laymon CM (ed.): *The Interpreter's One-Volume Commentary on the Bible.* Nashville, Abingdon Press, 1971.

Kee HC: *Jesus in History: An Approach to the Study of the Gospels.* New York, Harcourt Brace Jovanovich, Inc. 1977.
Kee HC: Mark, Long Ending of. In Mills WE (ed.): *Mercer Dictionary of the Bible.* Macon, Mercer University Press, 1997a.

Kee HC: Muratorian Canon. In Mills WE (ed.): *Mercer Dictionary of the Bible.* Macon, Mercer University Press, 1997b.

Khan MM: *Sahih Al-Bukhari—Arabic-English: Volumes 1-9.* Ankara, Hilal Yayinlari, ---.

Kierkegaard S: The Journals. As quoted at http://paulv.net/theology/UC/ Paul%20Paradox.htm. See also www.jesuswordsonly.com/ Recommended-Reading/kierkegaard.html, ---.

Kierkegaard S: *Papers and Journals: A Selection.* London, Penguin Books, 1996.

Kingsbury JD: Matthew, The Gospel According to. In Metzger BM, Coogan MD (eds.): *The Oxford Companion to the Bible.* New York, Oxford University Press, 1993.

Knight GAF: The Book of Daniel. In Laymon CM (ed.): *The Interpreter's One-Volume Commentary on the Bible.* Nashville, Abingdon Press, 1971.

Koch A (ed.): *The American Enlightenment: The Shaping of the American Experiment and a Free Society.* New York, George Braziller, 1965.

Koch G: Clementine Literature. In Mills WE (ed.): *Mercer Dictionary of the Bible.* Macon, Mercer University Press, 1997.

Koester H: Gnomai Diaphoroi: The origin and nature of diversification in the history of early Christianity. In Robinson JM, Koester H (eds.): *Trajectories through Early Christianity.* Philadelphia, Fortress Press, 1971a.

Koester H: One Jesus and four primitive gospels. In Robinson JM, Koester H (eds.): *Trajectories through Early Christianity.* Philadelphia, Fortress Press, 1971b.

Koester H: *Introduction to the New Testament: Volume 2: History and Literature of Early Christianity.* Berlin, Walter De Gruyter, 1982.

Koester H: The Gospel of Thomas (II, 2). In Robinson JM (ed.): *The Nag Hammadi Library.* New York, HarperSanFrancisco, 1990.

Koester H: Thomas Jefferson, Ralph Waldo Emerson, the Gospel of Thomas, and the Apostle Paul. In Koester H: *Paul & His World: Interpreting the New Testament in Its Context.* Minneapolis, Fortress Press, 2007a.

Koester H: Hero worship: Philostratos's Heroikos and Paul's Tomb in Philippi. In Koester H: *Paul & His World: Interpreting the New Testament in Its Context.* Minneapolis, Fortress Press, 2007b.

Kohlenberger III JR: The *NRSV* Concordance: *Unabridged: Including the Apocryphal/Deuterocanonical Books.* Grand Rapids, Zondervan Publishing House, 1991.

Lee JW: Nazirites. In Mills WE (ed.): *Mercer Dictionary of the Bible.* Macon, Mercer University Press, 1997.

Leon-Dufour X: *Dictionnaire du Nouveau Testament.* In Prendergast T (trans.): *Dictionary of the New Testament.* San Francisco, Harper & Row, 1983.

Leslie EA: The Chronology of the Old Testament. In Eiselen FC, Lewis E, Downey DG (eds.): *The Abingdon Bible Commentary.* New York, Abingdon-Cokesbury Press, 1929.

Lindars B: Saint Paul, the Apostle. In --- (ed.): *Encyclopaedia Britannica 2003.* ---, Encyclopaedia Britannica, 2003.

Mack BL: *Who Wrote the New Testament?: The Making of the Christian Myth.* San Francisco, Harper, 1995.

Manuel FE: Deism. In --- (ed.): *Encyclopaedia Britannica 2003.* --, Encyclopaedia Britannica, 2003.

Marks JH: The book of Genesis. In Laymon CM (ed.): *The Interpreter's One-Volume Commentary on the Bible.* Nashville, Abingdon Press, 1971.

Marlowe M: A Brief Introduction to the Canon and Ancient Versions of Scripture. http://www.bible-researcher.com. ---
Marsh J: *Saint John.* Baltimore, Penguin Books, 1972.

May DM: Thomas, Acts of. In Mills WE (ed.): *Mercer Dictionary of the*

Bible. Macon, Mercer University Press, 1997.

May HG: The people of the Old Testament world. In Laymon CM (ed.): *The Interpreter's One-Volume Commentary on the Bible.* Nashville, Abingdon Press, 1971a.

May HG: The book of Ruth. In Laymon CM (ed.): *The Interpreter's One-Volume Commentary on the Bible.* Nashville, Abingdon Press, 1971b.

McDonald LM: *The Formation of the Christian Biblical Canon—Revised & Expanded Edition.* ---, Henrickson Publishers, 2005.

McKenzie SL: Cush. In Metzger BM, Coogan MD (eds.): *The Oxford Companion to the Bible.* New York, Oxford University Press, 1993.

McNutt PM: Kenites. In Metzger BM, Coogan MD (eds.): *The Oxford Companion to the Bible.* New York, Oxford University Press, 1993.

Meltzer M: *The Bill of Rights: How We Got It and What It Means.* New York, Thomas Y. Crowell, 1990.

Metzger BM: *A Textual Commentary on the Greek New Testament.* Stuttgart, United Bible Societies, 1993.

Metzger BM: *The Canon of the New Testament: Its Origin, Development, and Significance.* Oxford, Clarendon Press, 1997.

Michaels JR: Matthew, Gospel of. In Mills WE (ed.): *Mercer Dictionary of the Bible.* Macon, Mercer University Press, 1997.

Micklem N: First and Second Samuel. In Eiselen FC, Lewis E, Downey DG (eds.): *The Abingdon Bible Commentary.* New York, Abingdon-Cokesbury Press, 1929.

Milgrom J: The book of Leviticus. In Laymon CM (ed.): *The Interpreter's One-Volume Commentary on the Bible.* Nashville, Abingdon Press, 1971.

Moffatt J: The formation of the New Testament. In Eiselen FC, Lewis E, Downey DG (eds.): *The Abingdon Bible Commentary.* New York, Abingdon-Cokesbury Press, 1929.

Moffatt J: The Second Book of Maccabees. In Charles RH (ed.): *The Apocrypha and Pseudepigrapha of the Old Testament in English: Volume I. Apocrypha.* Oxford, Clarendon Press, 1971.

Mowry L: The intertestamental literature. In Laymon CM (ed.): *The Interpreter's One-Volume Commentary on the Bible.* Nashville, Abingdon Press, 1971.

Murphy RE: Solomon. In Metzger BM, Coogan MD (eds.): *The Oxford Companion to the Bible.* New York, Oxford University Press, 1993.

Neusner J: *The Babylonian Talmud—A Translation and Commentary on CD-Rom.* ---, Hendrickson Publishers, 2005.

Nineham DE: *Saint Mark.* Baltimore, Penguin Books, 1973.

Noth M: *The History of Israel.* New York, Harper & Row, 1960.

Origen: *Contra Celsum.* In Chadwick H (trans.): *Origen: Contra Celsum.* Cambridge, Cambridge University Press, 1953.

Packer JI, Tenney MC, White W: *The Bible Almanac.* Nashville, Thomas Nelson, Inc., 1980.

Pagels E: *The Gnostic Gospels.* New York, Random House, 1979.

Paine T: *The Age of Reason, 1794-1795.* In Blanshard P (ed.): *Classics of Free Thought.* Buffalo, Prometheus Books, 1977.

Paine T: *The Age of Reason, 1794-1795.* In Carruth G, Ehrlich E (eds.): *The Harper Book of American Quotations.* New York, Harper & Row, 1988.

Peel ML: Nag Hammadi. In Mills WE (ed.): *Mercer Dictionary of the Bible.* Macon, Mercer University Press, 1997a.

Peel ML: Thomas the Contender, Book of: In Mills WE (ed.): *Mercer Dictionary of the Bible.* Macon, Mercer University Press, 1997b.

Peritz IJ: The chronology of the New Testament. In Eiselen FC, Lewis E, Downey DG (eds.): *The Abingdon Bible Commentary.* New York, Abingdon-Cokesbury Press, 1929.

Peters T: Does the 1797 Treaty of Tripoli say that "The Government of the United States is not, in any sense, founded on the Christian religion?" http://candst.tripod.com/tnppage/tripoli.htm. 1996.

Pfeffer L: *God, Caesar and the Constitution: The Court as Referee of Church State Confrontation.* Boston, Beacon Press, 1975.

Pherigo LP: The Gospel According to Mark. In Laymon CM (ed.): *The Interpreter's One-Volume Commentary on the Bible.* Nashville, Abingdon Press, 1971.

Phillips G: *The Doctrine of Addai, the Apostle.* London, 1876.

Polhill JB: Goliath. In Mills WE (ed.): *Mercer Dictionary of the Bible.* Macon, Mercer University Press, 1997.

Price JL: The First Letter of Paul to the Corinthians. In Laymon CM (ed.): *The Interpreter's One-Volume Commentary on the Bible.* Nashville, Abingdon Press, 1971.

Quinn DM: *Early Mormonism and the Magic World View.* Salt Lake City, Signature Books, 1987.

Reeve JJ: Goliath. In --- (ed.): *International Standard Bible Encyclopedia.* In --- (eds.): *Ellis Maxima Bible Library.* Oklahoma City, Ellis Enterprises, Inc., 2001.

Reumann J: The transmission of the Biblical text. In Laymon CM (ed.): *The Interpreter's One-Volume Commentary on the Bible.* Nashville, Abingdon Press, 1971.

Richardson HN: The Book of Esther. In Laymon CM (ed.): *The Interpreter's One-Volume Commentary on the Bible.* Nashville, Abingdon Press, 1971.

Robertson AT: The transmission of the New Testament. In Eiselen FC, Lewis E, Downey DG (eds.): *The Abingdon Bible Commentary.* New York, Abingdon-Cokesbury Press, 1929.

Robertson AT: Paul, the Apostle. In --- (ed.): *International Standard Bible Encyclopedia.* In --- (eds.): *Ellis Maxima Bible Library.* Oklahoma City, Ellis Enterprises, Inc., 2001.

Robinson JM: Kerygma and history in the New Testament. In Robinson JM, Koester H (eds.): *Trajectories through Early Christianity.* Philadelphia, Fortress Press, 1971a.

Robinson JM: Logoi Sophon: On the Gattung of Q. In Robinson JM, Koester H (eds.): *Trajectories through Early Christianity.* Philadelphia, Fortress Press, 1971b.

Robinson TH: Genesis. In Eiselen FC, Lewis E, Downey DG (eds.): *The Abingdon Bible Commentary.* New York, Abingdon-Cokesbury Press, 1929.

Rohl DM: *Pharaohs and Kings: A Biblical Quest.* New York, Crown Publishers, 1995.

Romero F: A brief history of swearing in. *Time* Vol. 173, (3), 2009. Page 18 (January 26, 2009).

Ryle HE: *The Canon of the Old Testament.* New York, Macmillan, 1892.

Sampey JR: Elhanan. In --- (ed.): *International Standard Bible Encyclopedia.* In --- (eds.): *Ellis Maxima Bible Library.* Oklahoma City, Ellis Enterprises, Inc., 2001.

Sandison GH: Jewish sects and their beliefs. In ---: *The Holy Bible: Authorized King James Version.* Cleveland, The World Publishing Company, ---.

Sarna NM: Biblical literature and its critical interpretation: Old Testament canon, texts, and versions. In --- (ed.): *Encyclopaedia Britannica 2003.* ---, Encyclopaedia Britannica, 2003.

Saunders JL: Stoicism. In --- (ed.): *Encyclopaedia Britannica 2003.* ---, Encyclopaedia Britannica, 2003.

Sawyer JFA: Messiah. In Metzger BM, Coogan MD (eds.): *The Oxford Companion to the Bible.* New York, Oxford University Press, 1993.

Schafer P: *Jesus in the Talmud.* Princeton, Princeton University Press, 2007.

Schonfield JH: *Reader's A to Z Bible Companion.* New York, The New American Library, 1967.

Schonfield JH: *Those Incredible Christians.* New York, Bantam Books, 1968.

Schwartz B: *George Washington: The Making of an American Symbol.* New York, The Free Press, 1987.

Seldes G (ed.): *The Great Quotations.* Secaucus, Citadel Press, 1983.

Seymour BJ: Lord's Prayer, The. In Mills WE (ed.): *Mercer Dictionary of the Bible.* Macon, Mercer University Press, 1997.

Shaw G: Barabbas. In Metzger BM, Coogan MD (eds.): *The Oxford Companion to the Bible.* New York, Oxford University Press, 1993.

Shepherd MH: The First Letter of John. In Laymon CM (ed.): *The Interpreter's One-Volume Commentary on the Bible.* Nashville, Abingdon Press, 1971a.

Shepherd MH: John. In Laymon CM (ed.): *The Interpreter's One-Volume Commentary on the Bible.* Nashville, Abingdon Press, 1971b.

Siddiqi 'AH: *Sahih Muslim: Volumes #1-4.* ---, ---, ---.

Silberman LH: The making of the Old Testament canon. In Laymon CM (ed.): *The Interpreter's One-Volume Commentary on the Bible.* Nashville, Abingdon Press, 1971.

Smalley SS: John, The Gospel According to. In Metzger BM, Coogan MD (eds.): *The Oxford Companion to the Bible.* New York, Oxford University Press, 1993.

Smith DA: Phinehas. In Mills WE (ed.): *Mercer Dictionary of the Bible.* Macon, Mercer University Press, 1997.

Smith RH: The Book of Joshua. In Laymon CM (ed.): *The Interpreter's One-Volume Commentary on the Bible.* Nashville, Abingdon Press, 1971.

Smith T (trans.): The Recognitions of Clement. In Pratten BP, Dods M, Smith T (eds.): *The Writings of Tatian, and Theophilus; and the Clementine Recognitions.* Edinburgh, T. & T. Clark, 1880.

Smith TC: Septuagint. In Mills WE (ed.): *Mercer Dictionary of the Bible.* Macon, Mercer University Press, 1997.

Snyder GF: Didache. In Mills WE (ed.): *Mercer Dictionary of the Bible.* Macon, Mercer University Press, 1997.

Soards ML: Paul. In Mills WE (ed.): *Mercer Dictionary of the Bible.* Macon, Mercer University Press, 1997.

Stegemann H: *Die Essener, Qumran, Johannes der Taufer und Jesus.* In -
-- (trans.): *The Library of Qumran: On the Essenes, Qumran, John the Baptist, and Jesus.* Grand Rapids, William B Eerdmans Publishing Company, 1998.

Stendahl K, Sander ET: Biblical literature: New Testament literature. In --- (ed.): *Encyclopaedia Britannica 2003.* ---, Encyclopaedia Britannica, 2003.

Strecker G: The reception of the book. In Bauer W: *Orthodoxy and Heresy in Earliest Christianity.* Philadelphia, Fortress Press, 1971.

Sundberg AC: The making of the New Testament canon. In Laymon CM (ed.): *The Interpreter's One-Volume Commentary on the Bible.* Nashville, Abingdon Press, 1971.

Sundberg AC: Canon Muratori: A Fourth-Century List. *Harvard Theological Review* 66: 1-41, 1973.

Talbert CH: Luke, Gospel of. In Mills WE (ed.): *Mercer Dictionary of the Bible.* Macon, Mercer University Press, 1997.

Toombs LE: The Psalms. In Laymon CM (ed.): *The Interpreter's One-Volume Commentary on the Bible.* Nashville, Abingdon Press, 1971.

Tomson JEH: Ebionism; Ebionites. In --- (ed.): *International Standard Bible Encyclopedia.* In --- (eds.): *Ellis Maxima Bible Library.* Oklahoma City, Ellis Enterprises, Inc., 2001.

Tregelles SP: *An Account of the Printed Text of the Greek New Testament.* London, 1854.

Turner JD: The Book of Thomas the Contender (II, 7). In Robinson

JM (ed.): *The Nag Hammadi Library.* New York, HarperSanFrancisco, 1990.

Walker J: Little-known U.S. document signed by President Adams proclaims America's government is secular. http://www.earlyamerica.com/review/summer97/secular.html. 1997.

Washington HA (ed.): *The Writings of Thomas Jefferson: Being his Autobiography, Correspondence, Reports, Messages, Addresses, and Other Writings, Official and Private: Volume VII.* Washington, Taylor Maury, 1854.

Werblowsky RJ: Judaism, or the religion of Israel. In Zaehner RC (ed.): *The Concise Encyclopedia of Living Faiths.* Boston, Beacon Press, 1967.

Wever JW: The first book of Samuel. In Laymon CM (ed.): *The Interpreter's One-Volume Commentary on the Bible.* Nashville, Abingdon Press, 1971.

Wilken RL: Tertullian. In --- (ed.): *Encyclopaedia Britannica 2003.* --, Encyclopaedia Britannica, 2003.

Williams PW: *Popular Religion in America: Symbols, Change, and the Modernization Process in Historical Perspective.* Englewood Cliffs, Prentice-Hall, 1980.

Wilson I: *Jesus: The Evidence.* London, Pan Books, 1985.

Wilson RF: James. In Mills WE (ed.): *Mercer Dictionary of the Bible.* Macon, Mercer University Press, 1997.

Wingren G: Irenaeus, Saint. In --- (ed.): *Encyclopaedia Britannica 2003.* ---, Encyclopaedia Britannica, 2003.

Yeoman RS: *A Guide Book of United States Coins, 38th Edition*. Racine, Western Publishing Co., 1984.

---: *The Lost Books of the Bible*. ---, Alpha House, 1926.

---, Hirsch EG: Goliath. In --- (ed.): *Jewish Encyclopedia*. Jewish Encyclopedia.com, 2002.

---: Maps. In Laymon CM (ed.): *The Interpreter's One-Volume Commentary on the Bible*. Nashville, Abingdon Press, 1971.

---: *The New Revised Standard Version Holy Bible*. Nashville, Thomas Nelson Publishers, 1989.

--- (eds.): *Ellis Maxima Bible Library*. Oklahoma City, Ellis Enterprises, Inc., 2001.

---: James Madison. In --- (ed.): *Encyclopaedia Britannica 2003*. ---, Encyclopaedia Britannica, 2003a.

---: Barabbas. In --- (ed.): *Encyclopaedia Britannica 2003*. ---, Encyclopaedia Britannica, 2003b.

---: Nubia. In --- (ed.): *Encyclopaedia Britannica 2003*. ---, Encyclopaedia Britannica, 2003c.

---: Jethro. In --- (ed.): *Encyclopaedia Britannica 2003*. ---, Encyclopaedia Britannica, 2003cd.

---: Matthew, Saint. In --- (ed.): *Encyclopaedia Britannica 2003*. ---, Encyclopaedia Britannica, 2003d.

---: Sin. In --- (ed.): *Encyclopaedia Britannica 2003*. ---, Encyclopaedia Britannica, 2003e.

---: Zealots. In --- (ed.): *Encyclopaedia Britannica 2003*. --, Encyclopaedia Britannica, 2003f.

---: Samaritan. In --- (ed.): *Encyclopaedia Britannica 2003*. --, Encyclopaedia Britannica, 2003g.

---: Talmud. In --- (ed.): *Encyclopaedia Britannica 2003*. ---, Encyclopaedia Britannica, 2003h.

---: Judah ha-Nasi. In --- (ed.): *Encyclopaedia Britannica 2003*. ---, Encyclopaedia Britannica, 2003i.

---: Gamaliel I. In --- (ed.): *Encyclopaedia Britannica 2003*. ---, Encyclopaedia Britannica, 2003j.

---: Gamaliel II. In --- (ed.): *Encyclopaedia Britannica 2003*. ---, Encyclopaedia Britannica, 2003k.

---: Epiphanius of Constantia, Saint. In --- (ed.): *Encyclopaedia Britannica 2003*. ---, Encyclopaedia Britannica, 2003m.

---: Lucian of Antioch, Saint. In --- (ed.): *Encyclopaedia Britannica 2003*. ---, Encyclopaedia Britannica, 2003n.

---: Tacian. In --- (ed.): *Encyclopaedia Britannica 2003*. ---, Encyclopaedia Britannica, 2003o.

---: Cyril of Jerusalem, Saint. In --- (ed.): *Encyclopaedia Britannica 2003*. ---, Encyclopaedia Britannica, 2003p.

---: Tarsus. In --- (ed.): *Encyclopaedia Britannica 2003.* ---, Encyclopaedia Britannica, 2003q.

---: Saint Clement I. In --- (ed.): *Encyclopaedia Britannica 2003.* ---, Encyclopaedia Britannica, 2003r.

---: Ebionite. In --- (ed.): *Encyclopaedia Britannica 2003.* ---, Encyclopaedia Britannica, 2003s.

---: Nazarene. In --- (ed.): *Encyclopaedia Britannica 2003.* ---, Encyclopaedia Britannica, 2003t.

---: Gnosticism. In --- (ed.): *Encyclopaedia Britannica 2003.* ---, Encyclopaedia Britannica, 2003u.

---: Attis. In --- (cd.): *Encyclopaedia Britannica 2003.* ---, Encyclopaedia Britannica, 2003v.

---: Adonis. In --- (ed.): *Encyclopaedia Britannica 2003.* ---, Encyclopaedia Britannica, 2003w.

---: Dionysus. In --- (ed.): *Encyclopaedia Britannica 2003.* ---, Encyclopaedia Britannica, 2003x.

---: Osiris. In --- (ed.): *Encyclopaedia Britannica 2003.* ---, Encyclopaedia Britannica, 2003y.

---: Persephone. In --- (ed.): *Encyclopaedia Britannica 2003.* --, Encyclopaedia Britannica, 2003z.

---: Tammuz. In --- (ed.): *Encyclopaedia Britannica 2003.* ---, Encyclopaedia Britannica, 2003za.

---: Baal. In --- (ed.): *Encyclopaedia Britannica 2003*. ---, Encyclopaedia Britannica, 2003zb.

---: Clementine literature. In --- (ed.): *Encyclopaedia Britannica 2003*. ---, Encyclopaedia Britannica, 2003zc.

---: Sanhedrin. In --- (ed.): *Encyclopaedia Britannica 2003*. ---, Encyclopaedia Britannica, 2003zd.

---: The Pew Forum on Religion and Public Life: U.S. Religious Knowledge Survey. http://pewforum.org/Other-Beliefs-and-Practices/U-S-Religious-Knowledge-Survey, 2010.

Other books authored by Dr. Jerald F. Dirks
and published by amana publications

THE CROSS AND THE CRESCENT

ABRAHAM, THE FRIEND OF GOD

UNDERSTANDING ISLAM: A GUIDE
FOR THE JUDAEO-CHRISTIAN READER

THE ABRAHAMIC FAITHS: JUDAISM,
CHRISTIANITY, AND ISLAM

MUSLIMS IN AMERICAN HISTORY:
A FORGOTTEN LEGACY

LETTERS TO MY ELDERS IN ISLAM